The Elephant in the Room

A combat manual for Democrats

By Ralph Lopez a.k.a. the blogger "Polis"

Bonus essay: "Mom, Apple Pie, and the Iranian Revolution."

This is the case against BushCo! Keep it by your side when you're talking to your congressman, speaking on the radio, or running for office yourself!

Searchable companion website at www.ralphlopezworld.com

"A treasure-trove of sources for getting your facts straights, and damned fun to read too..."

"I oughta be there dammit, an old man safe while my little brothers are dodging car bombs, what's wrong with me? Writing this crap no one is ever going to read, hoping it might wake people up, so we can impeach the man and get our boys out of there." –From the book

As numbness in much of the country wears-off from the 2004 election, many people are still left with the question: What happened? Pushing past the taunts of – "You lost, get over it!" – comes the blogger Polis, an underemployed, self-proclaimed "smart-aleck" who frantically watched this most historic election unfold.

"I promise I'm not an egomaniac, who am I to tell Kerry how to "get his act together?" I'm saying that almost anyone who's not a complete half-wit could be doing a better job," he says of John Kerry's campaign to beat George Bush. He worries, frets, and tears his hair out at what he sees as horrible message management by Kerry.

> "Everything on the line right now. Greenhouse gases, jobs, terror, the suspense is so bad I'm a nervous wreck. I'm a hundred-percent sure that if Kerry doesn't win we'll have another terrorist attack. Every moderate Muslim will begin to hate each one of us, personally. The connection will be solid: Americans are vicious Nazis who will kill hundreds of thousands of civilians to lash out at shadows. Now the guilt will not be the government's. Bush's sins will become ours."

But as the author says in his introduction, "There would be no justification for this book if it were just my diatribe against what went wrong. Who cares? It's done. My hope is there is a blueprint here for the future, a battle plan. I'm not interested in Existential hand-wringing. I want to win."

Based on a real blog that had the ear of the Kerry campaign, this book reads as a manual for combat with the Far Right. Could Polis have won it for Kerry? Can we win in 2006? Half the country is extremely unhappy. That's not okay with Polis.

2

"Explosive…"

"A battle plan for the future."

"A handbook for all Democrats who never want to lose that way again."

Dedicated to Hunter Thompson, 1937 – 2005;
Truth-teller.

Table of Contents

"Liberty lies in the hearts of men and women, when it dies there, no constitution, no law, no court can do much to help it."

-Judge Learned Hand

"A book is now more important than a weapon."

-Mikhail Kalashnikov, inventor of the AK-47

Boston, November 2nd, 2004

Eleven PM, Copley Square, and all I can think of is Mohammed Naeem Noor Khan. The Al Qaeda double agent who could have led us to bin Laden. Bush blows his cover, the Brits and Pakis are ballistic, and it's John Kerry people don't trust. Incredible. An incredible time, this Year of Our Lord; 2004. How many generations have witnessed the Constitution in its death-throes? The inauguration of the Permanent Enemy? The haunting, surreal images of 9/11? 9/11. The horror of the Post-Modern World crystallized into three digits and a slash. A number laden with cabalistic mystery since the beginning of time, a Rosemary's Baby waiting to hatch from the collective subconscious of man on a sunny Tuesday morning, to reveal its hidden and awful meaning. Nine. Eleven. Third square, sixth prime.

Only an hour ago it felt like a big street party here. Copley Square is bounded by the Romanesque Trinity Church on the east (Episcopal), the Neoclassical Public Library on the west; the five-star Copley Plaza Hotel with its black-caped, top-hatted valets; and nineteenth century Historical Register oddities that are home to restaurants, bars, clubs, and a CVS where you can buy your condoms in case you get lucky. Bon Jovi just played and it seems the bad dream is about to be over. But I can feel the air slowly going out of the crowd, like an invisible leak in a giant inner-tube. A sudden reversal of the charge. And I'm supposed to blame Jesus Freak rednecks in Ohio.

Somehow it doesn't feel right. I'm not sure exactly why. Who but John Kerry could lose this race to an incompetent war criminal, whose own people were singing against him along with generals, admirals, and Howard Stern? The Shrub couldn't do a damned thing right except slime anyone who got in his way, starting first, last, and always, of course, with John Kerry. The DNC honchos will point fingers at everything and everyone – homophobes, religious nuts, NASCAR dads – everyone but themselves. It means that on top of losing the most important election since there have been elections, they didn't learn a goddamn thing.

7

Wed, 8 Sep 2004
From: "Ralph Lopez"
<ralphlopez_2003@yahoo.com>
Subject: Rebuttal to Cheney "a vote for Kerry is a
vote for terror"
To: augie_grace@kerry.senate.gov
bcc: recipient list suppressed

Kerry People;

Dick Cheney's remark that "a vote for Kerry is a
vote for terror" is breathtaking and really needs
to be rebutted. From outside the campaign
"bubble," I can tell you your response "they
crossed the line" is weak. Crossed the line? They
burned the village, killed all the livestock, raped
the women, and sold the children into slavery. Or
the political equivalent. Tom, are you out there?

> **Polis**

It's not as if Kerry didn't have help. One scandal after another, 380 tons of HMX explosives stolen from right under Bush's nose in Iraq, to outright treason in the case of Valerie Plame. One scandal after another and each time Kerry's the one who manages to look bad. He's a Houdini in reverse, could tangle himself up in a roll of toilet paper from what started as a little piece stuck on his shoe. How does he *do* that? Administration dissidents, Richard Clarke, Paul O'Neill, General Eric Shineski all come out for Kerry. Al Franken Ambassador Joe Wilson and half the CIA. The Boss Springsteen. How can you lose with the Boss on your side? "Farenheit 9/11," 9/11 widows, retired brass and didn't they support the troops? A unified and furious base. There were "Bush Relatives Against Bush": a slew of second and third cousins out to recover the family's good name.

Boston Herald, August 29, 2003:

'It hurts my feelings that my son, who was a good

and decent person, was used as a front for Bush's agenda," said [the mother of a 9/11 victim.] "All these kids (in our military) are dying, and for what? We went in there for oil and military supremacy in the region and our own corporate interests. If anything, we're breeding far more people who hate us because they see us as bullies. And if they can't beat us standing up, they'll beat us any way they can. They'll beat us with many more Sept. 11th's, and many more innocent victims like our soldiers and my son.'"

Even Bush's hometown paper, the Lone Star Iconoclast, endorsed Kerry. Just proves what every high school football coach knows: no fancy gear, no spiffy uniforms will help the team that doesn't go out and fight. *You* have to want it and want it bad. It was over when the Democrats decided not to Lewinski Valerie Plame.

"Lewinski": When a minority party attacks a president in order to stop his agenda, in a coordinated and persistent assault. All Monica all the time. Usually involves presidential wrongdoing but the appearance of it will do. Synonyms: hardball, playing-for-keeps, to do a Gingrich. A Contract on America.

They didn't Lewinski any of it, Noor Khan or Plame, or Cheney's business with Saddam Hussein. The high crimes and misdemeanors elephant was in the room, gurgling and snorting and burping, but the Democrats perfected the art of talking past it so they could pretend it wasn't there. Farting, slurping, raising an unholy smell.

Elephant? What elephant? Can't hear you, there's chewing sounds coming from somewhere. Come again?

What a job these Democrats have. Give a blustery speech every now and then, to show the folks back home you still have a pulse, then off to the next lobbyist party, especially that guy with the great call-girls. Most discrete. Very important in this business.

When the Republicans wanted to stop Clinton dead in his

9

tracks, they didn't attack his agenda. They attacked *him*. Over nothing.

Then that other stuff, Dick Cheney's nexus-lexus of terror, never let a threat materialize, Iraq is where it all comes together, blah blah blah. Kerry didn't remind them that Al Qaeda doesn't *need* a nexus. They're international. Bush is trying to fight Hitler when it's Al Qaeda 2.0. If they're going to get a nuke, they'll get it from the old Soviet Union or better yet our good buddies in Pakistan. Democratize the Middle East? Give me a break. We would have started with Saudi Arabia, *without* starting a war, if we gave a good goddamn about that.

Mohammed Naeem Noor Khan. When the Financial District terror alerts hit the news, people asked Bush just what are these based on? Besides the election coming up? Bush dusts-off threats that are over three years old. Oh right, sure George. People were *laughing* at him. Boy, he hates that. So to show he's fighting terr' he tells the papers that the Pakis had secretly picked up Noor Khan. So it's not a secret anymore. Noor Khan is the prize double agent we had big plans for, up to him taking us to the mass killer himself. We didn't want Khan to get antsy while we rolled up a batch of his pals, but now everyone knows who the rat is. Including bin Laden.

The Pakis, the good ones, and the Brits were bullshit. Another elephant walks into the room, the Democrats say nothing. Except funny how it's feeling so crowded in here.

The problem with pinning the blame on these rednecks is they are my people. Hating them would spark an identity crisis of devastating proportions. This adds a dimension to the gonna-move-to-Canada thing. I *can't* move to Canada. I'm *from* here. A born-in-Texas, gun-loving, liberal-loathing good-old-boy myself. Limousine liberals, that is. The Ted Kennedys of the world who are happy to raise your taxes but never touch the corporate hog troughs; bail-outs, special treatment and pillaging of federal lands for a song. An old man in my neighborhood, he's probably dead by now, told me that Kennedys of the world want to help the poor as long as it's always with *your* money, not theirs. I didn't know what he was talking about. I was young then.

Mark Twain quote: "When I was a boy of fourteen, my father was so ignorant I could hardly stand to have the old man around. But when I got to be twenty-one, I was astonished at how much the old man had learned in seven years."

I'm not even drunk, at the biggest block party since the Red Sox won the World Series. Too much of that lately. You drink to forget your financial situation which in turn worsens your financial situation, which makes you want to drink more. A vicious trap. The hope is the Sox will rub off on Kerry. I smell beer on breath everywhere. For me the moment is enough. Watching Bush get booted back to Waco or wherever the hell he's from is its own special high. No chemicals necessary. I actually want to be straight for this.

College kids swarm a truck cab parked on Boylston Street, one of a solid wall of sound trucks, satellite dishes, command trailers, bleachers, and a stage thrown up at the last minute by Hizzoner the Mayor and the Kerry campaign to celebrate the victory. They're even balancing on the truck's gigantic tires, a good trick, I'm thinking. They have placards that say "no war." The words are inside a red hexagon, like a stop sign. By the library, Jersey barriers block-off a long stretch of Boylston Street so the Kerry motorcade can roar right up to the stage when the time is right, bypassing the ocean of jostling, swaying Bush-dislikers. The entertainment includes Sheryl Crow, the Black Eyed Peas, Carole King, and James Taylor. A projector throws the stage action onto the side of the side of the Westin Hotel in giant relief.

I try hard to take it all in. I want to remember this. Until a while ago I never saw so many different-looking types looking so happy. It's my idea of what a good bar should be. Not college, not older, not yuppies or blue-collars, well-dressed, shabby, black or white. A little bit of everyone, all having a good time. I'm feeling so proud of my country for shoving that man back down the gopher hole he emerged from; for showing the world that all Americans are not fear-crazed warmongers. We, at the end of a nail-biting movie, still do the right thing. It has a happy ending, and the good guys win.

Bush called Kerry a flip-flopper so much he mainstreamed it.

I heard a couple arguing on a bus and the guy was saying: "No honey you're flip-flopping. You're flip-flopping."

Everything on line right now. Greenhouse gases, jobs, terror, the suspense is so bad I'm a nervous wreck. I'm a hundred-percent sure that if Kerry doesn't win we'll have another terrorist attack. Every moderate Muslim will begin to hate each one of us, *personally*. The connection will be solid: Americans are vicious Nazis who will kill hundreds of thousands of civilians to lash out at shadows. Now the guilt will not be the government's. Bush's sins will become ours.

And you're damned right you don't need an assault rifle to hunt deer. That's self-defense and a last resort against a tyrannical government. The Constitution guarantees it. Believe me, they ain't for shooting Bambi.

Everyone trying to stay positive. I'm listening for far-off eruptions of cheers, which mean good news, another state turns blue, another optimistic projection. Where the hell are they? The temper is changing. Everywhere knots of people are glued to people who are glued to cell phones, who are talking to people on the other end who are glued to the television or "the Internets," as Bush called it. "What's wrong with that?" – my old man would say, "Isn't it the 'Internets?'" Part of Bush's rural swing state magic.

Drained from working seventeen hours straight as an exit pollster in East Boston, I go home to get some sleep. We'll know soon enough. The counting could go all night. On the subway a kid sees my Kerry button and gives me a thumbs-up. He says: "Kerry."

Two other college kids next to me argue in detail about swing state electoral vote arithmetic. This impresses me: everyone suddenly into politics. People think they can change things. It's a far cry from my generation. We didn't know what the Electoral College *was*. Or how you could lose even with more total votes than the other guy.

Back in my office, my bedroom, I throw myself off my throbbing feet. It's a good day's pay from ABC-CNN, and I'm happy to pocket the check. But I still think these exit polls ought to be outlawed. On the TV a map of Florida flashes onto the screen with a checkmark in the box next to "Bush." Not even 2 a.m. and they've called Florida. This is bad. It's all over. All over. I switch off the television and turn out the light.

An exit pollster. Joke job. But with a good view of the action on the ground. People came out of the woodwork to vote, saw a young Chinese cat drag his whole family to the polls. He harangues the crew outside on why they have to go in and do what he says, grandma and gramps and aunt Edna and the rest, all in their Sunday best, smiling with their hands clasped in front of them. Like, ok fine, so let's get it over with and go to dinner already.

Gobbleday taki noo yaktra! Glibberty do da BOOSH! Mu geep frigga num sik IRAQ! My gut feeling is he's not happy with our president.

Welcome to the Official Kerry-Edwards Blog!
Real security for America's future!

Polis,

Give it up, okay? You're not dragging Kerry over to be Dean-lite, particularly after Trippi and the angry-left Greeniacs did that to Dean and it killed him. Your ad nauseum prescription for how to win this race, which echoes Huffington and others on the progressive left, is a prescription for division and failure. We don't want to rip the country down the middle again and hope we get the most votes - we want to embrace the country and get the lion's share.

Posted by: Mark from Iowa on July 12, 2004 09:22 PM

Did they listen to me? No. We're neck-and-neck in the polls! We're doing fine! Do you understand the magnitude of that achievement? The Democrats are unified and Kerry is tied! Shut up! And if you want to help, send money!

It was High Noon and the good guys ran to the gunfight using sling-shots. Draft-dodgers making a war hero's medals the issue. Now that's ugly. The good guys were found shot down like dogs with their pistols and rifles holstered, clips full of ammo, and no one knows what to make of it. Why didn't they pull their guns? Why didn't they fight?

Welcome to the Official Kerry-Edwards Blog!
Real security for America's future!

kj, man! (I know you're not ;) ...Polis is right; we need some serious, down and dirty truth telling about Bushco NOW. And I'd like to believe that Kerry is doing everything exactly right, but I've seen Mondale, Dukakis, and Gore all go down for being "above all that." My experience and my gut tell me now is the time to start swinging.

Posted by: Moltar on July 12, 2004 09:05 PM

The vicious, the dishonest, the hypocritical triumph over the merely bad, but that's nothing compared to how you feel at the Red Staters lapping it up. Who are these people? What the hell are they thinking? That's the tough part. I thought I knew this country. Now some people aren't even speaking as we look across the Great Red-Blue Divide. Like waking up in the house you grew up in and suddenly feeling you're surrounded by strangers. For awhile I think maybe the time for civility is over. Time to tell it like it is. You've got to be plain dumb to vote for George W. Bush. Even advice columnists were at a loss.

Dear Prudie,

George W. Bush has won re-election, and I think he's a scumbag. His decision to go into an unjustified war that resulted in over 1,300 soldier deaths (at the time of this writing) and somewhere between 10,000 and 100,000 civilian deaths is

unconscionable.

I've already decided that I do not want to date or be friends with anyone who voted for Bush in 2004. This isn't a problem. The problem is what to do with two very close friends (a couple) that were Bush supporters. I still care about them and would have no problem helping them out if they were in a jam, but I no longer wish to spend any time with them.

My question is: What is the right way to drop them? My current plan involves phasing them out. I no longer call them. When they call, I'm friendly, but I decline all invitations. I figure they will get the hint. Is this the best strategy, or should I just tell them the truth?

—Trying To Stay Away From Bush Supporters [1]

Who on Earth cannot see exactly what he's doing? "There are *people* (snicker snicker) who think you can *negotiate* (snicker) with *terrorists*.   You don't *negotiate* with terrorists. You *defeat* them." Wild applause from the carefully-screened crowd. One time on the radio, a smart-aleck interviewer ambushed rock star Johnny Lydon with an unflattering question. *"It's been said that..."* the interviewer said, followed-on by something rude. Johnny shoots back, with that cool English accent: "Of course it's been said, *because you just said it!* No one else did! *Now shut-up and play some music!* "

There are people...It's been said...shut-up, George, and play some music.

Liberals are condescending? Bush sees you standing there in your bib overalls with your thumbs hooked in the straps, nodding

---

[1] *Boston Globe,* "She's phasing out friends who are Bush supporters," Dec. 7, 2004

your head and narrowing your eyes. *We, they, we will move forward, we will not go back...* The truth is, you can't take it away, George was born to be the world's greatest used car salesman.

So we look at them, the Red-Staters, and we can't believe it. My God! You poor dumb bastards! Do you know what you have done? This man is against your interests, don't you see that? The worst of it is they're the ones whose kids will be feeding the Green Machine in disproportionate numbers, bleeding and dying in Iraq. The whole thing just makes you want to cry.

"Thou salt not kill." – Exodus 20:1

At one time I got to know a few of my people a little better than I wanted. In Carolina there was Lewis. He was one of those tall lanky kids who should have been in seventh grade when he was in sixth. That's back when teachers did the kindness of holding you back if you hadn't learned anything, instead of passing you up through the grades to get rid of you. Lewis had an American flag sewn onto the back of his Levis jacket, with the sleeves cut-off, just like Peter Fonda in Easy Rider. Who was everyone's hero. We lived on dirt roads and he would whisper *hey Paco, Paco taco* at me in the back of class on account of that I was Mexican. But he didn't mean any harm. Not really. Dumb old Lewis. Good old Lewis. I thought he looked pretty cool, the jacket and the straight blond hair you could flip out of your eyes. And here I was stuck with this goofy curly black mop.

Pop was career Air Force and we were always stuck in these backwaters. Great places to grow up, but that's about it. Large chunks of Rural America are where kids have happy a childhood then get the hell out, if they have any wherewithal whatsoever. That's where I met some of the kindest, most generous people I have ever known. Black people, white people. These are the people who nurtured me and treated me as one of their own.

We all dug that scene, Peter Fonda and *Hey boy why don't you get a haircut? BLAM!*

16

It's easy to get the emails for some pretty important players if you follow the papers and are handy with Google. When they run out of things to write about, the newspapers do a who's-who-in-the-campaign filler piece. They report on things like who has the *real power*, who's the pinch-hitter, the mastermind, whatever. Campaign staff must split a gut laughing over these. Anyone can say anything. "Hey guys did you know we call Frank here the "Terminator?" Who was that? Kelly was that you? HA!"

Anyway the reporters will write where these people work, such-and-such law firm or consulting firm or college, and you just go to the company online directory and plug-in "Cam Kerry," for example, for John Kerry's brother Cameron, and boom, there he is. It's a wonder how easy it is to get a mainline to someone who has the ear of the next president of the United States.

John Kerry lives up on Beacon Hill, not far from my neighborhood, around the corner from a buddy who is on Myrtle Street. Kerry is kitty-corner in Louisburg Square. But it was hard to talk to him on account of the Secret Service who were always around his house. He was never home anyway.

Back where my people live now, one of the reddest counties in a red state, Fahrenheit 9/11 never even hit the screen. No, the big movie event in town, the one people went to see four and five times was Passion of the Christ. We're God-fearing folks. Whereas in other parts of the country many thought it was too violent, too bloody, we understand that His suffering infuses the entire theology of Christ. It's the whole p'int, dadblame-it. Jesus did not take the easy way out. No Suffering, no Gift. You've got to *understand* this.

From: "Tom Vallely" <---> Add to Address Book
Subject: Re: Getting together
To: ralphlopez_2003@yahoo.com

Dear Ralph,

Thanks for your voice mail. The campaign is aware of your blog polis and the language there is good stuff. I'm

on the road a lot so it's hard to get me. But in a few days you'll be able to get me in the Cambridge office and the number there is --- and ask for my assistant Amy --- to set up an appointment (it'll be after the election).

Tommy

Fri, 17 Sep 2004 13:56:05 -0700 (PDT)
From: "Ralph Lopez" <ralphlopez_2003@yahoo.com> Add to Address Book
Subject: Re: Getting together
To: tom_vallely@xxxx.xxx

Tom,

Then I'll keep pumping out language and cc you occasionally if that's ok. Sorry to be a wet blanket, but when Kerry says, "I would have done almost EVERYTHING differently," it sounds like he's calling himself a Monday morning quarterback. I urge the campaign to make the clarification between voting for the diplomatic "big stick" of the War Resolution, and actually condoning the attack and occupation. John is getting killed on the "he voted for the war but now he's against it" thing.

Ralph

Tom Vallely is one of Kerry's "dog soldiers," as they came to be called. They are the Vietnam veterans who, along with Kerry's brother Cam, have been Kerry's inner circle since he started in politics. Tom was a state representative in Massachusetts eons ago. I remember visiting him at the State House once. He was in a group called Veterans for Peace. This was in the Eighties.

VFP were doing work in Nicaragua. I liked what they were doing, so I wanted to meet Tom after reading about him in the papers.

See, in the Eighties Ronald Reagan was funding a murdering, raping bunch of thugs called the Contras, who attacked villagers in the Nicaraguan countryside to put pressure on the mildly socialist Sandinista government. It was part of Reagan's policy of getting a tiny dirt-poor nation to say "uncle." One for the Gipper. Veterans for Peace thought this was immoral, so they ran food and medicine in caravans to the Contras' civilian victims, which most all the victims were. I dropped in on Tom at the State House unannounced, and I remember his secretary starting to give me the polite brush-off when Tom stuck his head out of his cube and said howdy. He smiled and told me to drop by again. He was in a meeting. A warm, friendly guy I liked right away, though I never actually went back.

I never cared much for Kerry as a politician. I live in Massachusetts, and he's been my senator for 20 years. I know his record. He pushed for Most Favored Nation trade status for China right after Tiananmen Square, which got him a nasty letter from me. But I really didn't like it when he voted for NAFTA. If you can't depend on a Massachusetts liberal to vote against NAFTA, what can you depend on? He was selling-out the same as all the other Democrats. I don't really like either party. I got onboard when I decided Bush had dangerous dictatorial tendencies hard-wired into his personality. Kerry was lame, but Bush was a menace. He felt entitled to run our lives and made no bones about it. Someone that convinced of his rightness is a mortal danger.

One suggestion the campaign didn't take was that Kerry drop his "ought to" mode. "We're not as safe as we ought to be." New jobs aren't as good as they "ought to be." And the most uninspiring single line of political speech-writing in history: "We can do better." More like your mother lecturing you on your grades.

There would be no justification for this book if it were just my diatribe against what went wrong. Who cares? It's done. My hope is there is a blueprint here for the future, a battle plan. I'm not interested in Existential hand-wringing. I want to win.

The Right not only tells it's representatives when to jump, it tells them how high. If they don't, they get phone calls, angry visits, and exploratory committees pop-up to sense-out challenges. What happens when Democrats sell us out? We shake our heads and half expect it. The Right knows where the levers are. Finding them is our first job.

The Right has toll-free numbers for congressmen and senators posted on their refrigerators, a readiness to boycott, and lots of righteous indignation. Don't believe me? Ask one. The secret is democracy works. Not as in voting every four years. As in: using it all the time. The first thing to watch out for is politicians who don't give you your money's worth of hell-raising. You pay them. It's the least they can do.

This book is based on my blog "Polis," my pen name. I forwarded it often to people like Tom Vallely and Cam Kerry. Also people like Jill Alper, Art Collins, and Paul Rivera, and Mike Dukakis. Kerry had a sloppy message, and you didn't have to be a political genius to do better. I was just trying to give them ideas. Somewhere around July of '04 I discovered Michael Scheuer's book "Imperial Hubris; Why the West is Losing the War on Terror." Scheuer published under the pseudonym "Anonymous," because at the time of the book's release he was still the active-duty head of the CIA's bin Laden unit. He couldn't use his real name. He has since resigned. "Hubris" is an eye-opening experience in understanding the war on terror. You'll see a lot of Scheuer's thinking quoted in this book. It was common sense even before he said it. Coming from him, it's alarming. The CIA's foremost Al Qaeda expert thinks Bush is losing this war. He says our freedom has nothing to do with why they hate us. They hate for "what we do, not who we are."

Here's a sample of something I wrote in my blog shortly before it magically appeared in a Kerry speech:

Polis, September 22, 2004:

"The Iraq diversion" is Kerry's magic bullet. Boston Globe today: some Kerry advisors worry he'll be seen as the "anti-war candidate." How can he be the anti-war candidate if all he's saying is we should be fighting the right war? Al Qaeda runs free in the border regions of Pakistan and Afghanistan, and in cities around the world. Kerry is the one who wants to take the fight to the enemy, not Bush.

John Kerry, September 24, 2004, at Temple University:

"The invasion of Iraq was a profound diversion from the battle against our greatest enemy, al-Qaeda."

It doesn't matter who said it first. The point is it every time Kerry launched an attack along these lines, his poll numbers went up. But by the time Kerry decided the American people could handle the truth, it was too late. You don't spring a thing like that four weeks before election day, because the first stage is "shoot the messenger." An idea like that has to be worked. Bush spent a year honing the same attack. Kerry spent a year coming up with one.

The story of the Kerry campaign is a story of too little too late. This blog, which can be read randomly as short essays or front-to-back as a history, is an argument for opposition. All is lost unless Democrats do a Lewinsky, all-Monica-all-the-time on Bush on national security issues. No matter how much his fortunes dwindle in his lame duck term, another terror attack will revive them and those of next-in-line Jeb Bush. The enemy is not Bush, it is Bushism. This brand of politics in which up is down and left is right must be rooted out, not just clipped.

The idea of the party system in America is that all sides are represented in vigorous debate, until compromises are reached which leave all sides neither completely happy, nor completely unhappy. I'm no historian, but I do know the Founders were great scholars of the Greek and Roman classics, and they applied to politics the idea of the "golden mean." The system doesn't work unless all sides have real representation. It doesn't work when large numbers of people feel cheated. Democratic calls for "unity" and "compromise" are like a football team that has been pushed back to its own tenth yard line, then it splits the difference with the opposing team and moves the ball even further back to the fifth. All the compromise is on one side.

21

And if a nation is "too divided," as John Kerry told the president in his telephone call to congratulate him the morning after the election? Should we not be working to "heal" those divisions? Politics ain't beanbag, and it ain't psychobabble. The Founders suspected that no nation as far-flung as this would ever enjoy a unity of opinion on all or even most issues. Unity is everyone believing they got a fair shake.

Bad things happen when large numbers of people feel they aren't represented. Politicians complain that Constitutional checks-and balances and the filibuster seem designed to produce "gridlock," but some scholars suspect that was the intention. Of all the landmines the Founders worried about when they designed our democracy, few concerned them as much as the "tyranny of the majority." The whole idea of our system of government is to make it hard for politicians to do too much damage.

The kind of politics that worries about going "negative" is the kind of poll-driven, passionless politics that has made Kerry and the Democrats what they are: hopeless losers. The Right never worries about sounding negative, and they will taunt a wounded war veteran by putting band-aids over Purple Hearts. During the 2000 Republican primary in South Carolina the Bush campaign spread rumors that John McCain, who was pulling ahead of Bush, was the father of an illegitimate mixed-race child. Watching McCain give Bush a hug when he endorsed him in August 2004 made me think: McCain has either lost it, or he has some truly vicious payback up his sleeve.

Cut to the chase. The reality in Iraq is our troops are dying in the middle of a low-grade civil war that's pumping up Al Qaeda. The March of Democracy will be irrelevant when we get hit here again, this time thanks to George Bush. After 9/11 and the Afghanistan invasion, which I supported, we were ready to hunt down Al Qaeda with 100% of our force and worldwide support. Even Muslim militants were turning against bin Laden in disgust.

A Pakistani militant who was executed in 2002 for his attack on CIA headquarters, Aimal Khan Kasi, said before he was killed, that the September 11, 2001 attacks on the World Trade Center were "totally wrong." He discouraged attacks on civilians in retaliation for his execution, and said "I'm against attacks on civilian Americans. They are not responsible for my execution." Kasi believed that attacks against CIA headquarters and the Pentagon were legitimate because it was "retaliation against the U.S. government" for American policy in the Middle East and its support of Israel.

Men like Kasi are the men who must be appealed to, to put the terror genie back in the bottle. When we bombed Iraq, bin Laden couldn't have been happier. Sales of bin Laden tee-shirts shot through the roof. Scheuer says "Frankly, America does not have many friends in its war on bin Laden, and none are willing to share all they hold on al Qaeda." This will continue as long as Bushism reigns. We're oil-stealers and baby-killers, all of us now. Not the soldiers. *Us.* American-lovers are turning into American-haters.

> **"We arrested people in front of their families, dragging them away in handcuffs with bags over their heads, and then provided no information to the families of those we incarcerated. In the end our soldiers killed, maimed or jailed thousands of Arabs, 90 percent of whom were not the enemy. But they are now."**
> **–Colonel Douglas Macgregor**

And for this trouble, what do we get in the end? An Iraq-Iran Shiite theocratic alliance, armed with nuclear weapons. Our soldiers dying in the middle of a low-grade civil war at the cost of $100 billion a year, which could turn into a bloodbath if we leave. China busts a move on Taiwan, and since we're bogged down in Iraq there's nothing we can do about it. US debt soars and the dollar takes a plunge. With industrial Taiwan the Chinese economy leap-frogs us. US now second-class power, except our ability to bomb, which makes us hated and attacked even more. Martial law declared. Halliburton is the government. This is the scenario George Bush drools over.

All that is supposed to be better than Saddam in power. Good going, George. Strength deters. Bullying backfires.

"The more disturbing development is that some

Iraqi jihadis, hoping to take their fight beyond Iraq's borders, are threatening to launch a terrorist campaign in the U.S. "If America continues to shield its people from the truth," says an al-Zarqawi loyalist, "we shall transport the battle to where their public cannot but see it."

-Time Magazine, August 16, 2004

In the end, Kerry was the mama's boy and the Bushies were the tough kids with two-by-fours waiting to jump him for his lunch money. Bush was swinging a baseball bat and Kerry was flailing with his fists. Bush had Kerry, a brave man, on the run down the alley and trying to keep his jacket from getting stolen too. Kerry is brave, but no one taught him how to deal with bullies. The kind who don't debate anything but attack anyone who disagrees.

When you're on trial for your life, you don't want to be represented by a lawyer who worries about sounding "negative." You want the smartest meanest son-of-a-bitchin' lawyer you can afford, and you mortgage the house for it. The point isn't to be nice. The point is to have your fair day in court. Politics is life and death. Politics shapes our future, our children's future, whether we are sent to war, whether our children will experience a terrorist attack. You don't go to Washington to be liked. You go to Washington to represent the people who sent you there. If you don't have the stomach for a fight, get out.

Fifty-three percent of Americans believe we will be attacked in the near future with a weapon of mass destruction, according to a 2005 AP poll. The best thing we can do is build the consensus that we will allow no more encroachments on our Bill of Rights, no matter what happens. No more incommunicado American "enemy combatants," like Jose Padilla. No Patriot Act III. If Bush can't win the war on terror with the powers we-the-people gave him, then we'll find someone who can. I should probably end this book right here, since in a nutshell that's what I have to say. Read on if you want. You might like some of it, anyway. --RAL April 13, 2005

They gambled with a go it alone policy and our soldiers are paying with their lives...Neither George Bush nor Dick Cheney has ever heard a shot fired in anger. Never worried whether he'd ever see his family again or seen the destruction caused by the weapons he's wielded. The losses of war are permanent. The consequences are unpredictable.

--General Wesley Clark

September 2003 - December 2003

Monday, September 29, 2003

Busy re-hydrating and nursing a hangover. I can't believe I'm going to do gym tonight. But that's the one hard-wired rule. No skipping gym night in deference to debauchery. The agony will remind me like nothing else to go home earlier next time.

I can't believe about half of what I'm seeing these days, and the half I do, I don't like about three-quarters of it. Not one bit. To my small but determined mind, the unreasonable search-and-seizure parts of the Constitution, which include no-search-without-probable-cause, were put there because they had figured out that if you look real hard, you'll find everyone has done something wrong. My Google scholarship tells me that back in Magna Carta days the King's goons could break into your hut, and sooner or later they'd see the pheasant poached from the King's game preserve hanging in the corner. Then you were fried.

Probable cause says the government can't do "fishing expeditions," which is poking around you or your property just to see what they can find. That's from a link on the Magna Carta page, which brought me to a page on the Supreme Court which bought me to a page on Watergate. This is how hours disappear on me when I'm online. Damn. My head is like a grease trap-for random and useless knowledge. If a small town cop hates your brother, you know who's going to get searched. Not your brother. Too obvious. *You.* The more I see, the bigger a fan I'm becoming of the Founding Slave-Holders. Even if they did have slaves. They knew people, and they included themselves, and their view of people was not pretty.

Sorry, all I'm doing here is working up to a good quote I just read, which sent me scurrying to the Oracle of Google. Senator Ron Wyden (D-Oregon), leading the charge against the Pentagon's proposed Total Information Awareness program (TIA), says:

"Americans on American soil are not going to be targets of TIA surveillance that would have violated their privacy and civil liberties. The

government is not going to be able to pick Americans up by their ankles and shake them to see if anything funny falls out."[2]

I'd say that's it. Don't need a law degree to understand that. That's it right there, the whole thing.

Here's something else that perked up my ears: 27 Israeli Pilots Refuse Raid Duty.

JERUSALEM -- Twenty-seven Israeli air force pilots, who are considered the most elite servicemen of the Israeli Defense Forces, pledged in an open letter published yesterday that they no longer would take part in raids on Palestinian population centers in the West Bank and Gaza Strip, describing them as "illegal and immoral."[3]

Bloink. Message. Boss says pretty pictures are ready to be made into Powerpoint, come get them. This job lets you be quite creative, though I can never figure out what the pictures mean. I may not get to the gym until 9:30.. Oh my head.

..Polis 3:09 PM

I know next to nothing about Wesley Clark, but he's the only Democrat saying anything half thoughtful about terrorism. Career politicians most of them, and it's the four-star general who has been thinking. How do you figure that? A Newsweek excerpt from Clark's new book:

"And what about the real sources of terrorists? U.S. allies in the region like Egypt, Pakistan, and Saudi Arabia? Wasn't it the repressive policies of the first, and the corruption and poverty of the second, that were generating many of the angry

---

[2] "Pentagon Spy Office to Close," Associated Press, Sep. 25, 2003

[3] *Boston Globe*, "27 Israeli pilots refuse raid duty," 9/25/2003

young men who became terrorists?" [4]

The Boston Globe is a Republicrat rag, but every now and then they have a good background piece. Teddy Roosevelt was the last president who had to deal with a "war on terrorism." In September of 1901, terrorists struck in Buffalo, New York, then the heart of America's industrial empire. Historian Eric Rauchway says:

"Theodore Roosevelt established a plan for deflecting the hate that inspired such assaults. Even as Roosevelt denounced the evil of terrorism, he used it to invoke the better angels of American nature against the shortcomings of his own society. His methods were influential, though today, they might seem unfamiliar."[5]

The better angels of American nature. God do we need someone like Teddy now. In other words, he saw both sides of the problem. The trouble with Bush: he is one simple-minded son-of-a-bitch. There are lots of good jobs for people who see things in black-and-white, but president isn't one of them. The world is more like a creepy forest with shadows and trolls and weird creatures. Cutting off a head might cause three more to spring into place. Come to think of it, might this not be the idea behind the Hydra of Greek mythology? I want email! Were the Greeks trying to describe a complicated and counter-intuitive world? Survival meaning not just the biggest but the smartest, who can see that a temptation to act is a really a trap? Like a Venus flytrap. Alright, it's knee-deep, I'll shut up. Maybe I've just been watching too much Dragonslayer or whatever that TV show is. My real question is, who does their hair?

...Polis 4:36 PM

Thursday, October 02, 2003

Amazing. Two people in the White House call columnist

---

[4] *Winning Modern Wars: Iraq, Terrorism, and the American Empire,* by General Wesley K. Clark

[5] *Boston Globe,* "The president and the assassin," 9/7/2003

Robert Novak and strip a vital American intelligence network right out of the bottom mud of the war on terror. Prez calling it a "leak." Yea I'll say. The kind that should get you stood against a wall and shot.

Valerie Plame spent 30 years putting the eyes and ears in place that might have intercepted a weapon of mass destruction before it got to us. She was to Al Qaeda what Donnie Brasco was to the mob. Someone who's true identity and allegiance was a deadly secret. If we get hit, Plame is the kind of agent who might have stopped it. There will be blood on the hands of the Bush White House. From David Corn, The Nation:

> **"...a pair of top Bush officials told a reporter the name of a CIA operative who apparently has worked under what's known as "nonofficial cover" and who has had the dicey and difficult mission of tracking parties trying to buy or sell weapons of mass destruction or WMD material."[6]**

There are two kinds of leaks: the kind that embarrass politicians and generals, and the kind that put us in mortal danger. The latter kind is called treason. The Pentagon Papers leak was a big deal because it showed that the generals who were running the Vietnam War were, far from Patton, more like the Three Stooges. Plame was a deep-cover operative actually doing what everyone is talking about these days: making us safer. I.E. winning the war on terror. So when do we hang the guys who gave secrets to our enemies?

Larry Johnson, former counter-terrorism official at the CIA and the State Department, on the McNiel-Lehrer Newshour:

> **"This not an alleged abuse. This is a confirmed abuse. I worked with this woman. She started training with me. She has been under cover for three decades. She is not as Bob Novak suggested a "CIA analyst." Given that, I was a CIA analyst**

---

[6] "A White House Smear," *The Nation*, July 17, 2003.

for 4 years. I was under cover. I could not divulge to my family outside of my wife that I worked for the CIA until I left the Intelligence Agency on Sept. 30, 1989. At that point I could admit it. The fact that she was under cover for three decades and that has been divulged is outrageous. She was put undercover for certain reasons. One, she works in an area where people she works with overseas could be compromised...For these journalists to argue that this is no big deal... and if I hear another Republican operative suggesting that, well, this was just an analyst. Fine. Let them go undercover. Let's put them overseas. Let's out them and see how they like it...I say this as a registered Republican. [7]

It all started when Plame's hubby, former Ambassador Joe Wilson, was sent to Niger to check out reports that Saddam was trying to get uranium for a nuke. Report: negative. Nada. Nothing there. Bush puts it in his State of the Union speech anyway. Wilson writes in New York Times that it's a lie. Wilson on Bush shit list. Somebody in the White House calls Robert Novak, right-wing columnist, to tell him the only reason Wilson got the job of going to Niger was because his wife Valerie Plame is an agent, and pulled some strings.

Here's what Novak wrote in the now-famous column, "Mission to Niger":

> **"Wilson never worked for the CIA, but his wife, Valerie Plame, is an Agency operative on weapons of mass destruction. Two senior administration officials told me Wilson's wife suggested sending him to Niger to investigate the Italian report." [8]**

---

[7] Newshour with Jim Lehrer Transcript, "In The Shadows," September 30, 2003, http://www.pbs.org/newshour/bb/media/july-dec03/leaks_09-30.html

[8] "Mission to Niger," by Robert Novak, July 14, 2003, http://www.townhall.com/columnists/robertnovak/rn20030714.shtml

The idea was to suggest that Wilson wasn't credible, just a well-connected Bush-hater. A Bush-league smear that was hardly worth the safety of the American people, as far as good smears go. Nyah nyah nyah. Joe Wilson is just a nepotistic pooh-pooh head. Doesn't know nothing doesn't know nothing…

From the Boston Globe:

" The political relationships of two key figures in the dispute over whether a Bush administration aide leaked the identity of a CIA operative took center stage yesterday, as members of both parties contended that the case could be tainted by politics. Ambassador Joseph C. Wilson, who said a Bush aide disclosed that his wife is a CIA operative in retaliation for his criticism of the Iraq war, has worked since May as an unpaid adviser to Senator John F. Kerry…" [9]

Doing the Bush: smear, question motives, slime.

Blogger bust! Novak said at first that no one in the administration called him with a leak aimed at embarrassing Wilson. Blogger Josh Marshall heard Novak say on Crossfire:

"Nobody in the Bush administration called me to leak this. In July I was interviewing a senior administration official on Ambassador Wilson's report when he told me the trip was inspired by his wife, a CIA employee working on weapons of mass destruction."[10]

In other words, oops, it just kind of slipped out. Crafty bastards, these. But Marshall compared this to a July 22nd Newsday article where Novak said:

---

[9] In probe of CIA leak, two sides see politics, by Patrick Healy and Wayne Washington, *Boston Globe*, 10/2/2003

[10] http://www.talkingpointsmemo.com/archives/001980.php

"I didn't dig it out, it was given to me. They thought it was significant, they gave me the name and I used it."[11]

Busted. Blogger Dailykos.com brings it on home:

"So Novak is clearly a liar. Either he lied in the Newsday article, or he lied yesterday [on Crossfire"] when he defended the administration. Looking at motives, it's clear that yesterday is the most likely lie as he seeks to provide cover to his Republican buddies." [12]

Ambassador Joe Wilson says he'd like to see Karl Rove "frog-marched out of the White House in handcuffs." Al Qaeda now knows that anyone who was talking to that foxy American woman (Plame *is* foxy) is someone who has to be whacked sooner or later. Who knows what the son-of-a-she-goat might have told her? Best not take chances. If someone in the Roosevelt White House had told the Nazis where the main landing would be on D-Day, would that be called a "leak?" Maybe. But it wouldn't have saved him from the firing squad.

Tid-bit, from the Yale Alumni Magazine: An alum says he has turned his Yale diploma against the wall for as long as Bush is president.

Tuesday, October 07, 2003

Someone I talked to got me thinking. Here's the problem. Suppose the Plame Affair is Bush's one dirty trick too many, he gets impeached, now we're looking at......President Cheney? Blood-curdling scream here! But my friend said we should "Spiro" him. Remember Spiro Agnew? Nobody wanted Nixon, but they sure as heck didn't want Agnew either. So they ran him out of town first, on

---

[11] ibid

[12] "Shutting down wingnut defenses,"
http://www.dailykos.net/archives/004364.html

tax evasion charges. Nixon nominated Michigan congressman Gerald Ford as the next vice president, and Ford became the first vice president chosen under the 25th Amendment. Straight from the Oracle of Google.

Cheney has enough dirt to make Spiro blush. From the Washington Post:

> **"During Cheney's tenure at Halliburton the company did business in all three countries [Iraq, Iran, Libya.] In the case of Iraq, Halliburton legally evaded U.S. sanctions by conducting its oil-service business through foreign subsidiaries that had once been owned by Dresser."** [13]

In other words, while US pilots were getting shot at by Saddam, Dick Cheney and Halliburton were trading with the enemy. That's legal? It's amazing the stuff you come up with when you are just surfing around, and not on any SETI conspiracy websites either. The Austin Journal Star:

> **"Halliburton also had dealings with Iran and Libya, both on the State Department's list of terrorist states. Halliburton's subsidiary Brown & Root, the old Texas construction firm that does much business with the U.S. military, was fined $3.8 million for re-exporting goods to Libya in violation of U.S. sanctions."** [14]

Is there some kind of news black-out going on in this country?

From a flyer in my local coffee shop:

> **"Social Anxiety Group. This group is for**

---

[13]   *Washington Post,* "The Profitable Connections Of Halliburton, by Peter Carlson," February 10, 2004

[14]   *The Austin Journal-Star,* "Cheney's Business Dealings Make Denouncing Saddam Awkward," 9-6-02

individuals, from diverse backgrounds, who experience anxiety in interpersonal and social relationships. Many people with this problem find themselves avoiding situations and are isolated as a result. Some notice that this impairs their ability to perform at work or enjoy friendships and social situations. Often people experience physical symptoms such as panic attacks, and endure extreme distress from the fear of being singled out or recognized."

GODDAMMIT! THAT'S ME!

....Polis 2:34 PM

Thursday, October 09, 2003

Thursday night is a party night yee-haw! They say when you get older you get tired of this stuff. The problem is, I'm not getting tired of it. Big trouble. Well at least all the usual suspects, my buddies, will be out at the neighborhood bars.

> **What would we do without these jerks anyway?**
> **Besides, all our friends are here**
> **Down at the Sunset Grill**
> **Down at the Sunset Grill**
> **-Don Henley**

A paper written for the Army Management Staff College's program, "Sustaining Base Leadership and Management," says:

"HUMINT (human intelligence) reporting is key to winning the fight against terrorism. Without such sources, the Intelligence Community lacks the ability to obtain specific, credible information concerning terrorist operational planning. Without this reporting, the Intelligence Community cannot provide the necessary

34

predictive analysis to prevent the next terrorist strike." [15]

Another post - 9/11 report, "The Intelligence Community's Challenge in the War on Terrorism," agrees that it's not lack of technology, but a lack of human resources abroad and on the ground, HUMINT, that has hamstrung US intelligence efforts in the war on terrorism. [16] Valerie Plame was an intelligence operative in weapons of mass destruction, the *real* front lines in the *real* war on terror. Not a fireworks show like bombing the hell out of Iraq, George's Excellent Adventure. That Army paper says, "a covert HUMINT source faces death if discovered."

The paper pulls in Sun Tzu in "The Art of War":

"What enables the wise commander to strike and conquer, and achieve things beyond the reach of ordinary men, is foreknowledge. Now this foreknowledge cannot be elicited from spirits; it cannot be obtained inductively from experience, nor by any deductive calculation. Knowledge of the enemy's dispositions can only be obtained from other men. The end and aim of spying is knowledge of the enemy; and this knowledge can only be derived, in the first instance, from the double agent. Spies are the most important asset, because on them depends an army's ability to march." [17]

---

[15] "The Intelligence Community's Challenge in the War on Terrorism," by Thomas H. Greene, Writing Contest, Army Management Staff College, Sustaining Base Leadership and Management Program, www.blogstudio.com/Polis/army.htm

[16] In recruiting new intelligence officers after 9/11 the CIA under Bush is guilty of short-sightedness and outright racism, discriminating against the very people we need. Former CIA agent Lindsay Moran says: "a second-generation-American applicant of Middle Eastern descent, someone who might possess the needed language skills and ability to assimilate into societies to which the agency desperately needs access, is inevitably viewed less favorably than a white male candidate from the Midwest." *The New York Times,* "More Spies, Worse Intelligence?" April 12, 2005

[17] Note the words "double agent." This is exactly what Mohammed Naeem Noor Khan waws before the Bush administration announced his secret arrest. See post of August 16, 2004.

35

It all came clear after 9/11. Boston Globe on Sept. 17, 2001:

"The Bush administration, with virtually no good intelligence in Afghanistan, is in the awkward position of relying entirely on foreign governments in the Muslim world for information on the whereabouts of Osama bin Laden."

What will I do for Halloween?

…Polis

Tuesday, October 14, 2003

Required Reading - George Bush Versus U.S. National Security, Sowing the Seeds for Security Disasters, by Edward S. Herman, from October '03 Z Magazine:

"One of the remarkable phenomena in this crazy political environment has been the Republican administration's success in getting President George Bush portrayed as the person who the citizenry can rely on to protect their security interests. This is amazing, given the Bush record and plans. I will argue that he has been a calamitous failure on security issues up to now and that he is busily engaged in sowing the seeds for security disasters in the future. In saying this I am using security in the narrow sense, concerned only with threats of terrorist and military attack....Bush has gotten away with this image of security-savior by stoking fears, stirring up patriotic ardor, manufacturing wars, or rather invasions of small and virtually defenseless countries and strutting about looking very grave, pronouncing momentous words attempting to evoke Churchillian grandeur ("I will not yield; I will not rest; I will not relent in waging this struggle for freedom and security for the American people"), and acting his part in frequent photo-ops that portray the erstwhile draft-

dodger as an active warrior chieftain (his jet-landing in Air Force garb on the USS Abraham Lincoln)...continued, click here, George Bush Versus U.S. National Security."

Edward S. Herman is a professor at the Wharton School and the author of numerous books and articles.

C. makes up another saying: "There may not be a future but there will always be a past." She's on a Dylan kick again, "He not busy being born is busy dying."

...Polis 12:00 PM

Monday, October 20, 2003

I admit it, I'm obsessed with this Constitution-Bill of Rights thing. Is that bad? My alarm went off when Bush starting grabbing American citizens off the street, declaring them "enemy combatant" with no right to a trial and no right to a lawyer. Then saying the war on terror was going to take a long, long time. Oh really. How long? Maybe forever? As long as there's one kid to throw an M-80 firecracker in a mailbox, that might be a terrorist attack. Better be on the safe side and say the war is still on. It might be bigger next time.

Then Howard Dean popped-off and said, one of his many so-called "blunders," that even terrorists deserved a fair trial.[18] The wing-nuts busted their hemorrhoids over that one. A ten-year-old could have asked the question: If they don't get a trial, how do we know they're terrorists? Innocent until proven guilty unless accused of terrorism.

I feel bad for foreigners who got dragged in like oysters by a trawler and sent to Guantanamo to get tortured, to see if they know anything. You go to another country, something bad happens, and you're screwed. No rights, nothing. That's why I stay home. Now you're telling me that could happen to me here too? Careful. We play with guns where I'm from. I will submit myself to a jury of my

---

[18] *Boston Globe,* "Kerry urges N.H. to vote against Dean," 12/28/2003

37

peers for anything, folks, any day, as my rights read. I was born here. Try to haul me to Gitmo and you'll see what's coming. It would be nothing less than my duty as an American to resist. And my good-old-boys back home, they think the same way. We will not go without a fight.

What popped into my mind as I'm reading about Bush's neat-o power grab might seem a little off to you. ENRON. I'm thinking, that kind of power could be handy. Suppose somewhere, there is a scandal ten times worse about to blow. Old ladies died on the street because these people stole their retirement money, and it goes right to the top. The *very* top. And it's one punk junior accountant who's catching on before we can clean the books, asking questions and acting like he's better than everyone else. One of these wise-guys who's going to get us all into trouble. He disappears, and no one can talk to him. See him in the paper and damned if he wasn't going to take a shot at the president, part of a terror plan. Whaddya know. That quiet little guy. That also takes care of anyone else thinking of growing a conscience. Whoa, this is waaay bigger than me. I'm retiring in 5 years. I didn't see a damned thing.

They hold him for a long, long time, the war on terror, you know. And if he ever does get out (can't have him giving secret signals to the enemy, now, can we?) he won't be the same man. Don't you worry about that. Could anything that stinking rotten happen in this country? Naaaw.

You say I don't trust Bush with that power, that I'm a Bush-hater. Wrong. I don't trust *anybody* with that power.

Sir, that, uh, thing is taken care of. That ENRON thing. They're gonna pick him up in 2 hours.

Okay Polis, quit your blabbering, no one's interested in your dumb-ass theories. What have you got for me? Right. On the boss's time I found this and wanted to hook you up with the link, The Gun Owners of America analysis of Patriot Act II, called "The Patriot Act II: Terrorizing the American People." [19] Good report. As part of my

---

[19] http://www.gunowners.org/patriotii.htm

obsession I am also reading Nat Hentoff's "The War on the Bill of Rights." Hentoff writes for The Atlantic, The Nation, The Wall Street Journal and others. Here's a Hentoff clip:

> **"the over-broad terrorism definition [in the Patriot Act sweeps] in people who engage in acts of political protest if those acts [are] dangerous to human life...World Trade Organization protesters have engaged in activities that should subject them to prosecution as terrorists."**

> **"From now on, covert FBI agents can mingle with unsuspecting Americans at churches, mosques, synogogues, meetings of environmentalists, the ACLU, the Gun Owners of America, and Rev. Al Sharpton's presidential campaign headquarters (he has been resoundingly critical on the Bill Of Rights.) These eavesdroppers do not need any specific evidence, not even a previous complaint, that anything illegal is going on or is being contemplated...the FBI is now telling the American people, 'You no longer have to do anything unlawful in order to get that knock on the door.'"**

In case you don't know, "sneak and peek" is in the Orwellianly-named Patriot Act, which allows the cops to enter your home when you aren't there, download your computer files, and take anything they want (your vibrator, your favorite South Park coffee cup, anything). Hentoff says Bush is already planning special detention camps for American citizens accused of terrorism, 'enemy combatants.' No right to an attorney (he or she might spread a SECRET MESSAGE! "My client has a cold" means it's a GO!) Forget the jury, you won't even have the right to be charged with a crime. Is that a minimal expectation or what?

I have an idea for Bush Monopoly. Instead of "go straight to jail" and missing your turn, roll the dice ooooh! you are now "enemy combatant, go straight to Gitmo." Your piece stays in that square until the end of the game. And the next game, and the next game, and the next game... Anytime dad breaks out the board for a game just put your piece in that square and keep it there.

Three states and 190 cities and towns have passed ordinances and resolutions that, among other things, order local law enforcement not to cooperate with feds who are carrying out certain provisions of the Patriot Act, such as search without probable cause (Fourth Amendment.) [20] Rep. Dennis Kucinich and Texas Republican Rep. Ron Paul have introduced the Benjamin Franklin True Patriot Act (HR3171) to repeal the most controversial sections of the Patriot Act. Make sure your congressman or woman is a co-sponsor!

Conservatives such as Texas Republican Dick Armey emerging as key opponents of Patriot II. Hentoff criticizes the media for aiding and abetting Bush by its silence.

Bush never says "war on terrorism" anymore. He says "war on terror." "Terror" is an emotion. It's not over until we're never scared anymore?

Sorry if this is getting a little stream-of-conscious. I do that. Remember that book everyone had to read in junior high? Ray Bradbury's Farenheit 451? The hero, an enemy-of-the-state, is chased down by this mechanical dog, and the whole chase is broadcast as part of the mass entertainment. If you saw a recent Frontline report "Chasing the Sleeper Cell" you saw an American, Kamal Derwish, get zapped in Yemen by a Hellfire missile from a CIA Predator drone aircraft. He was traveling with an alleged "Al Qaeda ringleader." I thought we were supposed to get a trial before the government executes us. Silly me.

Last bit of info found on boss time. Did you know that before the American Revolution the British had a "general search warrant?" It allowed agents of the crown to invade and ransack the homes of colonials at any time, kind of like sneak-and-peek, or a cop going through your trunk and glove compartment just because you were speeding a little. The colonists demanded an end to it, and when it didn't stop the Declaration of Independence was the result. That's how we got the legal doctrine of "a man's home is his castle" and that of "probable cause." Fourth Amendment, Bill of Rights. In other

---

[20] As of print time this is now 4 states and 365 cities, towns, and counties, Bill of Rights Defense Committeee, http://www.bordc.org

words, "sneak-and-peek" is the sort of thing that started the American Revolution.

True story, Democratic power-broker Robert Strauss once advised the Shrub, "Just remember, Mr. President. You can fool some of the people all of the time. Those are the people you need to concentrate on."[21]

....Polis 4:44 PM

Wednesday, October 22, 2003

Latest from the eyes of this cash-strapped, deluded, far too frequently shit-faced blogger. Is anyone out there reading this? This one is personal, Horatio Alger is dead. Study hard, don't party, and the world is your oyster. Not. Just because I squandered a fine Ivy League education doesn't mean everyone would, and I feel somewhat responsible for keeping the door open that was open to me. For real yo. If you have the grades why shouldn't you go to a top-notch private school? *Especially* if your parents aren't rich? The news is, for the first time since WW II it's starting to matter again how much your folks make, when it comes to college. Even if you have the grades. From an old Salon.com article, "Darwinian Admissions":

> **"...many prospective students and their parents have no idea that over the past decade, more selective U.S. colleges and universities have been looking at some applicants' ability to pay as a factor in admission... By employing need-sensitivity in admissions, colleges and universities are supporting a more rigid class structure where the rich get richer and the poor have limited access to education. "Instead of breaking down the implications of birth," says [policy analyst] Thomas Mortenson, "higher education is now reinforcing that.""** [22]

I had a wonderful time going away to college. This country

---

[21] *Boston Globe,* "Bush talk a laughing matter," March 26, 2001.

[22] http://www.salon.com/it/feature/1999/01/18feature.html

boy had his eyes opened, and how. What did I do with it? I thought if you went to Yale it meant you had to run for office. So I did. Five times. And lost all five. No regrets. This town was good to me, but I never had the brains to get a campaign manager. Plus somewhere along the line I got it into my head that I was some kind of writer – poor dad! – The nightmare of hearing your kid say he or she believes he or she was born to be an *artiste,* so you know you are going to be worrying about him or her the rest of your life. Which is always repaid with interest when your own kid tells you that he or she wants to be an actor or film director. Which I will be bound to be supportive and positive about the way dad was positive for me. Why couldn't I have just found diffy-q's – differential equations - fascinating and known I wanted to be an engineer?

NEXT…A nice little item in the Washington Monthly, How to be a Chickenhawk. Starring George Bush, Dick Cheney, John Ashcroft, Tom Delay, Paul Wolfowitz, Richard Perle, and Elliott Abrams, Neocon tough guys, non-Vietnam veterans:

> **"Cheney, who explained that he "had other priorities" at the time, received two draft deferments --one for being a student, and one for being married. In 1965, the government announced a change of policy: Married men would now be drafted, unless they were also fathers. Nine months and two days after that announcement, the Cheneys had their first child." [23]**

The author has a different take on Vietnam draft-dodgers in this article, as he was one of the guys who couldn't or wouldn't go to Canada, get a college deferment, or be one of the lucky dogs who got into the National Guard. These were the draft-resisters, and there's a difference. Resisters went to federal prison in Lompoc, California, for their refusal to work the system. They just said no. Bad things happened to them of the prison sort. You guessed it. The author says:

> **"The anti-Vietnam War liberals and the pseudo-patriotic**

---

[23] "Prisoner's Dilemma," by Robert Poe, *Washington Monthly*, October 2003

Neocons were more alike than different. Both embodied a privileged elite claiming to be paragons of idealism and patriotism, while hiding behind college or medical deferments to avoid putting themselves on the line, either in rice paddies or in prison...with neocon draft dodgers now trying to prove their patriotism at the cost of American lives, that leaves anti-Vietnam War liberals with a lot to answer for." [24]

Still no ideas for Halloween. I'm really in the mood for it this year.

...Polis 8:08 PM

Wednesday, October 29, 2003

One thing I like about living in the city is you may be stressed-out, but you are never bored. Once I saw a woman running down the sidewalk with her sweatpants down around her thighs yelling, "My ass is hot! My ass is hot!" I looked harder and sure enough there were two brown cheeks a' flapping in the wind. This was summer. In case I thought I was only seeing things there was a repeat performance. She came running back the other way, in the same state of attire and with the same urgent message. It's hard to be depressed about things when you can never walk more than three blocks beyond your doorstep and see the latest street drama playing out. There's no room for melancholy when you are standing in a coffee shop line and someone is muttering a monologue behind you along the lines of "I woulda fucked him up I woulda ripped his face off you wanna fuck with me? That means war..."

I guess there was no real point to that. Just thinking.

This stuff about detention camps for American citizens accused of terrorism is bothering me. It sounds too much like conspiracy stuff. Where are the hard quotes, the major sources? Right here. I found them. From the Wall Street Journal (not exactly

---

[24] ibid

a liberal rag.) WSJ August 8, 2002, page A4: "More Terror Suspects May Sit in Limbo--White House Seeks to Expand Indefinite Detentions in Military Brigs, Even for U.S. Citizens":

> **"The Goose Creek, S.C., facility that houses Mr. Padilla -- mostly empty since it was designated in January to hold foreigners captured in the U.S. and facing military tribunals -- now has a special wing that could be used to jail about 20 U.S. citizens if the government were to deem them enemy combatants, a senior administration official said..."**

And from the LA Times, August 14, 2002: "Camps for Citizens: Ashcroft's Hellish Vision":

> **"Ashcroft's plan, disclosed last week but little publicized, would allow him to order the indefinite incarceration of U.S. citizens and summarily strip them of their constitutional rights and access to the courts by declaring them enemy combatants. The proposed camp plan should trigger immediate congressional hearings and reconsideration of Ashcroft's fitness for this important office. Whereas Al Qaeda is a threat to the lives of our citizens, Ashcroft has become a clear and present threat to our liberties..."**

You can't believe everything you read? Exactly. Nat Hentoff ("The War on the Bill of Rights") and other journalists have taken the trouble to ask the White House and the Justice Department to deny it, if it's not true. They haven't. You can call the White House and ask them yourself at 202-456-1414 .

Yesterday Pvt. Algernon Adams, Sgt. Michael Barrera and Spc. Isaac Campoy killed in Iraq, from South Carolina, Texas and Arizona respectively. It goes on and on and on.

...Polis 10:17 AM

Monday, November 03, 2003

44

Sixteen soldiers killed in Iraq, Bush: America Will Not Run? For Halloween settled on a green tee-shirt, a down vest, black winter boots, green pants, and a wildlands firefighter helmut. Which I thought would come close. I signed up to soak down fires in the West when I was broke and out of the job. Not a shameful condition in the Bush economy. I know lots of guys smarter than me in the same boat. Even programmers. It didn't used to be this way.

Met Kris on the corner, and asked him what I was. I thought the vest would look like a flak jacket. When anyone asked me what I was, my line was: I'm a draftee going to Iraq. You're next. Kris said I looked like a construction worker. Wrong. Around here that means you're gay and trying to look like one of Village People. I'm not, and I had no interest in getting hit-on. Cambridge is cool and I have gay friends. But you've gotta know the ropes.

So I made Kris take me all the way home to change. He wasn't too happy about that, but I had beer in the fridge and the party was on the way. Did a hippie thing, love beads, headband. Kind of boring but at least with some lame attempt at a costume you're not totally out of place.

So the draft-dodger has turned this mess he got us into, into a test of everyone's resolve. That's rich. Go in when everyone and his uncle are begging you not to, saying this is a bad idea. Don't do it, George. *Don't do it!* Even James Baker III. Then when it goes sour, say this is a test of America's will. Will to what? Follow a guy who's wrong? Fortunately it just so happens that I did all my homework for a night school class I took last summer. American Foreign Policy with Prof. Jeremy Pressman at the Harvard Extension School. I hear Harvard has some kind of regular day program too. Ha ha. The best benny at this job is they give you a free class there each semester. What the heck. I'm turning out to be the student I never was in college, when women, beer, and all the books in Sterling Library that weren't assigned but that I picked up and read anyway competed with classes for my time. Call me a nerd, I loved that library.

"Crucial throughout the process of Vietnam decision-making was a conviction among many policy-makers: that

Vietnam posed a fundamental test of America's national will." [25]

It's from a famous 1968 Atlantic Monthly article "How Could Vietnam Happen?" by former Kennedy and Johnson State Department analyst James Thompson.

I'm thinking there was a better case for this "resolve" game back then. The Russians did, after all, have thousands of warheads aimed at US cities, right? They had just rolled into Eastern Europe with tanks. A reasonable person might have thought, "well, it's lousy because the commies are taking advantage of real peasant discontent with a corrupt South Vietnamese government, but we can't just let them have all of Southeast Asia, now can we?"

And now? The world's lone superpower. But the Shrub thinks a bad man tried to kill his daddy. Bill Clinton, who I'm no fan of, took a more philosophical approach to this sort of thing. Talking about his executive order which authorized covert operations against bin Laden he said:

"we know at the same time he was training people to kill me. Which was fair enough - I was trying to get him." [26]

Politics is for big boys who don't take things too personal, I guess.

For some reason I'm thinking of that scene from The Shining where Jack Nicholson is pounding away on his typewriter for days on end the same words, all work and no play make Jack a dull boy all work and no play make Jack a dull boy...
...Polis 4:46 PM

Saturday, November 08, 2003
More Patriot Act Abuses. Hey maybe it's just me, but when the government says

---

[25] "How could Vietnam happen?" *The Atlantic Monthly*, April 1968.

[26] *Breakdown*, by Bill Gertz, (Regnery Publishing, 2002)

"The Patriot Act was not meant to be just for terrorism. A lot of the uninformed criticism was obviously misplaced" [27]

that is saying to me: We don't give a damn what you think. Come on, you guys, you can do better than *that*. This is what Justice Department spokesman Mark Corallo said when they got caught using the Patriot Act's powers to prosecute people who had nothing to do with terrorism, in Las Vegas. According to the newspaper:

"Top politicians [were] indicted on multiple counts of accepting hundreds of thousands of dollars in bribes from the owner of local strip clubs in exchange for looser regulations of what strippers can do."

.....Polis 4:41 PM

Monday, November 10, 2003

Wow! Whatever You're Doing, Keep it Up!

The pols are listening to YOU! Today's headlines could have been straight from our website. The Dems are finding some spine re the George Orwell Patriot Act. Al Gore says he wants to "challenge the Bush administration's implicit assumption that we have to give up many of our traditional freedoms in order to be safe from terrorists." Gore even touched on the detention of American citizens as enemy combatants. That's pretty good for old middle-of-the-road Al.

More of our influence: Democratic Candidates Urge More Student Aid in higher education. I may have to file for copyright infringement (see post Wed. Oct. 22.) But that's the whole idea. You and tell them what we want, then they tell it back to us as if it were their own idea. Keep those emails and polis links going to whoever will listen and some that won't. (Are we taking too much credit? Hey if Al Gore can take credit for inventing the Internet...)

---

[27] *Boston Globe*, "Patriot Act gets mixed review in Vegas," Nov. 8, 2003

...Polis 1:46 PM

Wednesday, November 12, 2003

The Draft Dodger is reportedly set to try and make a virtue out of his stupidest blunder, the hare-brained notion of pre-emptive attack. The way the doctrine reads is: we reserve the right to attack preemptively for our security, but only if the enemy is smaller and weaker, does not have a nuke, and you think he tried to kill your daddy. The Bush argument says that Saddam Hussein is an irrational madman on whom the doctrines of containment and Mutual Assured Destruction do not apply. Funny, he was sane enough for us to be buddy-buddy with in the Eighties. Right. That was then. Things change.

The hole in the Bush argument is, if Bush was sure enough he had WMD to start a war, he was sure enough to just have said, Looky, Saddam, if we get hit we'll just assume it came from you, do not pass go do not collect $200, and we'll clobber you, remove about the first 3 feet of topsoil from every square inch of Iraq. Even if he's crazy, the bastard's not suicidal. That's the new doctrine of Mutual Assured Destruction for the war on terr'.

...Polis 3:32 PM

Monday, November 17, 2003

Boy this city sure does something to people. Two months ago this nice Indian or Bangladeshi lady at the Store 24 down my street could barely speak English, was shy and easily flustered, and just now I saw her yelling at some lottery junkie: "I don't have time to hold your hand! I don't have time to hold your hand!" Her English has gotten quite a bit better.

My obsession coming through again. Today the 2nd U.S. Circuit Court of Appeals "considers whether an American suspect can be jailed indefinitely without being charged and cut off from access to lawyers" in the case of Jose Padilla. Padilla is the Shrub's first stab at declaring anyone of us he wants an "enemy combatant," and throwing us into a hole with no trial. For as long as he says we should stay there.

People rise. Remember names like Omaha Beach, and Juno Beach and Pointe du Hoc, where the American fighting man did not hang back once the ramp crashed down but rushed the machine guns of a regime that didn't believe in Constitutions, and we kicked their asses. The beaches ran red and the sand was slippery with guts but we kept coming, because we knew if these people weren't stopped our children would grow up in a world where you could be disappeared off the streets by your own government....Polis 11:18 AM

Tuesday, November 18, 2003

You can skip this post if you want, it's pure drivel. Script treatment, sci-fi movie of how America would lose its freedom. Mood: "Bladerunner" or "Soylent Green." Dark futurism. Giant corporate logos everywhere.

On the day a vital Bill of Rights case is heard in a high court:

CNN November 17, 2003 – "It is the latest legal battle over how far the Bush administration can go in holding [American] suspects as it fights the

war on terror. A three-judge panel of the 2nd U.S. Circuit Court of Appeals will hear two hours of oral arguments starting at 10 a.m." [28]

the leading newspaper in the land runs a movie star as top-of-the-news:

New York Times Nov. 17 — "Arnold Schwarzenegger completed an unlikely odyssey today, taking the oath of office as California's 38th governor after a historic recall election."

The people have bread and circuses. An attack by invisible enemies gives the president powers to detain his political enemies. The president's character comes off as an affable buffoon, but he is actually a studious and talented actor, who understands his appeal and power base. He's about to go to London on a state visit, so on this same day he says, "I've got my tails all set out and ready to go. Had to rent them, but just don't tell anybody." [29]

The scion of an elite Eastern family who has probably owned a closet-full of tuxedos since age 10. But it's Yesirree I got me them fancy duds goin' to London to see the queen, har har, nudge wink. His hayseed-from-the-sticks act is good. America will not run, these colors don't run, get him dead or alive. The president's ear is perfectly tuned to the Southern-Midwestern, good 'ol boy center of electoral college gravity, whose interests he is against, but they like him because he speaks their language. He gets more and more powerful every day, it's only a movie, it's only a movie.

...Polis 2:33 PM

Thursday, November 20, 2003

Why Do they Hate Us - Part ?? - Bush Supports Another

---

[28] http://www.cnn.com/2003/LAW/11/16/padilla.appeal/

[29] www.timesonline.co.uk, "I never dreamt that I would be staying in Buckingham Palace," Nov. 14, 2003

Ruthless Dictator

This guy, Karimov, has received about $600 million from Bush since 2001, has over 6,000 political prisoners, and surely his own mass graves.

From the St. Louis Post-Dispatch, Nov.8, 2003:

"THE BUSH ADMINISTRATION'S sole surviving rationale for invading Iraq is that by removing a brutal dictator who tortured his people, the United States was prosecuting the war on terror.

It turns out that to prosecute the war on terror, the United States has cut a deal with another dictator who tortures his people in a way that Saddam Hussein in all his infamy never imagined: Islam Karimov has people boiled to death.

Mr. Karimov is the neo-Stalinist president of the Republic of Uzbekistan, a place most Americans would be hard-pressed to locate on a map. The former Soviet state is just north of Afghanistan, and Mr. Karimov was only too happy to let the United States stage attacks on Afghanistan from one of his air bases. In return, he got a visit to the White House last March, and 45 minutes of face time with President George W. Bush.

The Uzbek leader took home to Tashkent a five-point "strategic partnership" agreement with the United States, along with $500 million in aid and credit guarantees. As they say in the Missouri Legislature, this was a "hold-your-nose kind of a deal." Mr. Karimov has long been criticized by the State Department for human rights abuses. In the wake of the Sept. 11, 2001, attacks, the urgency was getting into Afghanistan, even if it meant dealing with the devil.

But now the urgency there is over, and there are reports that Mr. Karimov, perhaps emboldened by his new ties

with Washington, is getting worse. Craig Murray, Britain's ambassador to Uzbekistan, presented forensic evidence which he said suggested Mr. Karimov had boiled two dissidents to death.

Mr. Karimov's enemies tend to be Islamic fundamentalists, which gives him common ground with the United States. He also arrests religious and political activists and homosexuals. According to human rights groups, the Uzbek state security service routinely subjects prisoners to gruesome forms of torture. This same state security service also received $79 million in U.S. aid, according to British press reports.

If U.S. foreign policy is to have any credibility in the Muslim world -- indeed in the world at large -- it must be based not on convenience, but on principle. It will be recalled that in the 1980s, the United States made a similar deal of convenience with another Central Asian tyrant. His name was Saddam Hussein."

...Polis 2:41 PM

Tuesday, December 09, 2003

News Blackout in Miami

FTAA conference in Miami last month, (Free Trade Act of the Americas.) Here is what happened in the streets. I love the pictures of the police provocateurs. These are undercover cops who keeps things boiling so they can arrest people, and you can always pick them out because they dress so silly. Don't believe me? Look at the pictures. Tell me these aren't cops. Beefy guys in beanies and tie-dye tee-shirts that no self-respecting anarchist would be caught dead in.

What's an anarchist? Isky says: "They're coool people who

do coool things."[30]

This cops beating peaceful people stuff happens all the time, you just don't see it on the tube. For that you have to go to the Indymedia websites, Indymedia.org. People with cellphone cameras and camcorders feed the action to the websites as it happens. Republican Convention 2000 comes to mind, so does Seattle November 28, 1999, and a 1000-person December 2001 rally for an Amnesty International political prisoner Mumia Abu-Jamal (yes, Martha, Amnesty says there are political prisoners in Amoor'ca.) Like I said, you won't see it on TV.

A talent for lying to rival his brother's. Governor Jeb Bush said:

> **"sincere protesters, who marched to Miami to express their concerns about FTAA, were afforded the respect and protection of the community. Those who engaged in criminal activity were arrested accordingly to secure a safe environment for the majority on both sides of the FTAA debate."**

What is the "FTAA debate?" Heard of NAFTA? FTAA is NAFTA-times-100, for the whole hemisphere. That giant sucking sound of jobs leaving the country, but LOUDER.

Right. The heroes here are the boys and girls who keep shooting pictures and video in the face of tear gas, rubber bullets, and beatings. Fearless patriots, I'd call them.

NOW, YOU DECIDE IF JEB BUSH WAS LYING.[31]
(These images and streamed videos are at www.ralphlopezworld.com)
"...the right of the people peaceably to assemble..."
- First Amendment of the US Constitution

"I may not agree with what you say, but I will defend to

---

[30] Steve Iskovitz, Indymedia.org reporter.
[31] These images and streamed videos are at www.ralphlopezworld.com

the death your right to say it."
- Patrick Henry

Video: Unprovoked pepper spraying.
Video: Cops go wilding
Video: Police use tazer stun gun on peaceful woman
Video: American War Zone
Protesting the unlawful arrests on Thurs, a large group gathered at the Miami jail. Walking backwards chanting 'we are dispersing' the cops surround, tackle and assault a group of unarmed US citizens. Note: this is a 20 MB download, to bad if you don't have broadband, but worth it. This footage is unbelievable.

Photos:
Police Disarm Dangerous Woman Protester in Miami
Steel Workers Lead March
Steel Workers Link with Youthful Activists
Here is an undercover snatch squad.
More shots of the undercovers.
Police infiltrators behind police lines
Wacko Anarchist?
Are we in Bagdhad or America? Armored personnel carriers
Inside the conference: US trade Representative Zollick
That'll learn 'em
A beautiful sight
Police marching into position
Hands
Police fire teargas and rubber bullets into crowd
Police fire paintballs with pepper spray
Nikki praying
Nikki shot in the back
Nikki 2
Nikki 3
Nikki 4
Nikki 5
Protesters man barricades
Woman in red
Helicopters over Miami
Miami Chief of Police Timoney

McCain Blasts Bloated Military Budget

Even Arizona Republican John McCain has had it with the Pentagon piggie. Of the all-time record $401 billion defense budget, McCain said "They are still trying to rip off the taxpayers....Dwight David Eisenhower must be spinning in his grave," referencing Ike's famous warning to "beware the rising power of the military-industrial complex." McCain said "This incestuous relationship between the contractors and the Pentagon and the lawmakers is just the worst."

McCain fingered the *next* $9 billion that will be dumped into the "Star Wars" missile defense scam, and the new generation of fighter aircraft. On Star Wars: "We have poured untold billions into it, and you still have not seen operational capability." Loren B. Thompson of the Lexington Institute in Arlington, Va. said defense companies "don't make a lot of money by going after terrorists. They make money on big ticket items." Now that's comforting.

From a letter in The New Republic, October 27, 2003 issue:

"One reason why the public can stomach casualties in Iraq...: Not every mother's child faces the possibility of being put in harm's way. Since the Selective Service abandoned the military draft, affluent families can concentrate on sending their children to college rather than seeing them put in uniform and marched into danger. The military does not represent the U.S. population as a whole but is heavily peopled with young men and women who come from homes that can't afford the luxury of going to college without the financial help the military provides. If all 18-year-old males were equally subject to a draft, I am skeptical that such a high percentage of Americans would be so cavalier in their acceptance of casualties--and U.S. foreign policy might be more closely aligned with the will of the electorate."

C.K. Blackwell
East Flat Rock, North Carolina

Include politicians' kids and roger that.

...Polis 3:37 PM

Tuesday, December 16, 2003

New York Times: Resistance in Iraq Will Increase

Saddam captured. Whoopee. Col. Ibrahim Mutlak, director of police patrols for Salahadin Province, to a New York Times reporter:

> **"Of course there will be violence, and resistance will increase. Lots of people did not want to join the resistance because they did not want to be called Saddam supporters. But now all the people who oppose the Americans will join."**

This came after two car bombs exploded at police stations in Baghdad on Monday. A police lieutenant said:

> **"Saddam does not have the power to do these things...Last night we saw him in a hole."**

Those dirty Saddam-lovers.

Go Howard Dean!

The Press says that unilateralism can be fine for defeating armies, but not for defeating borderless and invisible enemies. The Press, my night school foreign policy professor Jeremy Pressman. So Howard Dean seems to be the only candidate doing his homework. This week Dean said that to snuff Al Qaeda, we need international intelligence and cooperation. Why do we need pipsqueak countries like France and Germany? Answer: because they have more Arabic-speaking agents in one branch office than we do in our CIA and FBI combined (FBI: 45 full-timers on the day of the attacks. Count' em.

56

45.) [32]

Allow me to pontificate a bit. I know you don't like it R., but I'll keep it short ("drags down the blog" she says.) You cannot force whole-hearted cooperation. For that you need affection. After 9/11 the whole world was ready to jump through hoops of fire to help get the bastards who did it. Barely two years later, Bush has managed to piss-off the whole world with action figure publicity stunts only the Big Time Wrestling crowd could appreciate.

Terrorism is like the Mafia. For every psycho to pull something off, it takes a hundred fairly normal people to look the other way. Until you understand that, you can never beat terrorism. Freeper Neanderthals crack up at these "drain-the-swamp" theories.[33] Another "drain-the-swamp" theory! Social injustice! Boo-Hoo! I guess next we should be blaming ourselves for the attacks instead of killing terrorists! It's okay. Every grunt knows that a fool in your own company will get you killed as dead as an enemy bullet.

...Polis 12:00 AM

---

[32] "Arab experts desperately needed in Iraq," by Patrick Anidjar, *Middle East Online*, http://www.middle-east-online.com/english/?id=7767
[33] FreeRepublic.com, a right-wing website. I hesitate to call it "conservative"; it is more authoritarian, as dissent is often linked to treason.

April 2004 – November 2004

Friday, April 02, 2004

The National Emergency to Defeat George Bush

Disclaimer: this blog has no official connection to the Kerry campaign.

Okay, now we know. The lesson of the Madrid train bombings is that Al Qaeda wants Kerry to win. What I want to know is, what took these Neocons so long? When you finally reach the bottom of the sewer it's not enough to call your opponents sex fiends who prey on women with breast cancer. Hell, another couple of steps and you've got them working for Osama too.

Karl Rove should have worked for Marvel Comics. His villains are *excellent.*

After the bombings the Spaniards kicked-out their pro-Bush president faster than shit goes through a goose. Payback for following Bush into Iraq and bringing this upon them. But when the idea spreads that leaders might be held accountable for the carnage they have caused, that's got to be nipped in the bud. So last month Hoover Institution Cro-Magnon man Josef Joffe was dispatched to the pages of Time Magazine, to 'terpret things for us. A foul, greenish-brown substance smelling vaguely of stale bile dripped from Time, through which Joffe's words could barely be made out:

> **"[Al Qaeda has] scored beyond their wildest expectations. Spain is no longer ruled by a pro-US government..."**

A pro-US government. I guess that would mean pro-Bush. Meaning an anti-US government would be, well that about narrows it down. Better vote for Bush. We don't want to make Al Qaeda's day by voting for Kerry.

Despicable things coming out of these peoples' mouths doesn't surprise me. Not anymore. But turning the truth on its head is still a problem. Let's see, if Al Qaeda is sophisticated, and we always hear how diabolically clever they are, wouldn't they figure that the surest way to elect Bush would be to attack us? Wouldn't that kick-off the "resolve game?" We resolve to stay the course, even if it goes over a cliff. The difference between us and the Spaniards is they *punish* their leaders when they fuck-up. We reward ours, and the bigger the fuck-up, the better.

Resolve in the wrong situation is like pouring oil onto a fire, watching it flare, then trying to put it out with more oil. Like trying to stop a leak in a rubber raft by cutting out the hole.

If you ask me, bin Laden prefers Bush because Bush keeps the fires stoked. Invade a Middle Eastern country, kill lots of civilians. Darwinian selection, turn out lots of battle-hardened fighters who had a talent for nothing until they showed a special talent for killing. Turn them loose in the world, sort of like the Afghan mujahadeen. Remember them?

And so, welcome to the National Emergency to Defeat George Bush website, dedicated to the proposition that, whatever you think of the lame bastard, John Kerry must send Bush packing back to Waco, Texas. Or wherever the hell he's from. Or this country is in a world of shit. If we fail we'll be exposed to the greatest peril we have ever known. It'll be open season on Americans. If we re-elect Bush on this "pre-emptive war" platform, the world will believe, this time, that whatever we get, we deserve.

We're here to give Kerry his lines so he can beat Bush. God knows he needs the help. He doesn't have Howard Dean's gift for the one-liner: Dean said this shouldn't be about "God, guns, and gays." I don't remember, ever, a campaign spreading a rumor like Bush's did in the 2000 South Carolina primary, that John McCain was the father of an illegitimate mixed-race child. Why didn't they just come out with it? Hey ya'll rednecks! Sure and McCain been gettin' him some brown sugar. Yee haa! McCain and his wife Cindy are the adoptive parents of a little girl of Bangladeshi descent, Bridget. It worked. McCain's lead in the South Carolina polls vanished.

I'm mad and I'm scared. Bush's money is on the square that says enough people are dumb and gullible. I'm mad because it's there; and scared because it might work. In the State of the Union address Bush said America does not need "a permission slip to defend itself." Now only because I've done a little sales me-self, I did, I can tell you what that's about.

When you talk to your mark, er, prospect, you get around to popping the question, and Rule Number One is never ask if they *want* to buy, you ask *how many*. It's called the "implied close" (they even have a name for it) and the trick is to snooker the person into agreeing with you. Of course we don't need a permission slip to defend ourselves. While your mind was on "permission slip" you overlooked the word "defend." But was there anything defensive about the attack on Iraq? You just let it slip by and nodded your head, didn't you? Now you're on *his* side. Damn right we don't need a permission slip! The same as a good salesman has got you focused on what color you like best, when a minute ago you weren't even sure you wanted it.

Reading the papers in the Era of Bush is bracing yourself to feel your blood pressure rise. First you read it, then, slowly, you start to see what he is saying between the lines. Then you get madder and madder until you're done or you need a break and put the paper down. Bush makes your newspaper experience akin to feeling like you've been raped.

Last month in Detriot pushing "free trade" to a bunch of auto workers, Bush brought out the twelve-inch brush and tarred a big gooey stroke across anyone agin' him, they were "isolationist." That's it. Me: good. You: bad. Me: free trade. You: isolationist. Me: democracy. You: help Al Qaeda. Listen carefully to the man. He's good. He really is. Progress versus decline. We "move forward." They "retreat." State of the Union: We want to move "forward" into safety, Democrats want to "go back" to the "dangerous illusion that terrorists are not plotting." Unquote. No Democrat said that, but you were nodding your head, weren't you?

Scare, dumb-down, divide, dumb-down, scare, divide, lather, rinse, repeat.

The mere concussion from a bunker buster-bomb, from a half-mile away, can split you like a ripe tomato. Men, women, and children. I remember the first night of George's Excellent Adventure in Iraq, March 20, 2003, because when the first cruise missiles roared off the deck of the USS Abraham Lincoln, a reporter said how the mood of the sailors was "somber." That was his word. They stood on the deck and watched the missiles fly off toward a sleeping Baghdad. I wonder if any of them was silently asking forgiveness. I was.

Saddam was taking pot-shots at our pilots, sure. And we were shooting back, out in the desert. But somehow this didn't feel right.

State Department official:

"You chop off the head of Al Qaeda, and you get six more splinter tails that operate independently." [34]

Military action can be a "deterrent" to another nation's aggressive aims. But if that "deterrence" is perceived as aggression, further aggression will be the result. Night school class again. Reading: Robert Jervis, "Perception and Misconception in International Politics." During WWII no one seriously believed the United States was interested in taking over Europe, so we were a deterrent to Nazi Germany without being a threat to everyone else. In WWI, on the other hand, suspicion and mixed signals led to a world war no one wanted. See Press? "A". [35]

Jervis: the Iraq invasion was "foolish"; Saddam "did not pose a threat beyond the reach of normal statecraft." Americans think themselves "liberators" while Middle Easterners think we just want the oil. Bush says he will not "appease" another Adolf Hitler. Iraqis see another foreign invader and occupier of their homeland.

"Spiral vs. deterrence" playing out exactly as Jervis says it does, and he wrote this book thirty years ago. Bush's perceived aggressiveness is jump-starting nuclear programs in countries that are

---

[34] *Boston Globe*, "Role of possible Al Qaeda 'sleeper cell' probed in train blasts," by Charles M. Sennott, 3/15/2004

[35] Professor Jeremy Pressman, Harvard Extension School.

afraid of being next. The "spiral." North Korea says: "nuclear dismantling is a plot to overthrow the North's socialist system after stripping it of its nuclear deterrent." [36] Libya's Moamar Ghaddafi has given up his nuclear program, but the wiley old colonel is a special case. He never really had one. The Desert Prince still lives in a tent, is adored by his people, and is incorruptible. He gave Bush a badly-needed propaganda victory in return for aid and a lifting of sanctions. Bush got *used* by the Colonel.

From "All the Shah's Men; an American Coup and the Roots of Middle East Terror" by New York Times journalist Stephen Kinzer:

> **"It is not far-fetched to draw a line from [code name] Operation Ajax through the Shah's repressive regime and the Islamic Revolution to the fireballs that engulfed the World Trade Center in New York."**

Operation Ajax, the Original Sin, 1953 CIA overthrow of peaceful, democratic Mohammed Mossadeq in Iran. The CIA has a word for 9/11: blowback.

November '03, spokesman for Iran's Foreign Ministry:

> **"No individual, or group, has ever commissioned Mr. Bush to safeguard their rights...and basically, keeping in mind the dark record of the United States in suppressing the democratic movements around the globe, he is not in a position to talk about such issues."**

Arabic daily:

> **"all true democracies in the world came as a result of internal struggle, not due to foreign intervention,**

---

[36] *Boston Globe*, "N. Korea rejects US demand to dismantle nuclear weapons," March 28, 2004

particularly American." [37]

Multi-colored terror alerts, Rich says tell me something or tell me nothing. Are you out there Rich? Email me!

An Iraqi in Tikrit:

"Iraqis are attacking the Americans now because they have humiliated us. We feel if somebody trespasses in your home, breaks the door and beats the head of the household and cuffs his hands in front of his family, it is the greatest humiliation. It happened to Saddam. If it happened to me, I wouldn't hesistate to go and buy a Kalashnikov and look for an American to kill."

The new James Bond is an American Muslim.

Is the world a safer place because Saddam is deposed? It all depends on what replaces him. I always thought the answer to that was easy. Ariel Sharon killed the leader of Hamas. An Israeli politician who opposed the assassination says "without Sheik Yassin the world is a better place, but it is certainly not a safer place." That's an important distinction. [38]

Bush scares us with "big ticket" attacks like nukes and WMD. But I'm more afraid of lots of smaller attacks that go on forever. Anyone with fertilizer, a few blasting caps, and a heart twisted with hatred can do that. The problem with terrorism is that if someone really wants to hurt you, they'll find a way. Look at Israel.

This website is a come one, come all blog for you to submit your ideas on what John Kerry should be saying. The Kerry folks, who I'm sure aren't above ripping-off uncopyrighted material, can use what they want. That's ok: our reward will be having our country

---

[37] *Boston Globe* , "Middle Eastern governments tell Bush mind own business," 11/7/2003

[38] *Boston Globe*, "Israel pledges to kill more in Hamas," March 24, 2004

back. If we don't help John with his message, he might lose. We can afford that like we can afford a nice two-year lock-up without charges or contact with a lawyer in Guantanamo. We can afford that like we can afford another terrorist attack, courtesy of George Bush's pour-oil-on-the-fire foreign policy. Following Bush into Iraq is not a test of American will. It's a test of how far we will follow a misguided leader.

...Polis 4:47 PM

Thursday, April 08, 2004

Heading home to New Mexico to see the folks, after a prolonged fear of flying. It had nothing to do with 9/11. More like physics. The last time I flew I looked out the window and thought there was something un-natural about a hundred tons of steel hanging in the air. Then it dawned on me: I was riding Prometheus' Fire, stolen from the gods and never meant for man! And the five-square-mile carnage we get when a plane goes down is the occasional payment extracted by the gods! You never know when they'll take it, but they'll take it. There will always be another plane crash, somewhere.

I hear you all thinking. But wait, one more thing. It's just that the thought of dying doesn't bother me, but if you're 20,000 feet up that means you've got a full 7 minutes to have a good long think about what's about to happen to you. That's the part I don't like. Okay now you can say it: here's a dime, Polis, no make that a nickel. Call someone who cares. You can borrow the other nickel.

Saw a good quote: "Life is what gets in the way of blogging."

Ted Kennedy comes out swinging again, says Iraq is "Bush's Vietnam." Colin Powell said Ted should be "a little more restrained and careful in his comments because we are at war." No come-back from Democrats.

Excuse me, Colin, but this here is a United States senator you're talking to, and he can say whatever the hell he wants, don't you

65

threaten us, you asshole. What are you going to do, send us to Guantanamo? I hate to say it, but if I were in a fight I'd rather have Republicans covering my back. They'll jump in when you need them. Dems have a way of looking the other way when the fists start flying, like they don't want to get their St. Laurent suits dirty.

I know this will piss-off liberals, but I'm kind of on the anti-gun-control side of the fence. I think Kerry should split from the gun control do-gooders. Those soccer moms don't know an AK from an armadillo. Outlawing guns isn't the answer, it's sending gun outlaws to jail. Oh God, now you think I'm an NRA nut, but I really think this. Outlawing guns is fuzzy-headed liberals being used by the Trilateralists in a steady drive to disarm a free people.

Scared you didn't I? Well just because I don't believe *that* exactly doesn't mean there is no conspiracy. Remember when it was the Right-wingers who you'd associate with conspiracies, black helicopters and militias and all that? Now it's the right-wing nuts who say "conspiracy" like it's a dirty word. "Illegal plotting." That's the dictionary definition of conspiracy. What a relief to know *that* never happens.

Inside baseball on the gun platform: Kerry opposes gun-maker immunity from victim lawsuits. Bush supports immunity. Kerry should too, and they'll have exactly the same position; there are lots of gun nuts who don't have much use for Bush. Those lawsuits are just a windfall for trial lawyers, anyway.

The liberals won't like this either, but there are lots of things they won't like about Bush winning. There are times to charge and times to fall back. And there are times when you're charging into an ambush. I'm for gay marriage in my state, my question is *why now?* I'll never understand that one. Too many people aren't even making it. You throw a rope to the people drowning before you re-arrange the chairs on the deck. And now I'm shutting up on that before my compromised views get even more of my gay friends mad at me.[39]

---

[39] See www. cheryljacques.org for internal debate within the gay community on political strategy and the timing of the gay marriage issue.

Kerry was a prosecutor. Why doesn't he play that up?[40]

On a roll with unwanted advice. Democratic base voters are already so ballistic with Bush they would show up to vote for Donald Duck. They don't much like Kerry, but Bush waves a red flag. The battle is over NASCAR dads who think gay marriage is kind of silly, but their job just moved to China and they don't know for the life of them how they're going to pay the mortgage or help the kids with college. A Kerry College Opportunity Act that guarantees every American student the financing to attend any college for which he or she is qualified and admitted to. Think big!

Where to get the money? Star Wars. Even McCain hates it. Kerry can say if he's "weak on defense" because of he doesn't like Star Wars, so is McCain. Let Bush explain that one.

Bush keeps handing Kerry beauties. Cut out time-and-a-half for overtime? How beautiful can it get? Kerry stands at the plate and lets these slow dream pitches float by without swinging. Now I know what these out-of-control Little League dads must feel like.

Howard Stern gets booted by Clear Channel. Stern comes back from vacation reading Al Franken's book "Lies and the Lying Liars Who Tell Them" and goes from being pro-Bush to against him. When he talks politics Stern is everything he isn't the rest of the time: factual and well-spoken. Trouble for Bush. Stern reaches the hard-to-get, prized demographic of 18-34 year-old white male meat-heads. You'd have to spend millions in Playboy advertisements to get the same kind of coverage.

A nice, simple platform:

-stop paying companies to move jobs overseas

---

[40] Note: In that Fall's hunting season Kerry did make hunting trips to show he was not knee-jerk against guns, but they were met with ridicule from the Right, which believed a "cowboy" from Andover and Yale. My advice was simple: challenge Bush to a friendly shooting match. It's well-known that Kerry is not just a good shot, but a dead-eye.

-I like the FREE MARKET; I WISH WE HAD ONE! cut-off corporate welfare bums with their grubby hands stretched out to the American taxpayer, timber mining agribusiness telecommunications Halliburton[41]

-train American workers

-Kerry College Opportunity Act

-whatever happened to 10 million new jobs? That was good, haven't heard it in a while. Kerry's message jumps around like a kid with Attention Deficit Disorder. We could fix bridges, build schools, hire teachers, build light MAGLEV rail, in other words sweet union jobs with OT and good bennies. Build the new wind-solar-geothermal energy infrastructure.

MORE BRIGHT I-GODDAMN-DEAS FOR KERRY:

-"Put Kevlar on soldiers' backs, not pork in defense contractors' pockets."

-Unveil a "soldier's defense budget" from someone who has actually taken live fire.

The troops have a name for it now, BYOB - Bring Your Own Bulletproofs. Nice graphic in June 23, 2003 Time Magazine shows a soldier's wish-list (CamelBak hydration system, GoLite undergarments, Magellan Global Positioning System...)

DOOH! DON'T LISTEN TO JESSE!

An article says Jesse Jackson urged Kerry to talk more about "education, housing, healthcare, poverty, and voting rights," the mantra centrist Democrats use to condescend to minorities when they want their votes. BORING! Take care of American workers and the rest falls into place. You can *afford* a house. You can *afford*

---

[41] For more on the real welfare queens see
http://www.progress.org/banneker/cw.html

healthcare. You *have time* to help the kids with their homework…

And as long as I'm showing my egomania for being in charge and having all the answers - so why can't he pay his rent? - you're asking. Fair enough, we bullshit artists are craven whores for anyone who'll by them another drink. Plenty of talk and no damned money. But as long as I'm at it, I may as well tell you my foreign policy if I were prezdent, which isn't so brilliant except maybe the way 2 and 2 equals 4.

Since if there were no enemies we'd need aliens to invade, to unite us and keep us from killing-off each other, why don't we just pretend the aliens are global warming, child prostitution, and population growth? Here's the new foreign policy if I were prez, on top of defeating Al Qaeda: No onboard with global warming, child sex slavery, and ZPG, Zero Population Growth, no tradey with US. Simple. No ticky no shirty. Make ZPG the new race to the moon. With ZPG everything else falls into place. Less people, less pollution, less of all the other problems. No rocket science there.

Ok, taking my pills now. All better.

What nice people these Bushies are. An historical airplane hobbyist digs an abandoned WWII Corsair out of a swamp where it crashed in North Carolina 60 years ago, and after months of "painstaking restoration," gets sued by Ashcroft's Justice Department. The airplane guy admits to being shaken and says: "I'm just a little guy. I have no wealth, work for a living, have four kids."[42]

John Dean, formerly of the Nixon White House dirty tricks department, says:

"I've been watching all the elements fall into place for two possible political catastrophes, one that will take the air out of the Bush-Cheney balloon, and the other, far more disquieting, that will take the air out of democracy."

---

[42] *Boston Globe*, "Navy sues man for plane he recovered in swamp," 3/28/2004

What does it say when a guy who worked for Nixon says Bush plays too dirty?

Please Teddy! Fade from the Pictures!

Unable to resist the spotlight a few doors down, Ted Kennedy keeps poking his head into Kerry's photo-ops, draping his big hairy paw across the junior senator's shoulders, jostling and grab-assing. Plus he knows that's where all the women are. The Repugs die for joy at every picture of them together.

Okay, someone has to say it: since Kerry is in the fight of his life to avoid being tarred as a Massachusetts liberal, you should fade from the pictures, Ted. Pretty please. He's a big boy now. Anyway, the White House is going to use that famous picture of you and George together, Bush signing the No Child Left Behind Act, that was never funded. So George can show voters he works in a bipartisan manner. You got used like a Senate intern in the private bathroom of your office. If you want to do some good, say 100 Hail Marys for challenging Jimmy Carter, your party's sitting president, for the nomination in 1980. That stunt probably weakened Carter just enough to make Reagan look good, and brought this right-wing scourge upon us.

White House: brilliant spin control on the 9/11 Commission. It has everyone focused on the April 6th memo, which doesn't say much.   But it has the words "explosives" and "hijackings." Goddammit don't you see what they're doing? This steers it away from the *real* story, whether the White House had information on terrorists using planes as missiles against targets like the WTC. Rove does it again. The administration will come out of this just fine, because Americans will forgive a failure to predict the unpredictable. Problem is, it *was* predicted. Blogger bust. Dug this up from the San Francisco Chronicle:

" Democratic commission member Richard Ben-Veniste disclosed this week that Rice had asked, in her private meetings with the commission, to revise a statement she made publicly that "I don't think anybody could have predicted that those people could have taken an airplane

and slam it into the World Trade Center ... that they would try to use an airplane as a missile."

Rice said she had "misspoken." Actually, she was repeating a lie she told last May:

> "I don't think anybody could have predicted that these people would take an airplane and slam it into the World Trade Center, take another one and slam it into the Pentagon; that they would try to use an airplane as a missile, a hijacked airplane as a missile,"

Lies. But what sticks in peoples' minds is what she said on TV, not what she retracted in private. The Bushies are happy to be arguing about the April 6 memo rather than how predictable was planes-as-missiles.

Sibel Edmund's testimony (when do we hear this on the news?) From the Toronto Star:

> "Edmonds, a Turkish-born U.S. citizen, said she was "appalled" by Rice's public statements, delivered in a number of television interviews, that there was no information indicating planes would be used on domestic targets. Had Rice indicated that she did not know, Edmonds may have given her the benefit of the doubt. "Then I would say maybe the FBI did not take the information to her, maybe she didn't know," Edmonds said. "But she's is saying `we' did not know, including herself, her advisers and the FBI. That statement is not accurate. I've never really been diplomatic in life. It's a lie and a lie is a lie." [43]

Sure let's talk flip-flops. In Feb. 2001 Colin Powell said of

---

[43] *Toronto Star,* "Ex-FBI worker challenges 9/11 'lie'," April 5, 2004.

Saddam Hussein "Frankly, the sanctions have worked. Saddam has not deployed any significant capability with respect to weapons of mass destruction. He is unable to project conventional power against his neighbors." Kind of opposite of what he said in front of the UN. Colin you sly devil...

More of Democrats playing dead; hey you Dems good stuff over here! Lookit Lookit!

From Craig Unger's book, "The House of Bush, The House of Saud":

- 50 recommendations made by the Gary Hart-Warren Rudman commission early in 2001 to address terrorism and Hart's words: "Frankly, the White House shut it down."

- How's this for "actionable" intelligence? In 2000 Richard Clarke urged attacking bin Laden and Al Qaeda camps with unmanned Predator drone aircraft. That and other plans never got anywhere for lack of interest and funding. But as late as Sept. 9, 2001 Donald Rumsfeld was on Capitol Hill threatening a veto of a $600 million diversion from star wars to counterterrorism.

Threatening to veto $600 million if it went to terrorism instead of corporate pork? Do you know what would be happening to Bill Clinton right now if it had been him? A videotaped crucifixion at Shea Stadium.

Trivia: On the record, George Bush to a Hartford Courant reporter at the 1988 Republican Convention:

"Reporter: What do you and your dad talk about when you are not talking politics?

Bush: Pussy." [44]

---

[44] "A Major League Asshole, In an embarrassing gaffe, George W. Bush insults a New York Times reporter," Salon.com, http://archive.salon.com/politics/feature/2000/09/04/cuss_word/

Tuesday, April 13, 2004

Got Mike Dukakis' email now too. It said in the paper that he works at Northeastern University. That's the guy who lost to Big Bush in '88. Anyone remember?

Kerry groping toward some kind of stance on the college thing, but he still can't hit the sweet spot. You know that sound when the ball comes flying off the racket or the bat with a nice dry POP that tells you you've nailed it? Kerry never makes that sound, always a *tink* or a plinky scrape somewhere. Don't whine about rising tuitions, *attack the very demise of the American Dream!* If you can't go to any college for which you have made the cut, what *can* you do in this damned country? [45] You want to talk about opportunity? Which the Neocons blather about like it's the Holy Grail? This is it! Don't do drugs, finish school, be Mr. or Miss Goody Two Shoes Good Grades and then...go to State. You can't afford anything else. Sucker.

President warns that comparing Iraq to Vietnam is "sending the wrong message to our troops and to the enemy." When it gets hot he can't stand on his own, drags in the troops and calls the other guy a traitor. First he uses the troops to settle his personal scores, then to give himself an aircraft carrier photo-op, and now to shut people up who are giving him a hard time. To borrow a pithy quote from Full Metal Jacket, this is the kind of guy who would f-- a guy in the a-- without even the goddamn common courtesy of giving him a reach-around.

...Polis 10:15 PM

Wednesday, April 14, 2004

Fallen Heroes Families Speak Out

Last Tuesday night the president said we should "honor our

---

[45] "Darwinian Admissions,"
http://www.salon.com/it/feature/1999/01/18feature.html

fallen heroes by finishing the job." Following, the families of some fallen heroes speak out;

FROM:
http://www.bringthemhomenow.org/sound/letters/040302_02_pritcha rd.html

March 2, 2004
Mr. Bush:

I am an aunt of William Ramirez, the Army private killed Wednesday by a bomb in Iraq. I have never supported you or your war. War never has and never will make peace. War kills kids like my nephew. Oregon has one of the worst economies in the union and, not coincidentally, the highest per capita rate of enlistment.

William was a high school dropout; obviously he must have been a child that missed your "No Child Left Behind" policy. The Army lured him with visions of a bright future, lured him to a year of misery fighting for a cause you are still trying to come up with and ultimately to his horrific death by incendiary bomb. His mother holds tight to her belief that he died for our freedom only because she knows she could not live with the truth.

I want answers.

I want to know why you lied, or chose to not investigate your intelligence sources about the information that you claim as the reason for beginning this war. I want to know why no one in congress or any of your affluent supporters have children fighting and dying in this war. I want to know why you joined the National Guard to avoid being sent to Vietnam and yet now, as

commander-in-chief, you feel free to order the National Guard to leave our country and fight on foreign soil. I want to know why you chose to disregard the input of our allies and the United Nations, creating enemies and bad feelings when we need all the help we can get. I want to know where you found a link between the 9-11 attacks and Iraq that no one else had uncovered.

Most of all, I want to know how much longer our soldiers and the Iraqi people are going to have to endure the hell you have created and how many more children are going to come home in unrecognizable pieces before you decide it's over. You owe me and America answers and I am going to do everything in my power from now until election day to see that you are forced to come up with some.

> **Annette Pritchard**
> **Oregon City, Oregon**

FROM: http://www.mfso.org/
On November 2nd, 2003, Brian Slavenas and 15 others were killed when the Chinook helicopter he was flying crashed in Iraq. Rosemarie Dietz Slavenas, Brian's mother, wrote this letter to President Bush:

> **February 2, 2004**
> **Rockford, Illinois**
>
> **George Bush**
> **1600 Pennsylvania Avenue**
> **Washington, D.C. 20502-4259**
>
> **Dear Mr. Bush,**
>
> **In response to head weapons inspector David Kay's statement that he believes there are and were no weapons of mass destruction in Iraq**

(Associated Press), you are quoted as saying, "There is no doubt in my mind that Saddam Hussein was a grave and gathering threat to America and the world is better off without him."

My beloved son Brian died for your red herring in the sand. He was an honorable, restrained, talented, caring man, and the world would be better off with him alive and well. He resigned his commission in the Illinois National Guard when assigned to duty in Iraq as a matter of conscience. He served nonetheless, and he bled for 1/2 hour in the desert sand before any help arrived, though the helicopter he was flying was only 5 minutes off the ground when it crashed, according to witnesses.

After his death, I received two letters from him telling me he hoped to be home in April, 2004. On Christmas day I visited his grave. He did not give his life. It was cruelly taken from him by your rush to war -- against the United Nations, old allies like France and Germany, western religions' "Just War Doctrine," the entire Arab world, and most civilized nations.

You inherited peace and prosperity and created murder, mayhem, and massive debt. According to the ongoing investigation of the helicopter crash that took Brian's and 15 other American lives, the Illinois National Guard aircraft were sent into the field without basic survivability equipment, to accommodate your "shoot and bomb first, think and investigate later" brand of foreign policy. We don't need a trigger happy president.

Finders keepers, losers weepers. While we who have lost our loved ones have only tears to fill the empty space where love and laughter lived, you and your Halliburton cronies have found the oil wells and will undoubtedly keep your blood stained gains. Our sorrow, your gain. Brian was conscientious; someone wasn't. Brian was faithful; someone wasn't. Brian was thoughtful; someone wasn't. Brian was considerate; someone wasn't. Brian was truthful; someone isn't. Brian wasn't sloppy. Someone is.

Sincerely,
Rosemarie Dietz Slavenas

FROM: http://www.bringthemhomenow.org/sound/main.html

April 5, 2004

I almost wish the draft were reinstated at this point, to wake up the US public. Not much else seems to be waking them up, the press is gagged by the White House, and my husband cries all day, sometimes collapses when he sees the newest round of civil war engulfing the country. I can proudly say I marched against this war 3 times in DC and was always in opposition of it, as was my husband. They still took his son, my stepson, to hell, and when we don't hear from him for more then a day by email, we lose our minds. He has been in Baghdad since February, and he will be there for a year. God help us, we can barely get thru the day now. We try to get by one day at a time, but we can barely get thru one day.

May God damn all of the politicians, media, and bastards who forced this bloodbath on us, on our child Michael who is only 21 and just a scared kid who joined the reserves to help his country, and may God damn Bush, Cheney, and all the other bastards who took Michael away from us for their lies.

**Mrs. Marianne Brown
Michigan**

Polis 7:01 PM

Saturday, April 17, 2004

Just as he starts to say something the Republican moles inside the K. campaign yank his leash. Last week he promised free college to all American students in return for two years of national service – what we've been saying - but now he takes it back.

> **"Some education advocates got a rude shock last Wednesday when they logged onto JohnKerry.com: The candidate's much-touted plan to provide free college tuition to those who commit to two years of national service had been wiped off the screen, replaced with a scaled-down version. Gene B. Sperling, the former Clinton economic chief who coauthored Kerry's plan to reduce the deficit, helped press the delete key." [46]**

The centrists won no no that's a budget buster. But it's only a budget buster if it helps anyone besides their corporate clients. Why isn't Star Wars a budget buster, or the S&L bail-out?

Oh right, that sounds "lefty." Funny how that pops up whenever the Democratic lawyer-lobbyists see that starter-castle slipping away. We owe it all to old Bill, old Bubba Clinton, who came up with the playbook. Pull the wheel hard to the right on big business while fish-tailing left on the social things, nail down the suburban soccer mom vote with one eye on the polls and the other on the blond in the front row. A tricky maneuver. And who will everyone else vote for? Fuck 'em, they're not trying to get the hell out of Arkansas. In a style befitting a man of ma' talents, of course.

---

[46] *Boston Globe*, "Deficit reduction takes priority in Kerry campaign," April 17, 2004

Kerry not defining himself. Now it's guaranteed that Karl Rove will do it for him. I may have to shut my eyes. This could get gruesome.

IN THE NEWS Wing-nuts trying to spin that the '70s hearings on the CIA have hurt the war on terror, because we can't assassinate anyone we want anymore. Baloney. The problem is we were assassinating the wrong people, the Che Guevaras of the world instead of the Pinochets.

...Polis 6:59 PM

Monday, April 19, 2004

Illigitemum non carborundum. Latin, translation, Don't let the bastards wear you down.

Memo to Kerry: An Imaginary Interview With John Kerry, With say, Tim Russert. I made this up.

Russert: Senator, in light of 9/11, could you tell us why electing you would keep us safer than the re-electing president Bush?

Kerry: President Bush did a fine job in the weeks after 9/11 and in the war against Afghanistan. I applaud him for it. But by invading Iraq, the president committed a grievous error. Yes I voted for the resolution, but that was based on a couple of contingencies that were not met. The president was to certify that Iraq had WMD and that it had ties to international terrorism. The resolution was to be null in the absence of these. To put it simply, we were duped.

I keep hearing the president say we Democrats want to 'revert to a law enforcement approach' to terrorism. But terrorism is not a law enforcement problem. Nor is it only a military one. Terrorism is an international intelligence problem, the who-are-they, what-are-they-doing, and where-do-they-live kind of stuff. And international intelligence requires wholehearted cooperation, and that requires full-court-press diplomacy. You've got to convince other governments to

79

risk the lives of their best people. Finding and infiltrating cells of stone cold killers. It's called HUMINT in the intelligence business, Human Intelligence resources. Unless you know where they are, you don't know where to send the Predator drones, for example, to try and kill them, or where to round them up in international police raids. Or how to follow them so they lead you to more terrorists.

I plan to make us safer by putting my political capital into HUMINT, not wars that lash out blindly. When you lash out without good intel you hurt a lot of people, and wind up creating more enemies than you started out with. That's what terrorists thrive on, this cycle of violence. You want to put a fire out, you use water, not oil.

Russert: You sound like you're talking about James Bond.

Kerry: I am talking about James Bond. The new James Bond is an American Muslim, our most lethal secret weapon. We must develop our intelligence resources to match the depth and breadth of other countries'. These are 5, 10 and 20 year jobs.

Russert: Now we know Saddam Hussein had rape rooms, tortured children, really nasty stuff. Regardless of WMD, isn't the world better off without him?

Kerry: Better off and safer are two different things. Of course the world is a better place. But whether it's a safer place depends on what comes after. This war has no end in sight.[47]

Russert: When?

---

[47] The idea of trading tyranny for chaos as a response to "he would have left Saddam in his palaces" is central to why Kerry lost. It was not until Sept. 20 that he staked out this ground, far too late for it to sink into the American consciousness. This left Kerry holding the "He's against freedom" bag for most of the election season. When Kerry did finally offer a rebuttal he said: "Saddam Hussein was a brutal dictator who deserves his own special place in hell. But that was not, in itself, a reason to go to war. The satisfaction we take in his downfall does not hide this fact: We have traded a dictator for a chaos that has left America less secure." *Houston Chronicle,* "Kerry: We traded dictator for chaos," Sept. 21, 2004.

Kerry: As soon as the logistics can be set up. We should engage all factions to enforce a cease-fire while elections take place, and say to them, as soon as you guys have got it together, we're out of here. We pull back divisions to the borders, Kuwait and Saudi Arabia, and keep troops confined to bases ready to restore order if they have to. With a truly international coalition. No more patrols to show we own the place, which is like running around with a target on your back.

What we really have to do, Tim, is think outside the box, both in the war on terror and in Iraq, which keep in mind, are two different things. By going into Iraq we have united factions which hate each other, against us. That doesn't make us safer.

I'm going to be the president who thinks outside the box of the quagmire game, which there has never been a good way out of. Once you're in, you start to say now we have to stay in for reasons of national pride, until people hardly even remember how it got started. That's what got 58,000 guys killed in Vietnam, and it's not going to happen on my watch.

And From a Real Interview, Ralph Nader with Wolf Blitzer

BLITZER: Because four years ago, you suggested, when you were running with Gore and Bush the last time around, that there wasn't a whole lot of difference between Gore and Bush. You do believe there's a lot of difference between John Kerry and President Bush?

NADER: Not as much as I would like, but yes, of course, there's a difference. I mean, Bush is just such a messianic militarist. He's a big business toadie. He has cut taxes for the wealthy and created a massive deficit that's infuriating conservatives in his own ranks, along with big brother Patriot Act, and subsidies to big business, and the sovereignty-shredding effect of WTO and NAFTA. All of this is breeding a fury among

**conservative voters. And if the Democrats were
smart, they would try to appeal.** [48]

True fact: Colin Powell once called the Bush gang a bunch of
"fucking crazies."[49]

....Polis 7:03 PM

Thursday, April 22, 2004

Kerry adviser Michael Meehan: "We've known all along this
will be a neck-and-neck race."[50] Excuse me but can I ask a question?
Why? Big players turning against George left and right, news not
good from the Excellent Adventure in Iraq. Seems to me that his only
hope for staying even with Kerry is, well, Kerry.

Last Tuesday in Tampa Kerry told people he'd be better on
the environment than George Bush (duh.) [51] Bush was in a huge
swing state, Pennsylvania, 23 electoral votes, with a banner
"Protecting the Homeland" as big as a barn behind him. In case
anyone missed the point he flanked himself with a dozen cops at
parade rest on the stage.

Meanwhile Kerry flubs his soundbite on the Patriot Act to
some parts are ok, we'd submit our own version that was even
stronger in some places without violating civil liberties or something
or other - ugh. Bush hammered home his claim to have already foiled
acts of terror.

Sure, by stripping-out Valerie Plame's WMD intelligence

---

[48] CNN LATE EDITION WITH WOLF BLITZER, Aired April 18, 2004
[49] *The Observer,* "Colin Powell in four-letter neo-con 'crazies' row,"
September 12, 2004
[50] *Boston Globe,* "Bush team confident in steady poll results," April 21,
2004
[51] "Kerry blasts Bush on environmental laws," Associated Press, April 20,
2004.

networks?

Republican James Sessenbrenner: the Patriot Act will be extended "over my dead body." With covering fire like that Kerry still gets blown out of the water?

The scoop on the Patriot Act according to my best lights is you could keep a couple of parts about roving wiretaps and letting the CIA and FBI share information, and shit-can the rest, and you wouldn't miss a thing. Except being able to bypass those pesky warrant judges to *just do it! Flip the switch!* Find out what that major league asshole reporter is saying about you across town, and fix his little red wagon when you catch him cheatin' on his wife.[52] Hey, why don't we put his little cutie on the no-fly list? Just for laughs? Wait till he finds out he ain't gettin' any this weekend! You saw how mad Ted Kennedy got when we put *him* on the list...[53]

The Bush war room has the fastest fax machines in the West. Why doesn't Kerry's war room blizzard-fax Leon Sigal's op-ed "How Not to Disarm Korea?"[54]

Arrgh!

Republican insider John Dean says that the Iraq War Resolution came with conditions that were never met: the president's certification of the presence of WMD, and a link to Al Qaeda. When the time for certification came, in a move that blows away even former Nixon dirty trickster Dean, Bush:

"relied on information the White House provided Congress for its draft resolution; then turned

---

[52] At a speech in September 2000 Bush gaffed with the microphone still on and was overheard saying to Dick Cheney that Adam Clymer of the New York Times, in the audience, was a "major league asshole." Cheney was heard saying "Yea, big time."

[53] Kennedy was on the no-fly list for some weeks in 2004, and had trouble getting himself off. This is a US senator; how would the ordinary person fare?

[54] *Boston Globe,* April 17, 2004

83

around and claimed that this information (his information) came from Congress."

Dean says it was like "a dog chasing its tail."

Bush advance men send people in Flipper dolphin costumes to Kerry rallies, the flip-flop thing, especially the 'first he was for the war now he's against it.' Shouldn't John Dean's accusations be making headlines?

John Dean (and I still say he was Deep Throat, it's those shy-looking preppies you've got to watch) says that Bush's lies about WMD and about Iraq's ties to Al Qaeda constitute an "impeachable offense." Dean is staggered that Bush gets away with things his old boss Nixon would have been impeached for many times, never mind Clinton. He says blowing the cover off Valerie Plame is worse than Nixon's persecution of his enemies list "because it was immediately life-threatening and damaging to the national security."

Bob Woodward's "Plan of Attack" shows a Bush who fusses about getting across to "Joe Public." In December 2001 after a presentation on whether Saddam had WMD Bush says "Nice try, but that isn't gonna sell Joe Public. That isn't gonna convince Joe Public."

If Kerry just read random passages from these books out loud instead of his boring speeches, he'd be doing better.

More?

Former FBI Acting Director Thomas Pickard told the 9/11 Commission that after two briefings on terrorism, Ashcroft said he "did not want to hear this information anymore." Ashcroft, under oath, has denied saying this. No further investigation. One man or the other is lying. It's seems kind of important. [55]

Even Bill Buckley's National Review is turning on Bush, says the administration has "a dismaying capacity to believe its own public

---

[55] *Washington Post*, "Ashcroft Says He Backed Anti-Terror Efforts," April 13, 2004

84

relations." Bush has "an underestimation of the difficulty of implanting democracy on alien soil, and an over-estimation...of the sophistication of what is still fundamentally a tribal society."

Why the hell should this be neck-and-neck?

Republican Representative John Duncan of Tennessee: We should seek an exit soon:

> **"I think we should announce to the world that no country has come close to doing as much for Iraq as we have, but there are a significant number of people who don't appreciate what we have done...we should get on out, we should celebrate victory and we should leave."**

In his press conference last week Bush called Democrats racist again. Apropos to nothing, Bush suddenly launched a tirade against "those" who think Middle Easterners are not ready for freedom. "Is it because their skin is brown?...I don't accept that."

"Those?" Who's "those?" Who said anything about their skin? The worst is that the Democrats don't even make Bush say thank you for the stroke.

...Polis 9:24 PM

Saturday, April 24, 2004

Friendly Coaching for Kerry on Ads

Kerry made an ad called "Risk." Message - weak to medium, Kerry says we should share the burden in Iraq by reaching out to the UN. Not a barn-burner. Bush replies maybe Kerry "doesn't read the papers." If I voted based on who's funnier I'd definitely vote for Bush. Everyone knows the UN wants nothing to do with this debacle. Remember "freedom fries?" Kerry doesn't look at the camera. Dull interview format. Bush ads always have him firing up large audiences. Kerry blinks too much. Body language experts say

85

blinking looks like you're lying. Needs to achieve a comfort level with the camera. Better one-on-one. I'll send you guys my bill.

Been (ouch!) thinking again. Write me. Seems like some people live according to what they can get away with, and make up the rules as they go along, then you have those who believe the rules exist for a reason. Who try to apply some kind of watered-down ethics to their living, not much, but a little. Hell, I'm not saying I'm Jesus f-ing Christ, but some people actually get bothered by little things, and others never give them a thought from the day they are born. And these two main factions have been warring since the beginning of mankind, and who will win is still far from clear.

Polis 11:16 PM

Tuesday, April 27, 2004

Tonight we're out looking for Young Republican Junior Gestapo-types to beat up. The kind of pencil-neck geeks who might have been Karl Rove or Paul Wolfowitz 40 years ago. Smart, educated, and free of all qualms over whether their actions could ever get people hurt. Send the poor boys to get their guts blown all over the place. Someone has to stay here to run the show, Biffster. Plus this is where all the liquor, cars, and white women are.

The idea is to flush them out at some college bar by talking real loud about what an asshole Bush is. Then one will break cover, look at you and say "FOUR MORE YEARS!" Now you see him and you can lock-on. We beat them black-and-blue, focusing on the kidney area where he'll feel it for weeks. Let it serve for the beating he'll never take in the jungle or the desert. It's also important to have them ID'ed. These will be the ones who'll call the Gestapo to tell them you're home so they can drag you off to Guantanamo in the middle of the night. For holding an anti-Bush sign at a Bush speech.

This is what my homies do for fun. Some of it is true. We do talk loud in bars.

My little corner of the world, Central Square, is a mix of

86

cheesy bargain shops, a few yuppie stores getting a foothold, lots of ethnic restaurants, Korean, Indian, Ethiopian, Greek, Irish – Irish? – those are where you drink your lunch. It's great fun and everything you need to survive is in Central Square, a Walgreens, food market, a Blockbuster, and quite a few rowdy clubs.

And on Mass Ave. in front of the insurance agency is a tree that you'll see flowers tied to now and then. And a bicycle helmet. That's where Dana died. I still think about it though I never knew her. One day I happened across the street taped-off with police tape, both lanes, and what stands out is how quiet it was, with hundreds of people standing along the edge of the tape in a big circle. Everything was said in whispers, like in a church, and the cops and firemen where going about their business very quietly. Someone told me a bicyclist had gotten doored there a short while ago. She flew into a bus. By the nature of her injuries it's certain she was killed instantly. She 36. It was a beautiful summer day.

They had already taken her away, but I briefly saw the man who had inadvertently opened the car door that she hit, and a man standing next to me told me the man had been crying. That's a detail I can offer to Dana's family. And also my sense that everyone, hundreds of people, had the family in their thoughts, knowing that at any time they were going to get the news if they hadn't already. This was no cold city street your daughter died on that day, Mr. and Mrs. Laird. I was there, and you could feel the love and the reverence, in a big circle around the spot, after they had taken her, and after the accident scene had been cleared of all traffic. There was something holy in the air. I didn't think a city street could quiet down and be so somber. But it did. No one walked away unaffected that afternoon.

I didn't think I was going to write all that. I'm glad I did. When you talk about what is our community here in Central Square you can't not talk about Dana. She belongs to us too now. [56]

---

[56] For more on the bicycle safety issues involved and on Dana, see the website "Dana Laird Day," http://www.webmerchants.com/spectrum/Dana_Laird_Day.htm There is a moving photo of a police officer obviously having a very hard time, leaning against the back of the bus that hit Dana.

87

Polis 12:19 PM

Friday, May 28, 2004

Note: Technical difficulties had me shut down for about a week but all seems well now, I'll be ranting again with a vengeance. I think it was the CIA, cutting too close to the truth and, oh, here's those nice men in clean white coats...

Iraqi Insurgents getting better all the time, firsts it's AK-47 ambushes, then it's roadside bombs, then it's roadside bombs followed by AK fire to try to pick-off a few more. Guerilla warfare is a learning curve like anything else. Yet another thing no one told Bush? They are getting all that great training in Iraq, the same as Osama got his fighting the Russkies in Afghanistan. Only a matter of time before they bring it here.

Gore getting the religion, Old Al trying to redeem himself:

"There was then, there is now and there would have been regardless of what Bush did, a threat of terrorism that we would have to deal with. But instead of making it better, he has made it infinitely worse. We are less safe because of his policies. He has created more anger and righteous indignation against us as Americans than any leader of our country in the 228 years of our existence as a nation -- because of his attitude of contempt for any person, institution or nation who disagrees with him.

He has exposed Americans abroad and Americans in every U.S. town and city to a greater danger of attack by terrorists because of his arrogance, willfulness, and bungling at stirring up hornet's nests that pose no threat whatsoever to us. And by then insulting the religion and culture and tradition of people in other countries. And by

pursuing policies that have resulted in the deaths of thousands of innocent men, women and children, all of it done in our name." [57]

Wing-nut columnist Maureen Dowd throws the "wackodoo wing of the Democratic party" stuff at Old Al, but Bush's poll numbers are softening.

Only the most fear-crazed, wild-eyed monster could stomp indiscriminately on this many civilians to try to stamp out a few rats. Former Carter National Security chief Zbigniew Brzezenski said the Iraq war has made us: "less secure. I think we have increased the number of enemies."[58]

Why did Bush attack Iraq? If you ask me, it was personal. No other way to explain that smirk. No grown man acts that way unless he's a ruthless punk. "This is the guy who tried to kill my dad." "Saddam Hussein now knows I mean what I say." Heh heh. The aircraft carrier stunt. "Bring them on."

Happy birthday to me. Two days ago. For my birthday I want a new laptop, a bag of reefer, and a gas mask.

...Polis 5:06 PM

Sunday, May 30, 2004

Come on now. I posted the following rant on Kerry's blog (the subject was Karl Rove.) It was deleted before the cyber-ink was dry. Is it that bad? Okay maybe the Father Porter stuff is a bit vulgar. I was trying to be funny. Read it, tell me true - should it have been deleted? Okay, maybe I'll tone it down...Here's what I wrote...

Kerry's Quandry

Kerry has a problem. He can say the war has

---

[57] Al Gore Speech, New York University, May 26, 2004

[58] *Newshour with Jim Lehrer*, "One Year Later," March 19, 2004

been run badly, but he can't say it was a bad idea. He knows Bush is waiting around the corner with a baseball bat: Kerry, you voted for this war.

Bush will launch a last minute ad blitz that will leave Kerry feeling used like a choirboy in Father Porter's parish. He won't be able to sit for weeks. Between stripping the body armor off our heroes in Iraq (the truth is the opposite), to stomping on his medals and probably a flag too for good measure, to wanting married homosexuals to rule America, what the Rove Machine is going to do to Kerry will leave him looking like he got the short end of a scrape with the Tasmanian Devil.

Then Bush will run ads with himself in front of the biggest American flag you have ever seen. He'll flat-out out-flag Kerry.

Bush Ad Announcer: It's easy to be an armchair quarterback when you aren't responsible for America's safety. But sometimes a president has to make hard decisions.

[corny music, images exploiting 9/11]

Announcer: The course to safety is hazardous. It needs a steady hand and a steady head at the helm (hint hint: that Kerry guy is a left-wing wacko.) Our prezdent has led our nation through trying times. Don't let the nuts take over. (Okay, maybe they won't say this exactly, but that will be the idea.) [END]

If they can tar John McCain as the father of an illegitimate mixed-race child (gettin' some!) there's no telling what they'll do to Kerry. [59]

---

[59] Also posted at DNC blog "Kickin' Ass," http://www.democrats.org/blog/comment/00010692.html

A comment from the Kerry blog on this post (before it got deleted of course,) from raysharbutt:

"polis:
I agree. I think JK needs to make a 30 second ad looking straight into the camera D-bunking all (ok, some is all you can do in 30 seconds) of the right-wing Rovian lies about his votes on the Defense budgets.

The answer is NO. No, it is Hell, NOO! I did not vote against body armor. I voted to fund this war with a fair tax. I voted against more outrageous tax breaks for Duh-bya's friends while he is trying to fight this unprovoked war. I voted to fund the US military, but asked that we not use Iraqi oil funds to support Dick Cheney's Halliburton retirement fund. I voted to be open and honest with the people of the United States of America. I voted to be fair to all of the tax payers, by asking the richest 1% to give up their ill-gotten gains under these previous tax cuts. I voted for fiscal sanity. I voted against this continuing fiscal irresponsibility that has been the hallmark of George Bush's presidency.

It is time for all American's to demand an accounting beginning with demanding that GW answer the people's questions in an open public forum, under oath. And, if GW is afraid to answer questions, under oath, then I invite him to show up for an open public debate. George Bush it is time to start talking about the issues facing America in 2004. It is time for you to tell your campaign that you are not going to allow any more lies about my record.

George Bush - the American People are ready to

hear the truth." [60]

What is failure? Kerry playing more catch-up ball in place of a platform, saying that, like Bush, he believes "failure is not an option" in Iraq. I may be just a blogger nobody, but can I ask a question? What's "failure?" Announcement: there will be no Disneyland in Iraq. The magic show has been cancelled. Now what?

The writing on the wall is that George's Excellent Adventure will turn out to be a theocracy with ties to Iran. Iraq will celebrate the day US soldiers go home as a kind of independence day. This could be good. The best way to take some steam out of Islamic extremism is to give the poor downtrodden bastards some pride. First the West takes Palestine without anyone asking them, then we corrupt their own useless governments in Saudi, Pakistan, UAE, Kuwait and the rest, then we bomb the shit out of Iraq and there's not a damned thing they can do about it. No wonder they're itching to kill us.

Kerry needs to say that this kind of war is fought in international cities, Third World bazaars, and the Pakistani mountains. 9/11 was plotted in Hamburg, Germany, not Damascus.

And to have deadly intelligence on these people, you need the rest of the world. This is where getting rid of Bush comes in. Kerry hasn't said, we need other governments to risk lives, to infiltrate terror cells. They're not going to get people wasted for George Bush. Yes, we, America, mighty military and don't mess with Texas, NEED other countries to win this war. It's that kind of war.

Bush will - what else? - dumb it down. "We will not return to treating terrorism as a law enforcement problem." Return, go back, retreat, no. Advance, move forward, yes. That's Kerry's cue for saying, what is this guy talking about? Intelligence work isn't "law enforcement." He's doing it again. Pulling the wool over your eyes. Snookering you.

We can keep Iraq from becoming a terrorist training camp if

---

[60] http://blog.johnkerry.com/blog/archives/001615.html

we improve relations with Iran and stop the self-righteous, wounded giant routine. In fact, we should be happy if Iran can even work with us after what we did to them.[61] I'm surprised they'll even talk to us.

NY Times's Paul Krugman on what is "failure," says "lost prestige is better than ruin."

C. asked me "what's the movie The Alamo about?" I told her it's about how the heroic Mexican army exterminated the Anglo invaders in Texas.[62] Damned straight. You don't ask a Mexican that unless you want the truth.

…Polis

Tuesday, June 01, 2004

Fate has placed me at Ground Zero for the Democratic Convention, in 2 months. Why Boston? Why not smack in the middle of Florida? That way if we're attacked, Florida voters will rally around the Democrats in sympathy. I remember when we didn't have to think like this. I propose a day when for five minutes we all pretend it never happened, 9/11, GWB showed himself to be a complete nincompoop on nearly everything and he's about to lose the election, and at the airport everyone walks through security with a smile and a wave because this is America after all and no one wants to hurt us. Then we see that awful gap in the Manhattan skyline. It's like one of those bad dreams where you can't wake up.

What about the generation that will never remember a different world? Taught from the crib to see their Bill of Rights as something that is balanced against safety? An historic opportunity lost by George Bush, after September 11. To say: it would be easy to declare a police state. But since that's what you terrorist assholes want, because it would mean you win, we're going to do exactly the opposite. We're re-affirming the Bill of Rights, you bastards. We'll catch you with the Constitution we've got, because it works; we're not

---

[61] See "Mom, Apple Pie, and the Iranian Revolution," a supplementary essay in this book.
[62] The average age of the Mexican soldier in Santa Anna's army was 16.

93

going to have anything creepy like a Patriot Act. That would mean you left your mark on America and we're not going to let you do that. *Look world! This is what a free people looks like!*

I'd be out campaigning for Bush right now if he had done that, and be a registered Republican. But no. After 9/11 the Constitution was the first thing Bush went after, even before he went after Al Qaeda. The Patriot Act was passed in days. It took him two months to go after bin Laden.

Madness everywhere here. The Boston subway, the "T", has a new message blaring over the P.A. "Taking any kind of photograph on this public property is now a FE-LO-NY" The woman's voice throws in, for good measure, that the flash from a camera could actually BLIND a *train drivah*, yes, BLIND. "We ah unduh the Terrorism Protection ACT." You can tell she actually believes this crap. Another sign of the Era of Bush; war gives always nobodies a new sense of importance. Suddenly the drop-outs are giving orders to the doctors. And it feels good.

Lady sitting next to me: "Thank you John Ashcroft". I ask what happens if some poor slob doesn't know English and snaps a picture of sis and ma in their new Boston souvenir T-shirts? I TLAKE PLICTURE BOSTON WHAT MATTA? he'll say. In a spread-eagle position eating subway dirt. Wouldn't any terrorist have the sense to use a hidden camera for a "secret mission?"

Here's a bigger laugh. Making national news. Boston is so retarded. The Transit Authority is doing random bag searches of people waiting on the subway platform. The rule is, a subway cop can come up and ask to look through your bag. You can refuse, but you'll be asked to leave the station under threat of arrest. Now let me get this straight: rather than blow himself to smithereens on the spot, cop and all, a terrorist is going to say "I refuse a search" and go get a cup of cappuccino at the Starbucks. *Darn it! I came that close!*

So what happens when a terrorist says, ok, I'll just blow myself up on a crowded sidewalk, okay? How do you like me now? I don't have to go into no subway. Now they do random searches on the sidewalk? You see where this is headed. I've got no problem with something that actually makes you safer, hell don't get me wrong. I could see *everyone* getting searched *before* they enter the station, like people getting onto an airplane. Or as in securing chemical plants. Oh right, that costs money that could go to Star Wars. No, better get the Munchkins used to cops all in their business. The goal is to change attitudes here, Bushie.

The bad news is there's not a damned thing you can do to stop a determined terrorist. You have to lower the temperature. Invading countries is not really the way to do that. Once given a power, no government ever gives it up on its own. They push to see what they can get away with, and screw safety.[63]

Ah, but Boston is where crosswalks flash "walk" while traffic to your left has a green light for a right turn into your path, where they give 50 mile-an-hour traffic a full ten feet to merge before they end a lane. If you don't know these things it means YOU'RE NOT FROM HERE SO F--- YOU DOUBLE! GO HOME! This is patronage heaven. The bureaucracy is every state legislator's nitwit nephew, who keeps his job so long as he holds a sign on election day. Rain or shine.

Brain-flush, this one is bothering me. Junior has said on a number of televised occasions that his most "solemn duty" is protecting the American people. Mrs. Hendrickson's 8th grade civics class kicked in, and I went running to the Internet to look up the presidential oath of office. What I found was, on Inauguration Day the president is required to say these words, according to Article II, Section 1, of the Constitution:

"I do solemnly swear (or affirm) that I will faithfully execute the office of President of the

---

[63] Case in point: although at first claiming it was only during the Democratic Convention that random searches would take place, there is now a permanent sign in the Boston subway which reads: "For the protection and the security of the riding public, all persons choosing to use the MBTA transit system will be subject to security inspections of their handbags, briefcases and/or other carry-on items. Any person refusing to a allow a security inspection will be either denied entry or requested to leave MBTA property."

United States, and will to the best of my ability, preserve, protect, and defend *the Constitution* of the United States." (Italics mine.)

That's it, all she wrote. Nothing about protecting us, the Oz's little Munchkins, as his "most solemn duty." His job is to protect the Constitution. I got lost in my little project and wound up reading the whole thing, the Constitution, and guess what? It's not in there, anywhere, anything about "protecting the people." The lying bastard. Look for yourself. The way I see it, Congress owes us one impeachment. You can base it on one case, Jose Padilla, the American rotting in a Navy brig as an "enemy combatant." Without his constitutional rights. The administration is hiding behind war precedents that have nothing to do with the present situation. This is the first war against an enemy with no army, no one from whom to accept surrender. The dumbest shit-for-brains law school drop-out can tell you that the precedent doesn't apply if the facts aren't similar. But the whole Bush Justice Department can't see it.

One moment, Dave. One moment. Receiving transmission from Earth. Ah yes, through the alcohol-soaked, pot-scented haze of my college days I remember at least one other thing. Prof said: The Founders preferred to take their chances with common criminal-types; what they worried about more was when the bad guys WERE the government. Right. Checks and balances. I passed that class.

We're in the middle of a war, and declaring enemy combatant Americans is okay, looky here, there's a pree-cee-dent! Oh yes, by the way, this war is permanent, so don't whine about the Constitution ever again. Don't guys who would think that up sound like the kinds of guys the Founders had in mind?

What manner of men are these? From "Bearing Bad Tidings Can be Dangerous" by Donald Kaul at MinutemanMedia.org:

"Why speak to the truth when a personal attack is so much quicker?

"[Former counter-terrorism czar Richard Clarke] was the guy pushing hardest, saying again and

again that something big was going to happen, including possibly here in the United States. And it's disgusting to see the administration now putting a full-court smear on Clarke – for being right," said Thomas Maertens, former National Security Council director for nuclear nonproliferation.

Disgusting perhaps, but it's the Bush way.

Remember the case of Paul H. O'Neill a few months ago? O'Neill, who was dismissed as Secretary of the Treasury over a difference in economic policy (O'Neill wanted one), published a book saying pretty much what Clarke is saying; that Bush was all about Iraq all the time from the moment he took office.

A White House spokesman said that the administration was "simply not in the business of doing book reviews" then promptly threatened O'Neill with retribution for making classified material public. O'Neill folded like a three-legged card table."

A NYC blogger wrote: "Jesus is coming! And he's got a gun!"

...Polis 6:17 PM

Wednesday, June 02, 2004

Just another one of my "stupid opinions" in the words of some of my, ahem, fans. Kerry is making a BIG mistake by letting Bill Clinton be a star at the convention. Mr. "Depends on what you mean by the word 'is'" inspires a visceral, knee-jerk reaction in some ordinarily rational people. Don't ask me how come.

We walked into the middle of a street brawl, the mean kind

where they kick you in the teeth. Letting old Bullshit Bill get all those Hillary-haters riled-up is not the way to make friends. Say our platform is to end corporate socialism, get those corporate pickpockets out of our wallets, their hand-outs and bail-outs while the rest of us have to work for a living. Give the people some red meat. Bubba's lukewarm liberal bullshit will get us nowhere.

Iran making nukes for Fear of Bush. It's painful like watching a tennis player whose returns always just catch the top of the net. Kerry's rap on securing nuclear materials is a policy wonk's idea of hitting back hard. Meanwhile Bush hammers that pre-emptive war works. By attacking Iraq we got Libya to give up nucyular weapons, didn't we? Regardless of the mess there now, the world is safer, and the Kerrys of the world don't see the Big Picture. But what about North Korea and Iran?

Saw the ad aimed at Nader aired by Democrats "What's More Important Ralph? Your Ego?" Okay, now I'm going to go off a little. Warning: that's just going to piss us Greens off (ooo scared.) I'm only voting for your boy this time because Bush is so bad, but that doesn't mean we like to see Ralph dissed. I voted for Nader in 2000 and wouldn't have voted for Gore if he was the last man on Earth, at the time. Remember what he did at Kyoto? He took a 15% reduction in Greenhouse gasses and bumped it down to 5% as a gift to the corporate centrists. The lawyer-lobbyists who call themselves Democrats but who could give a shit who wins, as long as their Beamers are safe. Clinton/Gore's sell-outs on NAFTA, big timber/cattle/mining, and the biggest corporate rip-off of the decade, the $80 billion Telecommunications Act of '96. Hey no one's perfect, right? An old man in my neighborhood once told me, those Kennedy liberals want to help people as long as it's always with *your* money, not theirs. I didn't know what he meant at the time. I was young.

If you want to get Nader voters, Democrats, show some cajones: take on the Patriot Act, slam Bush on the Bill of Rights and the shut-down of free speech in America, starting with Howard Stern getting kicked-off Clear Channel radio stations after turning pro-Kerry.

Snarky attacks will get you nowhere. Stop caring about

nothing but money money money, like the Republicans. Take a stand. Surprise us.

....Polis 11:36 PM

Friday, June 18, 2004

A Speech for Kerry

Five weeks before the convention. I have written this speech for Kerry.

"Some Lines for Kerry"
copyright Ralph Lopez 2004
applause lines in italics

A Kerry administration will not hesitate to use force against America's enemies. But force tempered with wisdom.[64] I will lead our armed forces into battle only when absolutely necessary. We face important challenges on the homefront. Too many of our children are growing up without a proper education, without the skills necessary to succeed in life. Some of our elderly are forced to choose between heat and eat, too many families struggle to make ends meet. A Kerry administration will expend the political will necessary to accomplish real advances in education, in the war against poverty, and in strengthening the middle class. A Kerry administration will work to create not only minimum wage jobs but the kinds of jobs you want your children to have, jobs with futures, jobs with good benefits. We will do this by fully harnessing the greatest assets in our economy, the productivity, ingenuity, and skill of the American worker. We will not reward companies for sending good jobs overseas. *Those days will be over.*

There are some in the other party who will say the Democrats want to engage in class warfare. But wanting better for your children than you had is not class warfare, it is the very essence of America.

---

[64] In his convention speech Clinton used the line "strength and wisdom are not opposing values."

99

College costs are skyrocketing. Financial aid goes up but not enough to prevent you from having to mortgage the house or dig into the retirement fund. A Kerry administration will not fear a political battle in order to place the rungs of opportunity within reach of every young American. This is not class warfare. *This is the American Dream! And a prosperous, healthy, and fair America, is a strong America.*

As to the war on terror, the opposing party says we Democrats labor under the illusion that there is no enemy, that we do not know who he is. But we labor under no illusions. We understand this enemy. They are cunning, ruthless, and invisible. It will require cunning to defeat them. It will require the full efforts of our dedicated intelligence community. We will undertake a massive initiative to bolster and expand intelligence so that no corner of the globe is out of the reach of the eyes and ears of America, and if necessary, the sword of America, be it Africa, Asia, Europe, or the Middle East. Our intelligence must remain above the corrupting influence of politics. *A Kerry administration will never blame our intelligence professionals for it's own policy failures! A Kerry administration will never reveal the cover of an American intelligence officer for political reasons!*

As we move into the year 2005, we must ask ourselves some questions. One is whether, in the future, the world will follow America because she is respected, and not just feared. Another is whether we will allow the terrorists to change our way of life, to erode our basic rights and freedoms, by the false trade of liberty for security. To the first I answer, America will be followed because she is wise, decent, and just, and not only feared. As to the erosion of our liberties I answer: *Never!*

...Polis

Monday, June 28, 2004

Flash! Qaeda Prefers Bush

Christian Science Monitor: a CIA insider spills the beans and says Al Qaeda wants Bush re-elected. Will attack to insure the country rallies around him.

> **"A senior US intelligence official is "about to publish a bitter condemnation of America's counter-terrorism policy, arguing that the West is losing the war against Al Qaeda and that an 'avaricious, premeditated, unprovoked' war in Iraq has played into Osama bin Laden's hands." This senior intelligence official, who writes as "Anonymous," also says that "Osama bin Laden may attack the US before the November election to ensure the re-election of President George Bush." [65]**

Stay tuned...

On the Charlie Rose Show yesterday ambassador Joe Wilson refused to predict events in Iraq. Says the facts on the ground can change so fast that whatever you say can be worthless in 48 hours. That's what it feels like writing a political blog these days. Donald Rumsfeld gets a clue and says that terrorists may be getting created faster than we can kill them. He still blames religious ideology, but attacking Iraq is supposed to help that? Question: if the insurgency in Iraq is the work of a small minority rather than a popular movement, who are all those kids you see dancing around burning Humvees? [66]

It looks like someone actually reads this thing. Ted Kennedy questions a key claim of Bush, that the world is safer because Libya has renounced its nuclear program.[67] Bush says pre-emptive war works. The problem is Iran and North Korea have jump-started their nuclear programs. Bush makes them think they'll be next on the hit list, and they want a deterrent. It was all predictable.

---

[65] *Christian Science Monitor*, "Senior intel officer: Al Qaeda will attack US to ensure Bush win," June 21, 2004
[66] *Boston Globe*, "Rumsfeld fears US losing war against Islamic extremism," June 6, 2004
[67] *Boston Globe*, "Kennedy keeps drumbeat on Bush, Iraq, Says war obscures nuclear dangers in Iran, N. Korea," June 23, 2004

We owe it to Howard Dean. Remember the rafter of shit he took for saying the capture of Saddam didn't make us safer? Like saying the emperor has no clothes. It caught on. All because one man wouldn't be cowed by the Rush Limbaughs of the world. Rush: WHAT DO YOU MEAN THE EMPEROR HAS NO CLOTHES? YOU SHUT UP! YOU SHUT UP!

Damn I miss Howard.

Have to hand it to the Republicans. They are funny. Kerry wants to draw out the nomination process so he can spend more money later. I'm not sure how it works but the official nomination would come after the convention. Bush spokesman says "only John Kerry could be for the nominating convention but against the nomination."[68] Why can't we be that funny?

It's too bad Bush is going to win. To paraphrase one dear reader's email, I'm going to burden you with my stupid opinions.

Suppose there was zero link between Saddam and Al Qaeda. But Bush says, at the time, I was *really* sure that there was. *Really.* I had to decide. Since people can't seem to see by his gloating behavior that he's a lying little snot who had it out for Saddam, they'll give him the benefit of the doubt. This is no time for someone afraid to act, and you win some, you lose some. The lying? Aw shucks. That's part of being prezdent.

But acting in the wrong way is as dangerous as not acting at all. The trouble with saying "I'm not waiting to see a mushroom cloud over New York City" is starting a full-blown war might be what leads to that mushroom cloud. Al Qaeda understands the dynamics, if not Shrub. When you bomb you always kill a lot of the wrong people. It comes with the territory. They kill us back, then we kill more of them, kill kill kill. The cycle of revenge and it's as old as the hills, the Hatfields and the McCoys, Euripides, the Trojan War, the Bible.

We need a Kerry Doctrine. You had a Monroe Doctrine, a

---

[68] *Boston Globe,* "Hub's DNC melodrama churns on," May 28, 2004

Nixon Doctrine, a Carter Doctrine ("any attempt by any outside forces to gain control of the Persian Gulf region will be regarded as an assault on the vital interests of the United States of America," 1980.) Even a Reagan Doctrine, which was kind of lame ("anti-communist rebels must be supported because they oppose tyranny." But what if the anti-communist rebels *are* the tyranny?)

Just to show he's thinking, Kerry needs him a doctrine. How about: in the event of terrorist attack, the United States reserves the right to retaliate against any nation based on circumstantial evidence. And a terrorist attack on any NATO country will be considered an attack on all.

One of the helpless feelings of the war on terror is we might have no hard evidence. This doctrine will tell them we ain't waiting for, and we don't need, no smoking gun. If we think you're behind it, we're coming. So don't even *think* about it.

...Polis @ 4:46 PM

Wednesday, June 30, 2004

It's happening again, that Bush head-rush from rage. Bush says we must "finish the job" so our soldiers "didn't die in vain." Why that arrogant, manipulative, shameless, slimy little son-of-a-bitch. Put his critics face-to-face with the parents of dead troops, then point to you and tell the parents, "*he* wants your son to have died in vain. *He* doesn't want to finish the job." In grade school this is the kind of kid we would have stuffed in a trash can so fast.

First of all, what's "the job," besides whatever he says it is? Let's keep it simple since the Disneyland-in-Iraq magic show has been cancelled. Say, no making WMD, no attacking your neighbors, no toxic anti-Americanism. Fair enough? And no switching to the Euro, dammit, like Saddam was going to do.[69] No harboring terrorists. Do all that and we'll leave you alone. And we'll be

---

[69] "The Real But Unspoken Reasons For The Iraq War," By W. Clark, Rense.com, http://www.rense.com/general34/realre.htm

watching.

So they didn't die in vain? I thought the Jesus Freaks knew that God has a plan. This tells me this Bush Jesus Freak doesn't read his Bible. The Bible, one of the greatest works of literature:

"You saw me before I was born. Every day of my life was recorded in Your book. Every moment was laid out before a single day had passed..." Psalms 139:16

Okay by now you have figured that I'm a deluded megalomaniac who thinks people read his blog. He thinks he's talking to the prezdent! Indulge me while I tilt at one more windmill. A "Bush" will someday be a synonym for one who preys on the feeble-minded. But the feeble-minded can stop being feeble, with a little effort. A lot of right-wingers are extremely intelligent people. They just haven't thought some things through.

Okay, fuck me, I'm an asshole. But let me make my point. Saying our government has done bad things around the world, like in the Middle East, does not equal saying 9/11 victims somehow deserved it. The minute 9/11 happened and folks started asking what mistakes might have brought this on, the logic-challenged came back with: *you're saying they deserved it!* Sorry but there is no other way to put this: that is really stupid. It's stupid because it doesn't see the distinction between a government and a people. If there were none, we'd have the warm and fuzzies for the IRS.

Let me get this straight. "A" is guilty. "A" is a subset of "B." Therefore all of "B" is guilty as well. That's like saying if one black person commits a crime then all black people are guilty. Forget the war on terror. What we need is a war on error.

I always wondered about folks who say it's un-American to criticize the government. It's about the most totally American thing I can think of.

There's an 80s sleeper named Revolution starring Al Pacino - see it! - where old Al is a citizen-soldier in the American Revolution. I know, Scarface plays British colonial peasant. Funny. Funnier is he actually does a pretty good job. Anyway, old Al is a reluctant revolutionary at first, but he gets with the program. Starts to believe in the Revolution. And at the end there's a scene where this numb-nut bureaucrat is giving old Al the brush-off as he tries to collect his back-pay from the new government. You know the type. Tells Al to go "tell it to the Congress." So Al says "*You're* the one sitting there so I'm telling *you!*" Good line. Remember it the next time you're trying to clear something up at the motor vehicle registry.

Did I have a point? Oh yes. The government is not the people, but when the government makes mistakes or commits crimes it's the people who wind up paying. What's so hard to understand about that? Oh right, the other right-wing line: the blame belongs in one place only, *with the attackers. Otherwise you're guilty of moral relativism.*

Freepers and wing-nuts hear this: There is always one dumb-ass lieutenant who'll walk everyone into an ambush and get them killed because he doesn't understand the nuances of the situation.[70] The dumb fuck.

Have read Stephen Kinzer's "All the Shah's Men: An American Coup and the Roots of Middle East Terror," and to quote him:

> **"It is not far-fetched to draw a line from [code name] Operation Ajax through the Shah's repressive regime and the Islamic Revolution to the fireballs that engulfed the World Trade Center in New York."**

The CIA's excellent adventure in Iran, 1953. You want to know how we got the Mullah's? Read Kinzer. Saddam had nothing on the Shah, who was our boy. Had methods of torture like forcing boiling water up the rectum, oh you know, stuff like that. [71] What's too bad is both Truman and Eisenhower, the prezes at the time, *liked* the guy the CIA overthrew, Prime Minister Mohammed Mossadeq.

---

[70] FreeRepublic.com, a right-wing website.

[71] *The CIA's Greatest Hits,* by Mark Zapezeur (Odonian Press)

Ike called him "the only hope for the West in Iran."[72] But the CIA had other ideas and free-lanced it behind Ike's back, until it got out of hand.

The CIA calls it "blowback." 9/11, the ultimate blowback.

There will always be strange creatures who foam at the mouth and spittle no matter what you say, the Freepers and the wing-nuts who don't want the bad news. But if I'm captain of a ship, then the people telling me the bad news are more important than the ones telling me the good. Uh, sir, we're all going to be in the drink in 20 minutes if we don't fix this thing.

I don't want any happy talk saying we aren't responsible. I want to know what the problems are. The bad news is our government made big doo-doos all over the world, and now we need a serious pooper scooper. They don't hate us for our freedoms. It would be simpler if they did. But it's just not true.

I never accepted that there's a whole part of the world that wants me dead for no reason, or because I'm free to starve or become a millionaire. And ready to blow themselves up in the bargain. That dog don't hunt. If you read Kinzer your eyes will open like a baby's at its first breath. William Blum, who wrote "Killing Hope: U. S. Global Interventions since World War II," will do that too. I'm always around for a beer and a bullshit session about these books. Email me. I can make anything into an excuse for a couple of pints.

...Polis 7:10 PM

Huzzah to Gun Owners of America for opposing Patriot II.

I'm a gun nut. Well not really. I'm just from someplace where you get a BB gun for your tenth birthday, and your folks hope you don't shoot your eye out.

GOA president Larry Pratt:

---

[72] *All the Shah's Men; An American Coup And The Roots Of Middle East Terror*, by Stephen Kinzer

"If **Patriot II** passes, a substantial number of political lobbies (including Gun Owners of America) could be declared terrorist organizations by an administration that simply dislikes their methods and goals." **FULL REPORT HERE** [73]

...Polis 4:03 PM

From the website Military Families Speak Out, mfso.com :

"My son arrived in Iraq on Tuesday and got another purple heart on Wednesday. He was shot in the helmet and the vest and has a concussion and broken ribs. Or course in the sick, diseased world of Mass-murderer Bush, that isn't enough to get sent home. They just patch you up and send you back to the field to be used as pawns in the Bush/Cheney war for oil and money. Bush is a monster from hell and he has created hell on earth. I guess it makes him feel more at home, knowing that people are dying ever day. He is a sick and evil moron. Sorry, just venting."

Last, good link. [74]. Ex- CIA station chief John Stockwell videostream from a talk in '87, "Crimes of the CIA."

...Polis 3:24 PM

Thursday, July 01, 2004

"Fahrenheit 9/11" fact check. I've been laying it on a little thick; people tell me to get back to work. Blog work. Bloggers are here to filter and dissect the news, to cut through the brown, filthy

---

[73] Link, http://gunowners.org/fs0307.htm

[74] http://www.peace.ca/stockwell.wmv

haze that is the major media, and do some real-time fact-check and unprofessional opinion. Meaning not bought-out. On the following, all corrections and cross-checks from the blogosphere are welcomed.

It's amazing how fast the wing-nuts cornered Mike Moore in the back of the school-yard and started pounding on him. Not for nothing. It's a textbook example of how these people operate. First accuse you of saying things you never said, then shoot down those things in a big show of unmasking the dishonest, unpatriotic, dirty hippie swine. That would be anyone who disagrees with them. Michael Isikoff in Newsweek says Fahrenheit plays fast and loose with the facts. Isikoff writes:

> **"The movie claims that in the days after 9/11, when airspace was shut down, the White House approved special charter flights so that prominent Saudis - including members of the bin Laden family - could leave the country. Author Craig Unger appears, claiming that bin Laden family members were never interviewed by the FBI. Not true, according to a recent report from the 9/11 panel."** [75]

Blogger bust. Three different claims are contained in this paargraph:

1. Moore says the Saudis left when the airspace was shut down
2. Moore says the White House approved this
3. Moore says the members of the bin Laden family among these Saudis were "never interviewed."

For the first point, here is the transcript of the movie. Of course the original source is the film itself, which you can rent at any video store. It's well-known that US airspace restrictions were gradually lifted on September 13:

MOORE (Voice Over): "It turns out that the

---

[75] *Newsweek*, June 28, 2004

White House approved planes to pick up the bin Ladens and numerous other Saudis. At least six private jets and nearly two dozen commercial planes carried the Saudis and the bin Ladens out of the US *after September 13th*. In all, 142 Saudis, including 24 members of the bin Laden family, were allowed to leave the country...." (italics mine.)

Isikoff's words "the movie claims that in the days after 9/11, *when airspace was shut down*, the White House approved special charter flights..." are a lie. The movie makes no such claim. Whether or not Moore implies something untoward going on in family members leaving *so soon* after the airspace is re-opened is subject to interpretation. But that's not the issue raised by Isikoff.

For the second point, who approved the flights, former counterterrorism chief Richard Clarke said "it was a conscious decision with complete review at the highest levels of the State Department and the FBI and the White House," supporting Moore's contention. [76]

Last and most blatant, Isikoff LIES when he has the film claiming that bin Laden family members leaving the country were never interviewed. Although this is what Craig Unger says, FBI agent Jack Cloonan differs in the film, and says that they were only briefly interviewed, and not in accordance with what would have been standard in any capital crime, never mind the greatest ever committed on US soil. Cloonan's exact words, watch the film yourself:

"If I had to inconvenience a member of the bin Laden family with a subpoena or a Grand Jury, do you think I'd lose any sleep over it? Not for a minute Mike... You got a lawyer? Fine. Counselor? Fine. Mr. Bin Laden, this is why I'm asking you, it's not because I think that you're

---

76 Testimony of Richard Clarke, before The Senate Judiciary Committee, September 3, 2003.

**anything. I just want to ask you the questions that
I would anybody."**

Cloonan thinks they should have been *subpoenaed*, not just asked a few questions. He puts this in the context of hundreds of Middle Easterners being rounded-up on the flimsiest of grounds in those days:

**"How many people were pulled by the airlines
after that coming into the country who were what,
coming from the Middle East or they fit a very
general picture?"**

See how it works? Isikoff "discovers" that bin Laden family members *were* interviewed before they were whisked out of the country, and he trots out the 9/11 report as his authoritative source. But the film never concludes that they *weren't* interviewed, although its sources seem to differ. Isikoff picks the part of the difference that suits him and ignores Cloonan. What we do know, and even Isikoff doesn't dispute this, is that the interviews were toss-offs, not real interviews. So it isn't Moore who plays fast and loose with the facts. It's Isikoff.

The real story is it's absolutely vital to quickly smear, misquote, and distort anyone who hints at the truth, in this administration's playbook. And in the playbooks of their hit-men, like Newsweek's Michael Isikoff. What might be a Hail Mary play in any other administration, to be broken out in desperation, is this administration's standard ground-game. That's the difference between them and all the other corrupt politicians we've gotten used to in the past. The slime doesn't come out last. It comes out first.

Go after the sayer instead of haggling over what's being said. It is the Bush Touchstone and his Mother Lode. His Grail. They're proud of it; they brag. Before Big Bush's first campaign, Karl Rove's mentor, Lee Atwater, summed up his strategy against Mike Dukakis. He said he was going to "strip the bark off the little bastard."[77]

---

[77] *The Nation*, "Bush's Hit Man," by Louis Dubose, March 5, 2001

Milan Kundera wrote that even when the Soviet Politburo airbrushed someone out of a state photograph, someone they wanted you to forget, there were always reminders of the reality. Even if it was only the hole where his picture had been, this weird grey gap the line-up. The most brilliant criminal still leaves a trail; it's the nature of physics and the universe, and it's why the Bushies will sooner or later get their come-uppance. It's why, as long as we keep the fires of liberty burning in our obese and alcoholic American souls, as long as we have people like Michael Moore, we will be free. Fuckin' A.

True quote from Ben Franklin: "Beer is proof that God meant man to be happy."

....Polis @ 5:18 PM

Friday, July 02, 2004

I mean I can't watch "Friends" with my kids without my ears burning, and I thought I was pretty open-minded. Why should Republicans be the party of not wanting your kids to see kids under the sheets with other kids? Man, back in my day they left something to the imagination. Geeez.

Ralph Nader says there's an issue here and Dems are missing it. In an interview with conservative Pat Buchanan, Nader said:

> **"conservatives are aghast that a born-again Christian president has done nothing about rampant corporate pornography and violence directed to children and separating children from their parents and undermining parental authority."**

Rampant corporate pornography. Branding for the pedophile market. Putting make-up on 12 year old girls and posing them, and the marketers know *exactly* what they are doing. The truth is Hollywood/Madison Avenue is everything the Evangelicals say it is. Corrupting. Venal. Downright dirty.

111

I remember years ago strange bedfellows on this, Evangelicals and feminists, together. Now there's a tag team you Don't want to mess with. Anyway, Kerry letting it slip by. The guy has no imagination whatsoever.

The rest of the news:

This is where I'll post amusing tidbits you won't hear on Fox News or MSNBC, for folks who don't have a Starbucks where you can steal the New York Times or other major newspapers (No dad, The Alamagordo Times doesn't count.) From a recent article in Boston's Weekly Dig:

> **"To help combat its drop in the polls, the Bush campaign has engaged in a genius scheme of memory-blurring...a practice used by little kids and hockey players to the extreme: One little boy calls another fat. They go back and forth calling each other fatso for a few minutes until an adult intervenes, and then they both get in trouble. To the adult, it doesn't really matter who started it or that one kid is plainly fatter than the other - they're both name-calling and need to shut up. Bush launched his campaign by attacking Kerry for taking special interest money..."**

Correction: In the previous post I said a true Ben Franklin quote is "Beer is proof that God meant man to be happy." It actually goes: ""Beer is proof that God wants us to be happy." Thanks guys. Intellectual honesty in these matters is important.

....Polis 1:11 PM

Saturday, July 03, 2004

Hit back, John

Put up your fists, like this. Now punch. Keep your guard up.

John, Mary Beth, rest of the Kerry crew, I'd like to get paid for this. It's copyrighted (well, it's going to be...)

A Kerry response to the latest Bush attack ad, "Strategy." It really should be rebutted. LIKE THIS:

KERRY: I'm John Kerry, and I approve this message.

ANNOUNCER: George Bush says "we have to take the fight to the enemy," but since 9/11, Al Qaeda has gotten stronger.

[Show Washington Times Headline, "Al Qaeda ranks boosted by war on terror, Iraq"]

The New Republic calls many of the president's reasons for going to war in Iraq "highly dubious." The war on terror is like no other, against enemies who are cunning, and pledge to no national flag.

[Computer generated graphic showing worldwide reach of terrorist bases, Indonesia, Philippines, South America, etc, in rapid succession.]

That's why John Kerry will add 5,000 more special operations soldiers to our military, to hit terrorists hard in every corner of the Globe, guided by massive new intelligence resources.

A combat veteran with 20 years experience on the Senate Foreign Relations Committee, John Kerry understands this war. He *will* take it to the enemy. John Kerry: Simply the best man for the job.

...Polis 2:36 PM

Thursday, July 08, 2004

You heard right, Al Qaeda prefers Bush

It's official. Top CIA expert says Al Qaeda prefers Bush to

113

win the election. What he says: the invasion of Iraq was a "gift" to bin Laden. Iraq sucked-in resources we need in the shooting war against Qaeda. We poured them down the drain for some Disneyland-in-Iraq fantasy. Bush made bin Laden's day when the chips were down for bin Laden. Bin Laden had lost Afghanistan, was about to lose his hideout in Pakistan, then Bush gave he and Zarqawi the welcome chaos of Iraq.

Zarqawi couldn't hide in Iraq before. Well *now* he can. Al Qaeda 2.0 has more applicants than it can handle. The CIA author of "Imperial Hubris: Why the West is losing the War on Terror" is known only as Anonymous. Because he's still in the agency they won't let him put his name on the book. He has over 20 years in the Company and has been chief of the bin Laden unit for 9 years. I'll share this book as I go along. It's mind-blowing.

"...the United States, and its policies and actions, are bin Laden's only indispensable allies. Persian Gulf oil and the lack of serious US alternative energy development are at the core of the bin Laden issue."

–From "Imperial Hubris"

....Polis 3:08 PM

Friday, July 09, 2004

Yikes! He was gassing "his own people!" The Shrub leans into the camera to make sure we heard him right. *His own people.* So why doesn't he say, "and my dad helped him and so did Don Rumsfeld?"

On March 16, 1988, Iraqi forces launched a poison gas attack on the Iraqi Kurdish village of Halabja, killing 5000 civilians. We knew Saddam had chemical weapons, because we have the receipts. Anyone can look this up, it's called "US Chemical and Biological Warfare-related Dual Use Exports to Iraq and Their Possible Impact on the Health Consequences of the Persian Gulf War," by the Senate Committee on Banking, Housing and Urban Affairs, in 1994. The Riegle Report for short. From Chapter One, part two:

> **"Records available from the supplier for the period from 1985 until the present show that [prior to the first Gulf war] pathogenic (meaning "disease producing"), toxigenic (meaning "poisonous"), and other biological research materials were exported to Iraq pursuant to application and licensing by the U.S. Department of Commerce."**

In other words, we gave him anthrax.

When Congress found out Saddam was gassing his own people it passed the Prevention of Genocide Act, which would have punished Saddam. But Reagan/Bush Sr. and special envoy to the Middle East Donald Rumsfeld had the sanctions squashed.[78] Maybe Saddam owed us money for those Bell 214ST helicopters that we sold him. The ones he used to drop the gas. Oh yes, I almost forgot that part. [79]

Then there's the other thing, in 1998, while Dick Cheney was CEO of Halliburton, his company was doing business with Saddam. Washington Post:

> **"During Cheney's tenure at Halliburton the company did business in all three countries [Iraq, Iran, Libya.] In the case of Iraq, Halliburton legally evaded U.S. sanctions by conducting its oil-service business through foreign subsidiaries that had once been owned by Dresser."** [80]

---

[78] Norm Dixon, "How Reagan Armed Saddam with Chemical Weapons," *Counterpunch*, 17 June 2004

[79] The Saddam in Rumsfeld's Closet, by Jeremy Scahill, http://www.commondreams.org/views02/0802-01.htm

[80] The Profitable Connections Of Halliburton, by Jane Mayer, *The New Yorker*, Feb. 16, 2004

What is Dresser Industries? In 1998, it became a FULLY OWNED subsidiary of Halliburton. Among the company's customers were some of the world's worst dictatorships, including Iraq.

Link here to a CNN report on George Bush Senior's and Donald Rumsfeld's happier days with Saddam, including a photo of the famous handshake between Rumsfeld and Hussein. [81]

From my "Imperial Hubris":

"...words of little consequence in US politics and society are heard and remembered in the Islamic world as threats and blasphemy, earning America increased Muslim hatred. When Pat Robertson says "Adolph Hitler is bad, but what the Muslims do to the Jews is worse; the Reverend Jerry Falwell refers to the Prophet as a "terrorist", Muslims believe that "never has Islam faced such a frantic campaign of insult for centuries." They are particularly troubled because the clerics "hold

---

[81] CNN Report, Regime change: From building ties to Saddam to removing him from power, September 30, 2002, http://archives.cnn.com/2002/US/09/30/sproject.irq.regime.change/

high positions at the church," [and] are close to the US government."

...Polis 2:27 PM

Sunday, July 11, 2004

More armchair quarterbacking, here's my TV ad on defense for Kerry, I call it "Illusion."

KERRY: I'm John Kerry and I approve this message.

ANNOUNCER: Last March, 49 retired US generals and admirals called the Star Wars missile defense program "untested" and a "poor use of scarce defense dollars." "National missile defense provides no defense against the most likely future attacks on U.S.", the generals said. They called ballistic missiles the "least likely" method of delivering an attack. [82]

[On-screen graphics: Star Wars missile defense imagery, hardcopy newspaper headline, highlighted portions of report]

These experienced officers recommended that the money spent on Star Wars be spent instead on securing nuclear weapons around the world, and better protecting US ports. They call this the "militarily responsible course."

[Graphics: Images of Coast Guard patrolling harbors, "militarily responsible course" highlighted from report.]

But the Bush/Cheney administration remains "committed" to pouring more money into Star Wars, $10 billion this year. No matter what the experts say, they're going ahead with it.

[from Bush/Cheney website: show "missile defense" heading, pan down to "committed."]

---

[82] *Boston Globe,* "Retired top brass say no to 'missile shield'," March 27, 2004

117

A Kerry-Edwards administration will value the expertise of the men and women charged with defending America. They know there's a difference between real security, and the illusion.

[various patriotic imagery here, soldiers, flags, etc.]

Bush-Cheney: wrong on defense, wrong on terr'.
Kerry-Edwards: real security for America's future.

...Polis 7:13 PM

Monday, July 12, 2004

You think Karl Rove wouldn't use that picture? Today's New York Times, a Penacola Beach, Florida man says "Bush is doing a great job. So what if there is no weapons of mass destruction?" Yikes. Mark Hall of Cedar River, Mich., wishes "we hadn't gone in, in the first place," but he still supports the president. And one person interviewed compared the failure to find WMD to "rushing into a house with a search warrant, and it's really for a house two doors down."

This is what we're up against. We bombed the shit out of your country, hey sorry 'bout that, we meant well. Too bad about your aunt's head.

My best swipe at this. Bush has color-crayoned a certain picture of the world, and he wins as long as enough people see only that picture. The picture has Bush as the good guy who always means well and the villain-of-the-week is always bad to the core. So what I want to know is, when does Kerry bring out the photo of Rummy and Saddam shaking hands and being buddies?

In that photo Rummy is smiling like a simpering idiot. He wants Saddam for his war games and Saddam knows it, and Saddam is rubbing it in. Then Saddam stepped out of line and got greedy. Tried to bite off more than he could chew. Sure, the Kuwaitis were stealing his oil, but you gotta get an okay from the Godfather to

118

whack a Made Guy. [83]   Maybe Saddam thought he had a green light when the American ambassador told him we have "no opinion" on an invasion of Kuwait.[84]   Then again maybe the Godfather was setting him up. We said take the oil fields, not the whole enchilada, dammit. In the mob you've gotta show you're someone we can do business with, slaughtered Shiites or no.

In January 1990 Congress barred Saddam from the Export-Import Bank, but James Baker III and Big Bush signed an executive order to over-ride it. Jimbo said "We were under no illusions about Saddam's brutality toward his own people or his capacity for escalating tensions with his neighbors."[85]   If it was a carrot for Saddam to behave, fine, but let's get off this good-and-evil crap. Did we give loan guarantees to Hitler after we found out about the camps? No. Then why give them to Saddam? Answer: Saddam wasn't Hitler, just your run-of-the-mill killer of the type we do business with all the time.[86]

Alex Cockburn of the Nation says the first Gulf war was more like a "fight between business partners" than a WW II good vs. evil thing. They say Bush Jr. has some kind of competitive thing with his dad. Maybe Junior wants to prove he can pull the trigger like daddy, since he chickened-out during Vietnam and the old man was a bomber pilot, and he always loved Jeb best and...hell I don't know. What's with these people, anyway?

What I'm saying is, it's a question of motives. Bush is going to win because his hands look clean and he has made Kerry's look dirty. An ambitious, troop-slandering flip-flopper. Punch a hole in the color-crayon picture of reality. There's Mob history here. Maybe

---

[83] "Who is the Madman Here? Bush's UN Non-Sequiturs," by Tom Gorman, *CounterPunch*, September 13, 2002

[84] ibid

[85] *Ackron- Beacon Journal,* "Baker Backed Loans That Added to Iraq Debt," Jan. 11, 2004.

[86] Read Larry Beinhart's 1995 novel "Wag the Dog." In contrast to the movie, which centers around Eastern Europe, the novel centers around a dictator in the Middle East. In his new introduction to the novel, Beinhart reveals that to his horror it has crossed his mind that his book may have served as an "instruction manual" for the Iraq Invasion.

119

scores are getting settled that we don't understand and it's just the poor dying for the rich like always. Use the picture of Rummy and Saddam, John. You think they wouldn't use it against you? You poor naïve fool…

"Imperial Hubris":

"...there is no record of a Muslim leader urging his brethren to wage jihad to destroy participatory democracy, the National Association of Credit Unions, or the coed Ivy League universities."

...Polis 4:13 PM

Wednesday, July 14, 2004

Back to my unhealthy obsession with the Constitution, Bill of Rights overturned. I feel like a wide-eyed child watching all this happen. It's slipping away and no one gets it. DANGER WILL ROBINSON!

Except Harvey Silverglate. He's one of those ACLJew lawyers (how quickly we learn our anti-Semitic terms here on the East Coast. When I came from California those jokes always drew a blank stare from me. I didn't get them. Mexican jokes are what we tell out there. What's the Mexican recipe for chicken soup? First, you steal a chicken...)

Harvey, a neighbor of mine, alone cut through to the real meaning of this week's Supreme Court decisions on how long you can hold an American without a trial. Bush's "enemy combatants." While the newspaper editorials stroked the Brethren for coming down on the side of rights, it seems only Harvey read the damned decisions. The key words of the court are:

"…the standards we have articulated could be met by an appropriately authorized and properly

constituted military tribunal...".

What that means, boys and girls, yes, I sound pissed because I am - I know I'm smiling but I'm boiling inside - what that means is now when you read your Sixth Amendment:

"In all criminal prosecutions, the accused shall enjoy the right to a speedy and public trial, by an impartial jury of the state and district wherein the crime shall have been committed"

For everything after "the accused shall enjoy" you can substitute the words "a military tribunal." Goddamn Harvey. Slam-dunk again.

Local graffiti: Alan Dershowitz is a self-promoting, Bush-apologist, plagiarizing dolt. Silverglate rules.

Remember Jose Padilla? He's that alleged "dirty bomber" they grabbed at O'Hare airport a couple of years ago, held incommunicado until he just now was allowed to talk to a lawyer. Two years later. With no attorney-client privilege. The government listens in. Bush says he has the right to hold him for the duration of the war on terror. Goddamn traitor. Bush, not Padilla. We don't know about Padilla; but we know Bush took an oath to uphold the Constitution.

Padilla has been rotting away nicely in a special Navy brig at Goose Creek, South Carolina. Why are these always in places like Goose Crick, South Carolina? You never hear about a secret prison in Westchester County.

The Booshies knew they won and could barely conceal their glee. Administration spokesman Mark Corello said:

"The Justice Department is pleased that the US Supreme Court today upheld the authority of the president as commander-in-chief of the armed forces to detain enemy combatants, *including US citizens.*" (italics mine.)

121

That's right, baby, now the war is on *you*.

It figures they would use someone like Padilla for a test-drive of Junior's new powers. He's dark and glowers at the camera. And in his mug shot, I know a bad hangover when I see one.

It's bad news when arch-conservative Justice Antonin Scalia is bothered that a decision goes too far in favor of Bush. Silverglate says:

"The erosion [of rights] was sufficiently silent to fool the news media, but not Scalia."

Scalia dissented. What's wrong with military tribunals? Besides just not liking the sound of it for myself, thanks, the Court also ruled it was okay to impose the heaviest burden on the accused to *prove the government wrong*, rather than the government having to prove you guilty. Yeeea I *really* don't like *that*.

If all this still isn't kicking-in that sixth sense that tells you you're being set-up on the street, last spring just before the Court heard arguments in these cases, the Booshies released new allegations against Padilla. [87] The guy has not once had a chance to speak for himself.

Pick-up some guy with a long rap sheet, make sure he's ugly and scary-looking (a convert to Islam? Too cool!), and float it. When the next attack comes, the groundwork is laid-out for the punks we *really* want to lock-up. NEAT-O! Of course the guy who lied about weapons of mass destruction would never lie again. And that kind of power can sure come in handy when you've got some punk ready to uncork another ENRON.

The Justice Department built *another* case based on the testimony of someone they threatened with "enemy combatant" status. The possibilities are getting very cool here, mien fuehrer.

---

[87] *USA Today,* "Authorities: Padilla plot included plan to blow up apartments," 6/1/2004

They can testify and tell us what we want to hear, or get designated enemy combatant. Like a Ponzi scheme.

Enter one Nuradin Abdi, charged with plotting to bomb a shopping mall in Ohio. Wait, isn't Ohio the Mother of All Swing States in this election? No Republican has ever won the presidency without Ohio? Let's do it! Kill two birds with one stone! Test the Ponzi and scare the hell out of Ohio! During his trial Abdi "slammed his face to a glass table, kept it there, and looked around the courtroom smiling at no one in particular." His lawyer said "What did they do to him for seven months and why is he a broken man?" [88] The FBI refuses to say which mall he was supposed to blow up.

Pick a mall, any mall. Maybe the one nearest *you*. Be scared. Be grateful to our Fuehrer-Protector. He saved your hick asses. Tell you what, why don't you all just lock *yourselves* up after work every day, save Bush the trouble. Then you can all be perfectly safe? Except from Bush, who's only an "arrested alcoholic," not a cured one, so he's prone to occasional fits of rage.[89]

"Imperial Hubris" fix, I lost my first copy so I had to buy it again. You know it has to be a good book if I'm forking out 24 bucks twice:

> **"As smoke billowed over al Qaeda's massive victories in New York City and Washington, DC, no savage, preplanned US military response was initiated; none had been planned in the eleven months since the attack of the USS Cole, or in the five-plus years since bin Laden declared war. Oddly, the National Security Council and FBI did**

---

[88] *Monterry Herald,* "Suspect in Mall Plot Sent for Evaluation," Jun. 16, 2004

[89] See the book by George Washington University psychiatrist Dr. Justin Frank, "Bush on the Couch: Inside the Mind of the President." Bush reportedly pumped his hand gleefully in the air as the bombing of Baghdad began. Frank's conclusions have been seconded by colleagues such as Dr. James Grotstein, Professor at UCLA Medical Center, and Dr. Irvin Yalom, MD, former Medical Director at the Stanford University Hospital Psychiatric Inpatient Unit.

move with speed to assist the "dead of night exodus" of twenty-plus bin Laden family members...The FBI did not "verify whether the fleeing bin Ladens were both personally and financially estranged from Osama."

..posted by Polis 6:43 PM

Monday, July 19, 2004

Raunchy joke crime! Raunchy joke crime! I didn't get it all but Whoopi Goldberg made a naughty joke at a private Kerry fundraiser. The joke was a predictable pun on the Bush family name, Bush, the bush, a bush, well you get it. That's not the news. The news is word got out to the Repug Thugs, the rabid dog wing, and they howled in feigned outrage at this injustice and disrespect for our prezdent. Tens of thousands of innocent Iraqi civilians getting splattered around by 500 pound bombs, no problem. Dirty Bush joke, NO FAIR! Who are these morally deformed hillbillies? These troglodytes? Goldberg got fired from her Slim Fast contract. Big deal. She's already filthy rich. GO WHOOPI!

> **"I tremble for my country when I reflect that God is just..."**
> **-Thomas Jefferson**

Tuesday, July 20, 2004

From the Guardian, Blair admits mass graves claim untrue:

"Downing Street has admitted to The Observer (UK) that repeated claims by Tony Blair that '400,000 bodies had been found in Iraqi mass graves' is untrue, and only about 5,000 corpses have so far been uncovered." [90]

---

[90] *The Guardian,* "PM admits graves claim 'untrue'," July 18, 2004

124

And another fluff piece on Cheney in this week's Time Magazine:

"No real evidence has emerged to prove that Cheney lifted a finger to win contracts for Halliburton since he came back into government."

A smoke bomb. So what if he did or didn't? They were expecting a receipt that said "one quid pro quo, signed D.C" maybe?

When Cheney was CEO of Halliburton in 1998, Halliburton was doing business with Saddam, when it was illegal for American companies. Halliburton. Helped Saddam rebuild. His oil fields. Profits from oil fields equal more rocket launchers. Equals dead American troops. Equals Dick Cheney is a traitor. Again…(see July 9, 2004 post)

...Polis 6:44 PM

Friday, July 23, 2004

I'm going on break before I start throwing things and get myself fired. How I hate Bill Gates. I'm not on a techie trip, or even a purist business trip that says there has to be competition in the free market. Anyone can look around and see the only thing business hates is competition. That's life. But when it actually starts showing itself in inferior products, no good. This is what caused the Soviet Union to collapse, tires falling off cars in the middle of the street, whole apartment buildings with no door knobs. Why can't I go from office computer to home computer and back again even if it's the same version of Windows? Plain text file. That's simple-ass.

No excuses. This damned document goes out tonight. Boss doesn't care that I goof around blogging all day as long as I hit homers when the bases are loaded. If I have to work until 4 in the morning re-inventing the wheel on this friggen thing I'll do it. I'm starting to think current Darwinian selection favors Type A's, people with sticks of dynamite up their ass most of the time who are actually happy under pressure. I'm like that a little. Then you wonder why people are so mean to each other on the street, pushing and shoving and raging against all the bigger forces we are helpless before. Well not me. I'm switching to Wordperfect.

STILL LOOKING..."Blair, Mass Graves Untrue" (see post above, July 20, 2004)   Has anyone seen this in an American newspaper yet?

Quote of Note, The New Yorker's Seymour Hersh:

"My youngest (child) is 23, my oldest is 36. This is about them. What right do we have to put them in a permanent war with people who are crazy? Here we have 9-11, and the whole Muslim world, 99 percent of them, even the true believers were horrified and said, 'What can we do to help you?' And these nuts drove them away. These ideologues drove them away. How can you live with people like that?" [91]

The Bill Gates computer god must have heard me. The file is opening now.

....Polis 1:13 PM

Saturday, July 24, 2004

Alice in Wonderland Chapter 9/11. I kept thinking about Seymour Hersh's October 27 New Yorker article "The Stovepipe." In the Era of Bush you must constantly remind yourself that you really heard what you thought you heard, saw what you thought you saw. Easy to think you're losing your mind.

The latest re-arrangement of Bush parallel universe: I thought it was clear as Waterford crystal that the Bushies heard only

---

[91] "Mr. Hersh Goes to War," by Tim Madigan,
http://www.truthout.org/docs_04/072404D.shtml

what they wanted to hear from the CIA. I read everything quite carefully. Now Bush blaming the CIA for bad intelligence?

Back through the Looking Glass. New Yorker article "The Stovepipe":

> **"What the Bush people did was dismantle the existing filtering process that for fifty years had been preventing the policymakers from getting bad information. They created stovepipes to get the information they wanted directly to the top leadership."**

In my foreign policy class I found out that we've seen this sort of thing before, leaders hearing only what they want to hear, who fire people who don't give it to them. Cold War: Secretary of State John Foster Dulles purged experts from the State Department who had different views on China. Arthur Schlesinger says:

> **"Dulles' purge of the old China hands in the State Department deprived Kennedy and Johnson of the expert diplomatic counsel...If men like John Paton Davies, Jr., and John Carter Vincent had been on tap in the 1960s they would have informed their political masters of the ancient enmity between China and Vietnam, and the U.S. government would not have succumbed to the illusion that North Vietnam was the spearhead of a concerted Chinese plan to take over Southeast Asia."** [92]

The rich lie the poor die. What's new?

NEXT...Bin Laden family newsletter! Sorry we've been out of touch! Now that we know that members of the bin Laden family were whisked out of the country after 9/11, after only brief interviews (See Thursday, July 01, 2004 post) maybe a better question is, does it

---

[92] "The Measure of Diplomacy," by Arthur M. Schlesinger, Jr., *Foreign Affairs*, July/August 1994

matter? Isn't Osama what you call estranged from the rest of the folks? Even if we had subpoenaed them, they'd have nothing to tell us. Right?

Enter bin Laden's sister-in-law Carmen Binladen (she changed the spelling, wouldn't you?) She says in her new book "Inside the Kingdom" that "I cannot believe that they have cut off Osama completely." Of the bin Ladens and the Saudi royals she says:

"The bin Ladens and the princes work together, very closely. They are secretive, and they are united. They have been inextricably linked for many decades through close friendships and business ventures."

You're getting homework, dammit. You know I wouldn't if it wasn't important. Professor Stephen Walt, author of the "bandwagoning versus balancing" theory in foreign policy, on whether Saddam was a "madman." In the Shrub's well-wrought conundrum this is the key Lego. You can talk about deterrence this or containment that, it doesn't matter. All that pointy-headed crap is out the window. Saddam was crazy. He would have done something, sooner or later, and Bush wasn't waiting. That's the Bush case in a nutshell.

We had the guy boxed-in on two-thirds of his country with no-fly zones, the place was crawling with UN inspectors, and Bush still said he was hiding something. Remember? The Shrub didn't say we're invading because he's giving 25 grand to the families of suicide bombers in Israel, or because he has rape rooms. If you listen to wing-nut radio they call that "icing on the cake."

Now the problem is there's no cake under the icing. No WMD, so all that's left is the guy was crazy and would have gotten his hands on it eventually. One reason that doesn't hold water is, if bad guys getting their hands on WMD were really the problem, Bush wouldn't have stripped-out the networks of Valerie Plame.

But there's more. Prof. gave us this to read in night school class, so now it's your bedtime reading too, "An Unnecessary War,"

128

by Stephen Walt. [93]

Excerpt:

"...both the hard-line preventive-war advocates and the more moderate supporters of inspections accept the same basic premise: Saddam Hussein is not deterrable, and he cannot be allowed to obtain a nuclear arsenal. One problem with this argument: It is almost certainly wrong."

Last, the feds are visiting damned hippies thinking of free-speechin' at the Dem and Republican conventions, man I wish some of those guys would come to my house and try that. GIT THE FUCK OFFA MY PROPERTY! GIT THE FUCK OFFA MY PROPERTY! Give em some rock salt shot up the ass to underscore your point if they do not seem to understand. Anyhow, in Denver and a few other places, the FBI knocked on doors this week, like that of one Sarah Bardwell's, 21. She said six officers arrived about 4:30 p.m. Thursday at the Denver home she shares with four other young people:

"The six officers identified themselves as four FBI agents and two Denver police officers, but declined to give their names after the young people declined to give theirs. One officer said he took the young people's refusal to give their names as "noncooperation" and said he would have to use "more intrusive efforts to get his job done." "We had really no idea what was going on," [Bardwell] said...The officers asked three questions: Are you planning to be involved in any criminal acts at the national conventions? Do you know anybody who is? Are you aware that if you assist or know anybody planning any criminal acts and do not report them, it's a crime?"[94]

---

[93] Prof. Jeremy Pressman, see post Nov. 3, 2003. Walt article published in *Foreign Policy*, Jan./Feb. 2003

[94] *Rocky Mountain News,* "Warnings precede party conventions FBI, police

Uh, yea. Now exactly why am I talking to you assholes?

...Polis 12:48 PM

Wednesday, July 28, 2004

I know you might be saying what the heck, all this guy is doing is giving me a lot of names, dates, and places. Think of this blog as a record. I truly believe this is an amazing time in history, and someday historians will go to these blogs to see how things looked to the man on the street. Someday people will not believe half of what went down in these days and they'll want to study it. We invaded *what* country? Because we thought they had *what?* And that was going to *fix* the problem? And the president did *what?*

It's just my long way of saying post a comment! You're part of history! A blogger will say or do anything for comments.

AND...It's party week here in Boston, holy Molly, this really happened. During a peaceful march Sunday before the Democratic National Convention, a dark, swarthy-looking foreign-type (you know, one of them there full beards and what the hell is *that?)* was arrested by the Secret Service as he marched. My man-on-the-spot Isky was in the shit and got the scoop for boston.indymedia.org:

> **"At some point during the march from Boston Common to the Fleet Center, Secret Service agents approached the a man who appeared to be in his early 20s and of South Asian (Indian or Pakistani) descent, and wearing a full beard, and said they wanted to ask him some questions. The young man refused to talk with them and kept marching. They followed him for about a half-mile along the march, then stopped him again and asked his name and identification. When he refused again, they**

---

visits to young people rile ACLU official," by Karen Abbott, July 24, 2004

130

detained and handcuffed him." [95]

What followed was a little light harassment of a colored man. So it's nothing serious. But in the meantime a lawyer had arrived and had a chance to talk to the Secret Service. The attorney, John Pavlos said, "The Secret Service was very clear that they observed him *looking around*." (My italics.) So be careful where you "look around" while brown.

No one going into the "protest pen," the giant cage next to the convention site where protesters can practice their "free speech." It's a huge rectangle of 50-foot high chain link fence topped by razor wire. A Boston judge says it looks like a concentration camp. The protesters are ignoring it, one guy said "I'm not going in there, did you see that thing?" It's popular with tourists, though, who are taking pictures of each other standing inside it. A pro-Palestinian rights group uses it as a backdrop for skits about the Israeli occupation.

More scenes from the Democratic Convention, this by William Rivers Pitt reporting for Truthout.org:

> **"When I got to the Vets for Peace convention, there was a barrel-chested man absolutely collapsing with laughter in the lobby outside the speaking hall. "You won't believe it!" he shouted to a friend by the door. "I got promoted! I got a letter in the mail! I'm a corporal now!" I didn't get the joke at the time, but that was because I had not yet been properly introduced to Michael Hoffman, the barrel-chested newly-minted corporal, who is a veteran of Operation Iraqi Freedom and now the founder of Iraq Veterans Against the War (www.ivaw.net.)" [96]**

---

[95] "Racial Profiling at DNC: Man Arrested for Protesting While Brown," by Steve Iskovitz, http://boston.indymedia.org/feature/display/24043/index.php For a fuller account see "Idling While Brown," *Boston Phoenix,* Sept. 3, 2004,
http://www.bostonphoenix.com/boston/news_features/other_stories/multipage/documents/04097838.asp
[96] http://www.truthout.org/dnc-pre.shtml

131

Time for Kerry to shit or get off the pot. Say the Iraq adventure was a mistake. The convention speech tomorrow night is his big chance. This is getting ridiculous. Watching him tie himself up in knots and letting Bush pummel him is a little like watching the last scene in "Rocky."

Kerry says he wouldn't have "rushed to war"? What the hell does that mean? He would have gone but he would have taken his sweet time? Of course the war could have been done better. What war couldn't be?

I know Kerry's afraid of being labeled a dirty pacifist, like George McGovern against Nixon in '72. The similarities are weird. McGovern was actually the war hero then, too, a WWII bomber pilot, while Nixon never heard a shot fired in anger. All Kerry needs to say is: "Look, the war was a mistake. This is not a sign of weakness. It's a sign of strength. I will get us out of Iraq and back to the real war on terror."

Even my boss, a Republican I think, says based on what Bush gave us, I could come to your house, shoot you, then tell the cops it was justified because I thought you were going to hurt me. I can hear Bush saying, what's wrong with that?

The polls say the American people have turned against the war.

So Bush attacked the wrong people and our very presence in Iraq is a failure. Now let's push through with the elections and get the hell out. Failure is not an option. That right, Mr. President. We mustn't fail to catch the people who attacked us on September 11th.

You can't let Bush/Cheney get away with these mindless lines. We must take the fight to the enemy. Sure, let's take it to the *right* enemy, George. We must deny the enemy sanctuary. But we have made Iraq *into* a sanctuary, for terrorists. Terrorism loves chaos. It hates it when someone is in charge. Even if it's Saddam Hussein. Someone in charge can turn on you in a minute. You don't have that

132

problem with chaos.

We must hit the enemy where he lives. That's right, they live in Saudi Arabia, Pakistan, Indonesia, not to mention Bonn, London, and Paris. Kerry's whole rap is "I could have done it better." God he's boring.

Under the leadership of George W. Bush, the enemy got a Christmas present he never expected. We stepped into the quicksand all by ourselves. Come on John! It's time for Rocky to start punching back! I'm on the edge of my seat already, and I'm starting to not like this movie.

...Polis 11:57 AM

Friday, July 30, 2004

Late casualties, Marine Gunnery Sgt. Shawn A. Lane, 33, Corning, N.Y.; died in an attack in Anbar province; Nicholas Zangara, 21, Philadelphia; killed in an explosion in Tikrit; Marine Lance Cpl. Vincent Sullivan, 23, Chatham, N.J.; killed in fighting in Anbar province; Army Pvt. 1st Class Torey Dantzler, 22, Columbia, La.; died in Samarra when an explosive detonated near his vehicle.

33. 21. 23. 22. What heart-sickness. What waste.

This is the time of year I sit at sidewalk cafes to read and to watch the wildlife in Harvard Square. Summer is over before it begins in this place. Overheard one of the grumpy old men who gab and play chess all day, his take on Iraq. He was saying the best thing we could do is "put him back." Ah yes, like the joke about the elephant's ass corked up for a year and the monkey trained to pull the cork.[97] "We should say, hey look Saddam, maybe we were a little hasty here, but we had to double-check on those weapons of mass destruction, you understand....and you're clean, so we're putting you back in. We don't want this mess. Then we can get the hell out...the

---

[97] The surviving scientists testify to what they saw, first says "piles and piles of shit." Second says "piles and piles of shit." Third one says "all I saw was that poor monkey trying to put that cork back..."

best thing is to PUT HIM BACK! PUT! HIM! BACK!"

Iraq isn't like Vietnam? Excuse me?

-As in Vietnam, the insurgents see anyone who cooperates with the government as a collaborator. In Nam the Viet Cong would go from village to village and kill all South Vietnamese government employees: mayors, police, school teachers, anyone who took a paycheck from the puppet regime.

-New York Times today reports a big problem is corruption among our appointed puppets. This sounds like Diem and his cohorts all over again. Just like the Viet Cong, the Jihadists are feared, but acknowledged as incorruptible. Whatever they're fighting for, it isn't money. The Cong ate rice and rat meat and lived only to kill as many GIs as they could before they bought the farm themselves.

-Improving tactics by the insurgents; why the war is really stupid. You take a country full of people just out of the Stone Age, where donkeys are a major mode of transportation, and by trial and error they find out what works against our mil'turry. Squint George. The Viet Cong started out fighting the French in the 50s, and built generations of guerrilla knowledge by the time we got there. By the end of Nam the average teenage guerilla could make a booby trap out of a Budweiser can, and knew where to put it. We're seeing the same learning curve in Iraq.

General Ricardo Sanchez, before he got sacked, said attacking Iraq was good because it's like flypaper for terrorists, who'll be too busy fighting us there to bother us here. An incubator is more like it, flies laying thousands of eggs that grow up feeding on a gruel of hatred and the killing arts. Okay, a strained analogy. But when you have people who can only understand comic books, this is how you have to talk.

Flypaper, Axis of Evil, us versus them. Killing for most people is not a natural thing. You have to be hardened into it. What do you think Marines boot camp is for? The movie Full Metal Jacket: I'm told by a Vietnam veteran that's exactly how boot camp was during the Vietnam draft, right down to the glass removed from the barracks windows. Look close. They got rid of it because too many guys tried to slash their wrists.

The Iraqi insurgents are dealing with the first problem of any insurgency ruthlessly: their own people who cooperate with the enemy. It's the IRA the PLO and the Cong all rolled into one, in a country the size of California. The goal is to eliminate any middle ground. You are with us or agin' us. Yes George, you bet they know about that. The Middle East was a civil war waiting to happen, and we stepped right into the middle of it.

...Polis 1:04 PM

Sunday, August 01, 2004

What a party! I've never seen a political convention before, but I remember one lady telling me that they were one big excuse for a week of drinking, hell-raising, and screwing around. A city council woman or something like that. Parties EVERYWHERE for a solid week, one end of town to the other. Like Fort Lauderdale at Spring Break, but for old folks. Some parties you could crash, some you couldn't. I kept a fairly low profile and went to an art exhibit of drawings by Iraqi children who were in Baghdad during the bombing. Afterwards there was a talk by Howard Zinn. The wine was cheap, but the drawings were unreal. Little kids' art but with arms, legs and heads scattered here and there.

Watched the actual nomination at a party hosted by the Young Democrats. My friend C. and I weren't *absolutely* the oldest people in the room, but pert near close. Anyhow the convention has come and gone relatively peacefully. Word on the web is we are saving the mass arrests for the Republican Convention in New York come next month.

If you're planning on getting arrested for a cd, civil disobedience, you want to choose your time so that you're not on already on probation for a previous cd arrest. That makes them tougher on you. You could even go to jail if the judge is a bastard.

The Washington Monthly finally picked up the Tony-Blair-admits-mass-graves-in-Iraq-untrue story. Nothing in the mainstream press.

I'm really into this book, no time to blog. Here are a couple of passages. From "Imperial Hubris; Why the West is Losing the War on Terror," the CIA guy says:

> **"Sadly, unless the Divinity rids our eyes of hubris, we are lost. There is no sign we can remove it, and, I fear, Al Qaeda sees the world clearer than we."**

On the "gift" George Bush bestowed upon Bin Laden by attacking Iraq, "Imperial Hubris" author Anonymous says that the terrorist al-Zawahari wrote in late 2003:

> **"We thank God for appeasing us with the dilemma in Iraq after Afghanistan. The Americans are facing a delicate situation in both countries. If they withdraw they will lose everything and if they stay, they will continue to bleed to death."**

There it is, from the horse's mouth. George Bush is an "appeaser."

...Polis 6:09 PM

Thursday, August 05, 2004

Kerry/Edwards on full rock-and-roll in Michigan last Monday. For once it was Bush/Cheney who couldn't mouth a coherent sentence. That's because their position on terrorism isn't coherent the minute you say the emperor has no clothes. Kerry must have gotten nervous. Polls show improvement in voters' confidence in him, but not enough and not fast enough. Bush/Cheney unveil the final slimy plan for the last lap. Go straight for the fear, and don't bother about subtlety. Hit them over the head. Bush/Cheney equals safety, Kerry/Edwards equals danger. This is from the people who opposed the 9/11 Commission.

136

Kerry team pumping out rounds, George's Excellent Adventure in Iraq has improved recruitment for Al Qaeda, has alienated Muslim moderates; we're "turning the corner" sounds a lot like "mission accomplished." Bush badly wounded. The firefight raged throughout the day.

Bush said from the Rose Garden, after hearing of Kerry's remarks, Kerry shows a "fundamental misunderstanding of the war on terror." Kerry fires back that "you have to take it to the terrorists, you've got to...get them before they get us, but to do that you've got to have the best intelligence in the world, and you've got to have the best cooperation with our countries you've ever had. This administration doesn't know that. I do."

Then Kerry said: "Working with other countries is not a sign of weakness, it is a sign of strength."

Bush lobs a mortar in Kerry's general direction hoping he'll hit something: "Evidently some must think that you can negotiate with the [terrorists.]"

Kerry squeezed off a few more shots after dark, said Bush is employing a favorite tactic, putting words in other people's mouths. No one said anything about negotiating with terrorists.

Good. Strip it down to the reality and Kerry wins. Let the Shrub's comic book morality play stand, and Kerry loses. It's not easy to rattle these bastards but rattled they were. Kerry was tugging at the cape a little too hard, and they were afraid the whole get-up would come apart at the leotards.

Question for ya'll. Is it semiotics? Was arguing this the other day with B.C., what's the branch of linguistics that has to do with artful mixing of messages? Email me if you know. Fer instance, Bush said: "It is a ridiculous notion to assert that because the United States is on the offense, more people want to hurt us. We are on the offense because people DO want to hurt us."

This guy is good. There are times I catch myself nodding,

137

almost ready to admit I have been wrong all along, ready to march down to my local Election Commission to register Republican.

B.C. says what Bush is good at is called muddying the waters. Statement: "The United States is on the offense." But where? We're on the offense in more than one place, some good for us (Afghanistan, against Al Qaeda), some bad for us (Iraq.) Bush casually lumps it all together and then follows it with: So "A" is not a result of "B," "B" is a result of "A." Huh? That's what I mean. He's good.

I guess the answer to the pop semiotics (??) quiz would be that this statement is incorrect because it treats two unlike things as like. Remember that Sesame Street game for kids? "One of these things is not like the other." Then they'd show, like, three Chinese kids and a Mexican, or something, and you had to guess which of the similar things was different. Bush might have benefited from that show. It would be more correct to say "The United States is on the offense against *Al Qaeda* because they want to hurt us, but we should not be on the offense against *Iraq* because more people will want to hurt us." The ugly bottom of the Bush doctrine is that all A-rabs are alike.

I give myself an A. Yay. A logic (semiotics ??) teacher would have a field day with Bush's speeches.

My own take, for what it's worth. If you're still reading this maybe I'm making sense. Maybe you're just having a good laugh at my pure drivel. All good. The New War is what I call a "milintel" war, not military, not intelligence, but both. Special Forces and other elite agents creep around the world's cities, towns and countrysides, acting on deep-cover, corroborated intelligence, to engage terrorists with back-up from traditional military. This week's Newsweek says, after 9/11, some people in the IC, what these guys call the "intelligence community," wanted to hit Al Qaeda cells in South America or Indonesia before Afghanistan. Just to throw them off-balance. This war is for people who can think outside the box, not for people who need a cartoon bogeyman like Saddam to hang everything on.

138

When he attacked Iraq George Bush made the problem worse in three ways. First it drew valuable military and intelligence people into an unwinnable quagmire. USA Today reports:

"In 2002, troops from the Fifth Special Forces Group who specialize in the Middle East were pulled out of the hunt for Osama bin Laden to prepare for their next assignment: Iraq. Their replacements were troops with expertise in Spanish cultures."

Great.

Second, it turned a run-of-the-mill dictatorship that we supported when it suited us into an incubator for future terrorists. If we want to stop torture and women being raped in front of their parents, or whatever, we could *not* create death squads in El Salvador and places like that. You think Turkey doesn't have torture? They're our ally. We're talking about *Turkey*. Forget rape rooms. In Chile that hideous freak Pinochet that we supported had *rape dogs*.

Lt. Colonel Tim Ryan to a Boston Globe reporter in Iraq:

"We aren't going to change the man we're hauling off. It's the 10-year-old boy in the living room, watching us, that will one day make a decision about whether he's going to attack us."

Third and worst, Iraq has robbed us of the moral high ground we had after 9/11, which, like it or not, translates into help we need. Those Nazis you hear on the radio who say they don't care about civilian casualties are not only repulsive; that attitude is what's losing us this war. It's easy to kill terrorists when you know where they are. If everyone hates you, no one tells you that. Iraq is turning America-lovers into America-haters. The thing that's hardest to measure is the most important.

Oh! Oh! Teacher! Me! Me! Civilian casualties! Saddam was already killing his people! Funny how the people not getting bombed will always say it's okay for the ones who are. Did anyone ask the dead if it was okay to kill them to liberate them?

A headline from the spoof newspaper The Onion: *Widow says husband would have enjoyed freedom if not killed by bomb.*

In Israel they have summer camps for children of terror attack victims. One at Moshav Hazora'im hosted 100 kids. Oh Lord, this is not how I want to live. Dump Bush now.

I never thought I would end a post by quoting Live Shot Kerry.[98] But I will, because underneath the slick I believe there's a man's man who should be president. "We are here to work God's will and pray we see it clearly. Not to judge whether or not we have succeeded."

...Polis 4:25 PM

Tuesday, August 10, 2004

Going off now, you have been warned. Today's topic: "In youth we learn, in age we understand."
— Marie von Ebner-Escherbach

Sounds good but BULLSHIT! I don't understand much more than I did when I was 20! I *don't* understand why dirt-poor children are being blown to bits, and don't give me this lots of children died on 9/11 too crap because these dirt-poor children didn't do it! How a human being can watch a cruise missile attack on a populated neighborhood and not feel his stomach turn is beyond me. I *don't* understand. You've got to be so frozen up it's eating you up inside, man buys shotgun kills wife children self, a complete mystery no one could have seen coming. Goddammit there's a *connection* here! From whence this rage?

There.

---

[98] Early in his political career Kerry got this nickname in reference to his fondness for the TV cameras.

140

New blog debut www.aliberaldose.blogspot.com. He doesn't really like Kerry but thinks he must win because:

"if Kerry wins, the ruination of democracy by paperless e-voting will have been averted. Conversely, if Bush wins, it is guaranteed that HAVA will be strengthened, DREs will be forced upon the American electorate and verifiable elections will become a permanent impossibility."[99]

Bush wins, packs the Supreme Court with justices who see things his way, young enough to do real damage. The new Supreme Court agrees that "enemy combatant" status can apply to American citizens for as long as the government likes, doing away with that pesky Bill of Rights once and for all. The permanent rigging of elections seems a little far-fetched to me, but I also never would've believed we'd be occupying Iraq.

Noticed that the Kerry campaign blog has a lively "comments" conversation but the official Bush blog doesn't allow comments.

...Polis 8:21 PM

Monday, August 16, 2004

Damned these Democrats. What do you have to do wrong to get their attention? I bet even Bush is thinking it. Does a tree fall in the forest if politicians pretend they don't hear it?

Bush just ripped the lid off the secret arrest of a Pakistani Al Qaeda double agent, Mohammed Naeem Noor Khan. It sabotaged an investigation that "might have led to Bin Laden himself." [100]

---

[99] http://aliberaldose.blogspot.com/2004/07/from-left-field-so-why-kerry.html

[100] http://www.democracynow.org/print.pl?sid=04/08/10/149253

141

Reuters, August 7, 2004:

"Reuters learned from Pakistani intelligence sources at the weekend that computer expert Mohammad Naeem Noor Khan, arrested secretly last month, was working under cover to help the authorities track down al Qaeda militants in Britain and the United States when his name appeared in newspapers around the world."

> **"The revelation that a mole within al Qaeda was exposed after Washington launched its "orange alert" this month has shocked security experts, who say the outing of the source may have set back the war on terror."**

Christian Science Monitor:

"Pakistani intelligence officers said US officials blew the cover on an Al Qaeda mole last week, when the mole's identity was confirmed to The New York Times. The Times originally identified the source of their information as "senior American officials." The mole, computer expert Mohammad Naeem Noor Khan, was arrested secretly in mid-July in Pakistan. He had agreed to help authorities track down Al Qaeda militants in Britain and the United States...the revelation of Khan's name by US officials last week "exposed Khan and forced Pakistanis to move him to a secret location." [101]

Remember those New York financial district alerts? Pictures on the cover of Time, cops in black body armor carrying hardware that could stop a tank? A lot of good that will do. Bush was taking heat because when they asked him what he based these alerts on, besides the upcoming election, the stuff he brought out was over three

---

[101] *Christian Science Monitor* , "Did US blow cover on Al Qaeda mole?," August 9, 2004

years old. People were *laughing* at him. He hates that. One senior law enforcement official said:

> **"There is nothing right now that we're hearing that is new...Why did we go to this level [of alert]? ... I still don't know that."** [102]

So the Bushies tell everyone Noor Khan has been secretly arrested, which no one *but no one* is supposed to know. CS Monitor:

> **"The whole thing smacks of either incompetence or worse," said Tim Ripley, a security expert who writes for Jane's Defense publications [who was interviewed by Reuters]. "You have to ask: what are they doing compromising a deep mole within Al Qaeda, when it's so difficult to get these guys in there in the first place? It goes against all the rules of counter-espionage, counter-terrorism, running agents and so forth. It's not exactly cloak and dagger undercover work if it's on the front pages every time there's a development, is it?"**

If the Democrats acted like they had a pulse and Lewinskied this – people might stop trusting Bush. For damned good reason. CS Monitor:

> **"MSNBC reported Monday that the early exposure of Khan not only ended the sting that Pakistani intelligence was conducting, but it also forced Britain's intelligence service to move faster than it wanted to last Tuesday to apprehend terror suspects in England that had been e-mailed by Khan. Five other suspects were able to escape before British authorities could arrest them...CNN reports on Monday that several US senators said US officials should have kept Khan's identity a secret. They noted that Pakistani interior minister, Faisal Hayat, as well as the**

---

[102] *Washington Post,* "Pre-9/11 Acts Led To Alerts," August 3, 2004

British home secretary, David Blunkett, had "expressed displeasure in fairly severe terms that Khan's name was released, because they were trying to track down other contacts.""

University of Michigan Modern Middle East and South Asian History Professor Juan Cole:

"They dried up this potentially very rich well of further tracking and information which might have led to bin Laden himself." [103]

Plame-gate, trading-with-the-enemy-gate, now Khan-gate. And there are the Dems with a thumb up their butts and a big grin on their faces to pass the time of day. Lewinsky it, assholes! It was all-Monica-all-the-time!

....Polis 2:44 PM

Thursday, August 19, 2004

I give up. Going to the Middle East Cafe tonight to have a beer and not think about politics. The M.E. is where I went for a few nights after 9/11, just to be somewhere with people. After a few I even wrapped my scarf around my head, like a turban, hoping some thug on the street would say something. Then I had my line all planned out: this here is a Northern Alliance turban, maggot! Special Forces! Go before you die! Those guys can kill you six different ways with their bare hands. Special Forces, blue jeans, turbans, and machine guns. Fluent in Pashto or Farsi or some other far-out language. Most high-cool to be one of those guys.

We all did what we had to do in those days. You couldn't just sit home and cry. For the victims. For your country. I still didn't mind Bush back then. Didn't like him, but I didn't think he was that different from Gore. Not really.

---

[103] "Did the White House Sabotage the War on Terror by Leaking the Name of an al Qaeda Double Agent?," http://www.democracynow.org/print.pl?sid=04/08/10/149253

144

No one said anything about my head scarf. Cambridge is quite civilized that way. I did see people make a point of smiling and nodding at Muslims so they wouldn't feel paranoid and left-out. Can you imagine? To leave your house, wearing the badge of your faith, knowing a few Nazi thugs can't tell the difference between one brown person and another...

Kerry just said from the rim of the Grand Canyon that, even given what he knows now about no WMD in Iraq and no link to Al Qaeda, he would still have voted to authorize the war. Oh my God. The reporter was throwing him a softball, giving him a way to start untangling himself, giving him a chance to say, well son, now that you mention it, that vote came with conditions, and now that you mention it, those were them. WMD and Al Qaeda. We authorized force on *the condition* that the president *certify* there was WMD and a link to 9/11, and those conditions have not been met. He lied to us and he says I'm flip-flopping. I'm glad you brought that up...

There is just no helping some people.

Polls still put Bush on top in national security. Now you explain that one to me. Plame-gate, Cheney-trading-with-the-enemy-gate, now Khan-blown-chance-to-capture-bin-Laden-gate, but Kerry is the one who is suspect. It means you could have all the "gates" in the world, but someone has to pretend they notice. Would that be the Democrats? Does a tree fall in the forest...? Is there an elephant in the room? What elephant?

Fine with the lawyer-lobbyists. They've been cutting deals with Republicans for years, and whoever wins is okay as long as they keep their Beamers. The Constitution, the future of democracy, sending their kids to war and all that corny stuff doesn't keep them awake; it's what they'll bring in on the next billing cycle. Am I still in line for partner? Little twits. I have more respect for my homie rednecks who vote for Bush. The centrist-triangulators are at the absolute bottom of the invertebrate evolutionary scale. Squishy worms.

Where's attack dog Newt Gingrich when you need him? Is

there a party module transplant we can put in his brain and make him into a Democrat?

Republican Congressman Doug Bereuter breaks ranks and calls Iraq war a "mistake." Something Leslie Stahl on 60 Minutes tried over and over to get Kerry to say. Was it a mistake? Was it a mistake? Three times she tried. Maybe four. He wouldn't do it. "The president made a mistake in the way he took us to war" he said. Bush was loving it from his sofa eating pretzels. That's when he knew he was going to come out of this without a scratch. Knew that Kerry couldn't talk his way out of a paper bag. Michael Moore would have said to Kerry, "I'll take that as a 'No.'"

Doug Bereuter's letter. Referring to Saddam's links to Al Qaeda and the presence of WMD he said:

"Left unresolved for now is whether intelligence was intentionally misconstrued to justify military action..." [104]

"Mistake." You can do it John! Americans love nothing better than a repentant sinner!

More freedom and democracy in Bushland: West Virginia police report that the Secret Service had them arrest a couple wearing anti-Bush T-shirts at a public speech. The couple was standing quietly, listening to the speech.[105] Kerry should slam his opponent's Gestapo streak mercilessly.

And from an article in the Boston Herald by someone who I disagree with on nearly everything else:

"Yesterday, I noticed an ad in the Globe promoting a 25 percent off sale on ``Tommy Hilfiger Intimates" for girls. Because I am a

---

[104] *Lincoln Journal-Star,* "Bereuter: War in Iraq not justified," March 18, 2004

[105] "Thou Dost Protest Too Much ," Salon.com, http://slate.msn.com/id/2107012

trained observer, I figured that meant underwear. The ad cost about $25,000 and featured a kid - maybe 14 - who bore an amazing resemblance to Jon Benet Ramsey. She was the murdered 6-year-old from Colorado whose hideous parents made her dress like a pathetic teenage whore.

The little girl in the Hilfiger ad had a come-on look and a whole lot less than 25 percent on her frame. She was posed kneeling in bra and panties, staring into the lens, her mouth pouty, lips glossed and . . . well, you get the idea. It's enough to make any sane parent worry about how quickly kids have childhood stolen by the lurid life around us." [106]

Hey guys, can we be for something besides acid, amnesty and abortion? Being against this kiddie porn is a no-brainer and ought to be part of the platform. What I'm saying is, can we show we're normal though tolerant and open-minded people who worry about our kids the same as everyone else? Screw Hollywood. Screw Madison Avenue. What did they do for us besides make our kids hate us for not buying them CDs we can't afford?

Have been meaning to post this next thing from the Boston Globe on D-Day survivors' experiences. Some think attacking Iraq was a bad idea. Corporal Albert Skorupa of the First Special Engineer Brigade, who landed on Omaha Beach in neck-deep water carrying 30 pounds of C-2 explosives, said:

"As far as Iraq goes, we shouldn't be there. They're fighting for the oil fields. I don't blame France for being against the war. . . . Did they give us good reasons for why our guys are getting killed? I don't think so." [107]

---

[106] *Boston Herald,* "Kiddie porn sales pitches no real surprise," by Mike Barnicle, August 19, 2004

[107] *Boston Globe*, "D-Day Revisited," June 6, 2004

Mr. Skorupa is now 85. I guess Bush would say he doesn't support the troops, right George? Maybe he should shut up or he'll demoralize them.

Guest columnist Dahlia Lithwick for the New York Times last week says Bush is confusing protesting with terrorism:

> **"An account by Justin Rood in Salon last week revealed that at a recent rally in Duluth, Minn., Secret Service checkpoints were festooned with photos of men posing some ostensible physical danger to the president: one was a professor active in the Green Party, another a pacifist homeless activist. Both had plans to protest the war during Mr. Bush's visit."**

They had the Patriot Act on the shelf for years when they got 9/11 and said, Let's go for it! These protesting punks with all their blood-and-oil talk are upsetting my wife! Lithwick again:

> **"One section [of the Patriot Act] invented a broad new crime called "domestic terrorism" - punishing activities that "involve acts dangerous to human life" if a person's intent is to "influence the policy of a government by intimidation or coercion." If that sounds as if it's directed more toward effigy-burning, or Greenpeace activity, than international terror, it's because it is. International terror was already illegal."**

Is a sit-in at your congressman's office "coercion?" That makes you a terrorist.

....Polis 12:35 PM

Tuesday, August 24, 2004

Last Sunday, the Charlie Rose Show, PBS "the best television on television." Former CIA director James Woolsey versus former CIA analyst Ray McGovern. Woolsey, a high-domed, coke bottle-lensed Bush hit-man jumps right into they-hate-us-for-our-freedom. They hate "the very idea of freedom," they hate "the separation between church and state," they are out to "establish a worldwide theocracy." Pure, unadulterated, undiluted, fresh steaming horseshit.

McGovern politely differs, maybe our unrestrained support for the Sharon government was partly responsible for 9/11. Woolsey drones something mostly unintelligible but we *do* hear the word "anti-Semitic."

Woolsey keeps talking. McGovern, who looks and sounds like a tweedy English professor, starts saying "anti-Semite? An anti-Semite?" His voice kind of high and reedy, getting higher and reedier each time. It didn't take Woolsey long to bring out the slime. Woolsey backs down before it gets any uglier. McGovern was about to yank the old fool's chair out from under him and knee-drop him in the kidney. I could see it in the eyes. We'll never know what went down in the parking lot.

I believe this is what's called "poisoning the discussion." Are Jews who hate Sharon and his policies "anti-Semitic?" Or does it only apply to non-Jews? What if I'm half-Mexican and half-Jewish? This gets interesting. Can I say it if I wear a yarmulke under my sombrero?[108]

---

[108] My mother's maiden name is Elias, both an Arabic and a Jewish name. We aren't sure of the connection, but many Jews escaped the Spanish Inquisition by coming to Mexico.

This vile form of argument pops-up in surprising places. Harvard president Larry Summers once showed such Enlightenment Age reasoning skills when he said of students protesting Israeli policies:

> **"Where anti-Semitism and views that are profoundly anti-Israeli have traditionally been the primary preserve of poorly educated right-wing populists, profoundly anti-Israel views are increasingly finding support in progressive intellectual communities."** [109]

Flash: the president of Harvard is dumb. That's *Harvard*, yo. Can't tell the difference between protesting a policy and protesting a people. How embarrassing for all those professors who spent a life time trying to wind up at someplace with prestige. Are all Americans pro-Bush? Are all Brits monarchists? This is part of the SAT. The easy part.

Polis's book report: Anonymous "Imperial Hubris" says Woolsey is full of it. They definitely don't "hate us for our freedoms." Whatever they hate us for, that isn't it.

> **"We are defending ourselves against the United States," bin Laden said on behalf of the Islamic world in November 2001. "This is why I used to say that if [the Muslims] do not have security, the Americans also will not have it. This is a very simple formula..."**

"Imperial Hubris" says that bin Laden has built a case that Muslims around the world are under attack by the US; what we're dealing with is a "global Muslim insurgency." Anonymous quotes bin Laden:

> **"For God's sake, what are the documents that incriminate the Palestinian people that warrant**

---

[109] *Harvard Crimson*, "Summers Says Anti-Semitism Lurks Locally," Sept. 19, 2002

the massacres against them...What is the evidence against the people of Iraq to warrant their blockade and being killed in a way that is unprecedented in history. What documents incriminated the Muslims of Bosnia-Herzegovina and warranted the Western Crusaders, with the United States at their head, to unleash their Serb ally to annihilate and displace the Muslim people in the region under UN cover. What is the crime of the Kashmiri people...What have Muslims in Chechnya, Afghanistan, and the Central Asian republics committed to warrant being invaded by the brutal Soviet Military regime and after it communism's killing, annihilating, and displacing tens of millions of them...WE say that all the Muslims that the international Crusader-Zionist machine is annihilating have not committed any crime other than to say God is our Allah."

Anywhere you see Muslims massacred, you see that government allied with the US, including China (Xinjiang Province,) Burma (Myanmar,) and the Philippines. The problem is that whatever the reason, the pattern is clear. Anonymous calls bin Laden's case "pretty factual, although colored by his conviction of the West's malevolence toward Muslims."

"More important, [bin Laden's] portrayal of [these] as attacks on Islam and Muslims are completely plausible to Muslims worldwide. Faced with what he describes as the Crusader "onslaught," bin Laden is doctrinally correct in claiming that the proper Koran-based response for such attacks is a defensive jihad.... Posing the rhetorical question "Why are we waging jihad against you?" bin Laden responded: "The answer to that question is very simple. Because you attacked us and continue to attack us."

But highest on the list is Muslim anger at US support for corrupt regimes in the Middle East, who can torture whomever they

151

like as long as they keep the oil coming. We're disgusting junkies with tracks up one arm and down the other, and we shake and slobber if we think we don't get the oil fix. Anonymous says "we have nothing in common with the regimes; the tie is based overwhelmingly on the West's obsession with cheap oil." When the Israelis bomb Palestinian neighborhoods, they see American F-16s and Apache helicopters. When Saudi police keep a crowd from peaceably assembling, they carry American M-16s. Everywhere Muslims look, whoever is repressing them, the weapons are American. And they are fearsome weapons.

Yes, those insurgents behead people, but have you seen what an Apache helicopter can do to your head?

Anonymous finds no evidence that bin Laden wants a worldwide Muslim theocracy.

> **"So far as I have found, al Qaeda supports no Islamic insurgency that seeks to conquer new lands, notwithstanding the unsupported but media-pleasing claim of many in the West that bin Laden "makes very clear... [his] ultimate goal is to undermine Western civilization in its entirety...."**

The corrupt regimes include Saudi Arabia, Qatar, Kuwait, Pakistan, United Arab Emirates, and Egypt. Worse, Anonymous says these regimes fund organizations that:

> **"foster an intensely anti-American brand of Islam around the world...because they fear our example of representative government...[which] will inspire their people to rebel. It is the Gulf royals-not Osama bin Laden-who hate us for what we are, not what we do."**

Civilian casualties. Two conditions are met in order to justify large civilian casualties. The first is that a war is "asymmetrical," that there is no other way to get at an enemy that sits on aircraft carriers, rides in tanks, bombs from the sky against sling-shots, rocket launchers, and AK-47s. The second is that all attacks must be

152

intended to defeat the enemy, and not only to produce civilian casualties. [110]   Bin Laden uses the example of catapults in ancient warfare as a weapon that does not distinguish between soldier and civilian. He calls civilian casualties unfortunate but unavoidable.

Unfortunate? Can't be helped? Too bad? War is war? This bin Laden feller and George Bush sound a lot alike, if you ask me.

Anonymous informs us that bin Laden has left an extensive stream of warnings over ten years before mounting any attacks. Bin Laden

> **"went the extra mile in preparing Muslims for a WMD attack on the United States by turning America's democracy back on its own citizenry. "Many people in the West are good and gentle people," bin Laden said. "I have already said that we are not hostile to the United States. We are against the system [i.e., U.S. foreign policy] which makes nations slaves of the United States, or forces them to mortgage their political and economic freedom." Turning the absurd personalized war-making formula so beloved in the West -- "We are at war with bin Laden not Muslims," for example, or, "We are at war with Saddam not Iraqis" -- against the United States, bin Laden assures Americans that Islam is at war against their government and not them, and he explains that because he understands that America is a democracy, he also understands that Americans have the electoral power to change the leaders who are prosecuting an anti-Islam foreign policy."**

Review, they hate us *because*:

-the presence of US troops in the Middle East, where they prop-up corrupt and tyrannical governments,

---

-US financial and logistical support for these governments, which insures the flow of oil at sweetheart prices,

-lopsided US support for Israel,

-US alliances with Muslim-killers around the world, in Chechnya, Aceh Indonesia, the Kasmir, Bosnia, and China. Massacres of Muslims at Sabra, Shatila, in the Kasmir, Bosnia, Chechnya and China are cited.

All this has nothing to do with Sam Huntington smokescreens about young Muslim men angry because they don't fit-in. It has to do with swarms of street children in Cairo, in a country swimming in oil, because a few families steal it and can stay in power because of US guns. Anonymous urges:

> **"With [energy] self-sufficiency, the United States can disengage from the Persian Gulf regimes-especially Saudi Arabia-which are among the earth's most corrupt, dictatorial, and oppressive. They rule peoples eager to be free of their yoke and who think their torturers survive because of US protection."**

There's nothing complicated about it. We've been killing them so now they're killing us. Another thing Anonymous says:

> **"For bin Laden, the most effective recruiting tool imaginable is for the United States to keep doing what it has been doing in the Islamic world for the past thirty years. The invasion of Iraq and the subsequent insurgency there is icing on the cake for al Qaeda."**

The US attack on Iraq was a miraculous, "never to be hoped for gift" to bin Laden. Horror at his methods was causing his international support to dry up. In the long-run, bin Laden would have lost, because attacking the USS Cole was one thing, and the Towers were another. Even our enemies weren't buying into his civilian casualties argument. Not like that. And even people who hated us were disgusted at bin Laden. Then Bush attacked Iraq. Anonymous on page 212 of "Hubris" :

"Why is today's Iraq like a Christmas present you long for but never expected to receive? Give up? Well, there is nothing bin Laden could have hoped for more than the American invasion and occupation of Iraq...Think of it: Iraq is the second holiest land in Islam; a place where Islam had been long suppressed by Saddam; where the Sunni minority long dominated and brutalized the Shia majority; where order was kept only by the Baathist barbarity that prevented a long overdue civil war; and where, in the wake of Saddam's fall, the regional powers ...would intervene, at least clandestinely, to stop the creation of...a Sunni or Shia successor state...a land where al Qaeda or al Qaeda-like organizations would thrive...an invasion would sharply deepen anti-American sentiment in the Muslim world, a hatred that would only worsen as Muslims watched the US military's televised and inevitable thrashing of Saddam's badly led and hopelessly decrepit armed forces. And then, dreamed bin Laden wildly, things would get bad for the Americans. They would stay too long in Iraq, insist on installing a democracy that would subordinate the long dominant Sunnis, vigorously limit Islam's role in government, and act in ways that spotlighted their interest in Iraq's massive oil reserves. All Muslims would see each day on television that the United States was occupying a Muslim country, insisting that man-made laws replace God's revealed word, stealing Iraqi oil, and paving the way for the creation of a "Greater Israel.""

Anonymous says we should have gone in big around Tora Bora and those mountains while the televised images of the smoldering Towers could still be seen. Even countries against it wouldn't have dared say anything. Bin Laden was trapped. Instead, the two month delay before major ground operations began and our reliance on the easily-bribed Northern Alliance allowed most of the leadership to escape into Pakistan. The other fighters just went home, with their weapons.

These are rural people who just go back to farming and herding goats when they aren't fighting. Bin laden sent most of them home before the bombing began, and it wasn't easy. They wanted to stay and fight Americans. Anonymous:

> **"When combat began on 7 October, bin Laden and al Qaeda...moved fighters into the Afghan countryside and mountains, as well as to Pakistan and Iran...Few of the fighters wanted to leave. Senior al Qaeda field commander Abd al-Hadi has explained that "we had great difficulty persuading many of them to leave Afghanistan...I swear some of them wept when they were told to leave."**

The final chapter of "Imperial Hubris" is called "No basis for optimism." Anonymous believes Americans are so arrogant that we will dismiss his arguments, and equate a wise foreign policy to "surrender." He believes that because of this we're in for a hundred years war drenched in blood on our own soil, that will leave the nation bled dry of its economic vitality, constitutional rights, and democratic traditions.

To which I say, so what if it does? When global warming and the wars over water really ramp up, two things will insulate people who can afford islands, doctors, and private armies: money, and the social order. Think about the Halliburton billionaires being made this very minute. That kind of money will buy you an island and Blackwater Security for a 100 generations. During the Great Depression a few people had a *great* time.

There is a precedent for all this. Teddy Roosevelt was president. On another September, in 1901, anarchists struck Buffalo, N.Y., the heart of the new American empire. It was the latest in a string of attacks on Western nations.

156

Roosevelt hunted down the terrorists, but the Hero of San Juan Hill, gun-toting imperial warrior ordered a search for the grievances that turned people into anarchists, the terrorists of that day. Some wanted to dismiss anarchists as wild-eyed animals, the same as the Freeper Neanderthals now say just kill them don't think about what creates them. Almost alone Roosevelt favored a two-pronged approach of attacking enemies, and reforming the worst of the social injustices he saw. The speech in which Roosevelt addressed terrorism was entitled, get this, "The Regulation of Corporations."

> **"I see in the near future a crisis approaching that unnerves me and causes me to tremble for the safety of my country. . . . corporations have been enthroned and an era of corruption in high places will follow, and the money power of the country will endeavor to prolong its reign by working upon the prejudices of the people until all wealth is aggregated in a few hands and the Republic is destroyed."**
>
> **-- President Abraham Lincoln**

...Polis 4:44 PM

Friday, August 27, 2004

"The war is not meant to be won—it is meant to be continuous." -George Orwell "1984"

Follow this blog for baton-blow-by-baton-blow coverage of the Republican Convention this Sunday.   Meanwhile congrats to Lawrence Krakauer for getting this letter published in the current issue (Aug. 30) of Newsweek. Forward it to your conservative uncle:

157

Editor,
You did not speculate on why al Qaeda would want to strike in the United States before the election. Al Qaeda is sophisticated enough to understand that a strike before the election would rally Americans behind the president, who is perceived (rightly or wrongly) as being more hawkish than his challenger. So if Al Qaeda strikes in the United States before the election, it will be with the clear purpose of helping re-elect George W. Bush. After all, with the exception of Osama bin Laden himself, President Bush, with his ill-advised invasion of Iraq, has done more to benefit Qaeda recruiting than any other person on earth.

Lawrence J. Krakauer
Wayland, Mass.

I like this new blogger at www.aliberaldose.blogspot.com. Last Wednesday's post:

We Lose Our Shit Online

After dealing with a half-dozen of the asshole contingent online we throw in the towel and give in to our baser instincts, engaging in a little online flaming:

Q: Do you think Kerry should condemn Moveon.org and George Soros? Seems to be playing the same game?

Funny you should ask that, because Kerry did condemn them MONTHS ago. Well the ads, anyway.

Soros, as a private citizen, can pretty much say

whatever he wants. It being America and all, you know. Unless Bush steals a second term, people aren't jailed yet for speaking their minds.

But here's a nifty little update: seems Kenneth Cordier who coordinated the Shifty Whores for the GOP, was also on the Bush campaign's veterans NATIONAL STEERING COMMITTEE. What do you know; now isn't that the most amazing little coinky-dinky?"

The Swift Boat Liars Against Kerry. The height of it is not one of them was ever on Kerry's boat.

...Polis 2:24 PM

Tuesday, August 31, 2004

It's only the second day of the Republican Convention and already over 300 arrested. Even on a slow day, yesterday, 50 people, 4 times more than the total number arrested for the whole week of the Democratic convention. Last Sunday 500,000 anti-Bush demonstrators poured into the streets in a procession two miles long and taking six hours to pass by Madison Square Garden.

From the New York Times:

"A roaring two-mile river of demonstrators surged through the canyons of Manhattan yesterday in the city's largest political protest in decades, a raucous but peaceful spectacle that pilloried George W. Bush and demanded regime change in Washington...[they] denounced President Bush as a misfit who had plunged America into war and runaway debt, undermined civil and constitutional rights, lied to the people, despoiled the environment and used the presidency to benefit corporations and millionaires."

159

Activist group Code Pink borrows a theme from the Boston convention's "peaceful protesters" campaign, which gave food and drink discounts at local shops to protesters who promised to be peaceful. Code Pink designed a "peaceful New York police" button, which gives discounts to cops who wear it and promise to be peaceful. Officers who wear the buttons can receive discounts from businesses like ABC Homes and Carpets (20 % off); Axis Gallery (10 % off art work); The Culture Project (50 % off on any performance); Angelica's Kitchen (5 % off on meals); and screenings of the movie "Uncovered" at the Angelica Theater (10 % off).

264 Critical Mass bike riders arrested last Friday. They're those kids you see riding in a big pack sometimes on a Saturday or Sunday, to promote bikes, environmental responsibility, and to have fun. As they reached East Village the cops suddenly rolled-out bright orange plastic nets and encircled them, arresting anyone caught inside the net. At the holding area on Pier 57 people complain they aren't even protesters, there are Chinese food delivery men, German tourists, anyone in the wrong place at the wrong time.

This from Act Up website, a group of AIDS activists, breaking news:

07:14 PM
Marches are converging around Herald Square at 34th and 6th, heading towards the Garden. There are reports of police violence there. Multiple busses of riot police are around 32nd / 34th and 6th. Several police reportedly are not wearing badge numbers. Mass arrests are now occurring in Herald Square.

06:20 PM
Protesters from the library are at 42nd and 6th. 40 cops on scooters ran after protesters with nets. Apx. 50 have been entrapped with nets. Police attacked protesters within the nets. Reports of a cop using a bike to hit someone. Several hundred are in the surrounding area. Pepper

spray is being deployed at Herald Square. There are at least 1000 protesters there. Spray victims are being handcuffed.

07:45 PM
OVERVIEW OF CURRENT SITUATION: Action is taking place all over the city. There are 3 main points, where events are unfolding - 16th street and Irving (near Union Sq.): mass arrests are imminent, reports of beatings and people not being allowed to leave. Herald Square (6th ave. between 34th and 36th): people are being beaten, pepper sprayed and contained. 28th and Broadway: War Resisters League has been holding a die-in of 50 people in the middle of the street.

08:22 PM
About 100 people broke away from Herald Square, taking over the street on 28th just off of 5th. Police ran down Madison Ave chasing the group on bikes first then dropped bikes to pursue marchers on foot. People are being tackled and arrested. Protesters are now at park and 26th, shoved face-down on ground. Media is gathered at the corner, being pushed back.

09:21 PM
On the north side of west 35th street and 6th avenue reports of 50 violent arrests- people being thrown to the ground and against walls.

A New York judge is bullshit that floods of people coming before him look pretty normal and seem not to have done anything wrong. Carrying signs and chanting in the streets are still legal in this country, the last he checked. He orders the city to release 500 people immediately and when it doesn't he holds the city in contempt and charges it $1000 for each person not released.

The idea behind all this is simple. Chill speech by making it

161

costly and inconvenient. Cops say "you can beat the rap, but you can't beat the ride." Many people spending more than 38 hours in custody.

From a Republican conventioneer, today's NY Times: "You've got to give Bush credit. They attacked us when he was president, and he went after them."
No he didn't. He went after Saddam instead.

Baghdad Year Zero by Naomi Klein is a must-read.[111] Check out these excerpts and quotes:

> **"Even better, investors could take 100 percent of the profits they made in Iraq out of the country; they would not be required to reinvest and they would not be taxed."**

> **"a flurry of new consulting firms were launched promising to help companies get access to the Iraqi market, their boards of directors stacked with well-connected Republicans."**

> **"One well-stocked 7-Eleven could knock out thirty Iraqi stores; a Wal-Mart could take over the country."**

> **"Scott Erwin, a twenty-one-year-old former intern to Dick Cheney, reported in an email home that "I am assisting Iraqis in the management of finances and budgeting for the domestic security forces." The college senior's favorite job before this one? "My time as an ice-cream truck driver.""**

> **"In Baghdad the concrete barriers have been given a popular nickname: Bremer Walls."**

> **"The company's manager, on his way to work,**

[111] "Baghdad Year Zero," *Harpers*, Sept. 2004.

was shot to death. Press reports speculated that the manager was murdered because he was in favor of privatizing the plant, but Mahmud was convinced that he was killed because he opposed the plan. "He would never have sold the factories like the Americans want. That's why they killed him.""

"If people are shooting at each other, it's just difficult to do business."

NEXT...They didn't cut off heads? What are these?

"To make a long story short, we were not pleasant people and the war was not a pleasant business."

-Larry Heinemann, 25th Division, Vietnam 1966, winner of National Book Award for "Paco's Story"

In a conversation with J. about John Kerry, somehow we got to talking about Kerry's early opposition to the Vietnam War (we agreed his career peaked-out when he was 25.) This was at a party in South Boston, usually a lot farther than I like to travel for a party. But the dearth of social opportunities on the Cambridge side of the river that Saturday night forced me to take a bus for 25 minutes. Getting older seems to go hand-in-hand with my world shrinking. Now going a full 3 stops on the subway to Davis Square requires careful deliberation. I used to jump on a train to New York just for the hell of it.

When we got onto the controversy about Kerry saying, back then, that there was raping and cutting-off heads and ears and stuff by American soldiers J. told me about an old newspaper she had somewhere in her dusty attic. I was glad I made the trip because I ran into all my Cambridge friends. We were all in the same boat, and we were happy to be drinking M.'s free liquor.

What I don't understand is if people hate Kerry because they think those atrocities never happened, or because he talked about them. To my way of thinking it's not fair to put high-powered weapons into the hands of 19 year-olds, send them into terrifying situations, then hold them responsible when some start to flip-out. The anti-Kerry vets are using words like "slander," "smear," and "dishonor," which would imply that Kerry said things that weren't true.

I have a great solution to all this fighting among the vets, which is embarrassing the way it is when you see brothers fighting. You're instinct is to look down and look away. Shameful. Here it is: they should rent the biggest VFW hall in the country for a whole weekend, then both sides, Kerry and anti-Kerry, go there and get good and drunk, and then *get it all out!* The barroom brawl of the century! Up to and including trashing the place! Smashing the furniture!

There's only one rule: NO ONE WHO WASN'T THERE IS ALLOWED IN, UNDER ANY CIRCUMSTANCES! Especially little rich kids who snuck into the Guard. That would include chickenhawks like Shrub, Dick Cheney (5 draft deferments), John Ashcroft, Paul Wolfowitz, and fat-boy Karl Rove.[112]

Here are some scans of what J. dug up in her attic, a 1968 issue of a long-forgotten publication, "Vietnam GI." The point isn't whether or not these things happened. They did. The point is you don't send kids into places where they learn to shoot anything that moves just so they can make it to 21.

From the lead editorial in "Vietnam GI," 1968:

"The administration wants you to believe that anti-war feeling is limited to kooky college kids and a few far-out professors...Can they explain

---

[112] Two days later, Kerry did rip Dick Cheney's draft deferments, saying "I'm going to leave it up to the voters to decide whether five deferments makes someone more qualified than two tours of duty." *Los Angeles Times,* "Author says Cheney draft deferments weren't unusual," September 18, 2004.

164

how for the first time the Gallup Poll reports a majority of the American public opposed to our involvement in Vietnam? (original italics) In a special editorial this week, LOOK magazine calls the war a "mistake"...President Johnson would have us think that his policy is to seek peace in every possible way. Who can believe him? To speak plainly, he has lied about everything else, so why not about this too. We all know the negotiations that started in Paris this morning could have taken place years and many GI lives ago.[113] And vice-president Hubert Humphrey's remark that the talks could drag on for "years" is disgusting.

But are "twin doves", McCarthy and Kennedy, the answer? We don't think so. It's true that many good people have campaigned and voted for them, but we remember the last presidential elections, when all the liberals were running around crying that only Lyndon Johnson could keep us out of war in Vietnam. LBJ was a "peace" candidate then! There's a lesson there.

Robert Kennedy and Eugene McCarthy are politicians, in large part motivated by their personal ambitions. They've made many deals in "smoked-filled rooms", and have forgotten many promises. They do not lead, they follow: picking up votes a safe distance behind what is a spreading tide of popular opposition to the war.

Remember, neither politician has been willing to commit himself to simply getting out of the

---

[113] Compare this to journalist Seymour Hersh's words in an April 2005 issue of *The Nation*: "You understand that in 1965 during the Vietnam War anybody who said let's talk to the Viet Cong or the North Vietnamese would've been called crazy, just like anybody who says let's talk to the insurgents now would be called crazy."

Vietnam War. In fact, McCarthy has made a point of telling us that if the talks don't work out to our satisfaction, we'll just have to keep on fighting in Southeast Asia."

Sound familiar?

Here's one final excerpt, from the article "Wolfhound Brass: No Prisoners." I thought I was reading about Abu Ghraib.

"We don't have any textbook ideas about war - we were there. We know that war is ugly all the way around. But too much really brutal shit goes on in Nam, and the responsibility for this goes right to the brass....If the brass want troops to kill prisoners and stray civilians, then they should tell the American people that this is their policy. Of course, that is asking the brass to openly take responsibility for the dirty side of war, like men. As we know, most officers don't have the guts to do that! If anything goes wrong, they'll just see to it that some enlisted man pays for it."

Here is a picture from "Vietnam GI."

The above picture shows exactly what the brass want you to do in the Nam. The reason for printing this picture is not to put down G.I.'s but rather to illustrate the fact that the Army can really fuck over your mind if you let it.

It's up to you, you can put in your time just trying to make it back in one piece or you can become a psycho like the Lifer (E-6) in the picture who really digs this kind of shit. It's your choice.

Caption reads:

"The above picture shows exactly what the brass want you to do in the Nam. The reason for printing this picture is not to put down GIs, but rather to illustrate the fact that the army can really fuck over your mind if you let it. It's up to you, you can put in your time just trying to make it back in one piece or you can become a psycho like the lifer (E-6) in the picture who really digs this kind of shit. It's up to you."

Why Kerry is only neck-and-neck in the polls with a generally unpopular president. New Hampshire Greens, come on down! A NH Green sent me this:

"Bush came out very early for a sitting president and started slinging mud at Kerry. Bush's position was so weak he almost had to. But instead of Kerry duking it out -- thereby scoring some points and making the president look much less presidential -- he quietly sat and did nothing.

Ditto for the Swift Boat ads. Kerry should be crowing from the top of his lungs that Bush was a deserter and demanding his records. Hell, the Lt. Gov. of Texas just admitted that he arranged Nat'l Guard admittance for the sons of the rich (including Bush) during the Viet Nam War -- and what does Kerry do with it? Nothing; he sits and lets the media play "he says, she says" with the Swift Boat vets and he gets hammered."

Neither here nor there. Bloggers have a bad habit of writing whatever comes to mind apropos of absolutely nothing, and that's exactly what I'm going to do now. A distinguished-looking gentleman just walked past my table in the cafe where I'm blogging, about the same age as my dad. Which made me think of dads in general, which made me think of Elian Gonzales, which is why I'm putting you through this.

I promise it's short. Remember the Elian Gonzales thing during the Clinton years, when the little boy from Cuba was being fought over by his family? Uncles and aunts in Miami wanted him to stay here for a "life of freedom," and dad in Cuba wanted him back. Clinton gave dad a chance to move here, but dad *liked* Cuba. Said he liked his job as a mechanic and wanted Elian back. Which is what wound up happening. It got ugly. Anyway my thought was that it was the pictures that told the whole story.

You'd see little Elian with the head uncle in Miami, who seemed to love the publicity and always left the house holding Elian's hand and wearing leather bomber jackets and cowboy boots, like, in every single picture, and the aunts were always dressed to the nines with loads of jewelry. Bleached-blond hair. Elian's mother was dead – remember? - and this was the mother's side of the family that wanted to take Elian away from his father. So when they finally brought Elian's dad over from Cuba to fetch him back, here's a nice-looking young guy in sneakers, jeans, and a sweatshirt, and it hit me, That's his *dad!* That's what a *dad* looks like! They *belong* together!

Right away in the pictures Elian looked suddenly happy, in an inside-way, not in a I'm-going-to-Disneyland-again way, for the third time this week. They looked completely natural. Dad's are special like that. My own dad can build a house with his hands, and that's how he likes to dress. He says it's the man inside that counts. He would have dressed that way for my Yale graduation if my mom hadn't made him put on a nice sports coat. Only *over* the USC sweatshirt, though. That stayed. That's his football team.

...Polis 1:59 PM

Thursday, September 02, 2004

Republican Convention, something like 1100 arrests two days ago, this is already a record for any convention in American history, including Chicago '68. Postings like this on the web are rampant:

> **"Just got a call from a co-worker who was being penned in at Grand Central in front of Ciprianis. He indicated arrests were imminent and that there were no orders from police just quick and sudden encirclement. He was certain that he and 1 or 2 others were to be arrested for display of anti-RNC signage."**

From the ACT UP website:

> **"Yesterday thousands of protesters, waving pink slips, formed a symbolic unemployment line stretching three miles from Wall Street to the site of the Republican National Convention this morning, creating a 5,000-person strong "Unemployment Line" this morning on Broadway from Wall Street to Madison Square Garden,**

169

representing 1.2 million jobs lost under Bush."

Earlier Thursday, approximately 150 protesters chanting, "Fight AIDS, not Iraq," staged a brief demonstration near Grand Central Terminal's Information Booth. The protest began at 8:05 a.m. when a man strode into the middle of the terminal's concourse and blew a whistle, signaling other demonstrators to pour into the hall from its various entrances. Police quickly removed two banners that were unfurled at two staircases on opposite ends of the terminal and began making arrests.

A couple of days ago nine ACT UP aids activists arrested for stripping down to their birthday suits, to show-off the sign "Bush, Stop AIDS, Drop the [Third World] Debt Now" painted on their backs. One said "When it comes to fighting the AIDS crisis, Emperor Bush has no clothes."

Gimme a job! I have taken the trouble to compose and email the following remarks to the Kerry campaign, for a televised Kerry rebuttal to the Republican Convention. I'm not making it John, I need money. Hook me up with a consulting gig.

KERRY FACE-ON TO CAMERA. FULL 5-MINUTE AIRTIME BUY, BY POLIS:

KERRY: "The speeches at the Republican Convention are all very entertaining, after all these are funny and clever folks. All this flip-flop talk from the Mother of All Flip-Floppers: We don't do nation-building, yes-WMD-no-WMD, historic deficits from self-described fiscal conservatives - but now it's time to get down to business. You don't keep America safe by playing into the hands of America's enemies, you don't win the war on terror by creating new generations of terrorists. Catchy slogans about resolve and fortitude are fine, but we don't need lectures about fortitude. We need someone who understands what war is and what war does. My opponent does not.

The president has bungled the war on terror by taking it away from our real enemy, Al Qaeda. Yes, the tyrant Saddam Hussein is

170

gone, but we traded a tyranny for a hotbed of anti-Americanism, and though it's important to liberate oppressed people in far-off lands when you can, my first concern is for the safety of the American people. It always has been, and it always will be. No, we will not wait for a mushroom cloud over New York, but that is not the only problem. The terrorist are determined, and can attack in different ways. We continue to replenish the ranks of the enemy. We must be strong, but we must be wise. We the Democratic Party bring this message to you, as our party's response to the Republican Convention. We offer a different course for America than just war. A better course. And most importantly, a course to real safety, not just the illusion of it. I'm John Kerry, and I'd appreciate your vote for president on November 2."

[END. SMILE NOW JOHN! IT'S OKAY!]

From today's paper: "I said, "Look, we shot up a bunch of civilians. I don't want to put my life and my Marines' lives in jeopardy for a guy who's probably dead." –Sergeant Robert Sarra to his commander after an incident in which a Marine was Missing in Action.

"Imperial Hubris" fix:

"The Afghan Islamist leaders did not get along because of ethnic differences and political rivalry...Each, at times, took a break from killing communists to kill each other. The firefights and assassinations between Masood and Hekmatyar, for example, are legendary."

....Polis 1:43 PM

Friday, September 03, 2004

Over 1700 arrests so far of protesters at the Republican Convention. Action in the streets across the city.

I actually enjoyed Dubya's convention speech, very stirring.

171

Too bad it has nothing to do with reality. The boy has appointed himself the Messiah who brings freedom to the world, not obscene mega-profits to his buddies at Halliburton.

From that leftie news source, the Army Corps of Engineers: Halliburton Single Largest Recipient of Iraq Oil Funds. Bush also the largest single recipient of US oil and gas industry campaign contributions since 1998 - total stands at $1,724,579. [114]

More on the money trail, from AP: Big Iraq contracts went to big donors. [115]

Halliburton fined $7 million? Chump change.

Freedom? Whadda ya'll know 'bout freedom? (Remember the movie Platoon?) Command Sergeant-Major Charlie C. Carlson II's son gets Article 15-ed, court-martialed, for grumbling "Bush is no military leader." What the hell kind of freedom is that? From the father's letter:

> **"His crime involved nothing more than expressing his personal political opinion as guaranteed under the Bill of Rights, the very document that he had risked his life defending. Our government claims to be fighting for democracy, however those who risk their lives for democracy are being denied their basic rights of freedom of speech and opinion. My friends, the Bill of Rights and democracy are dead under the Bush Administration. This is only a sampling of what will happen if this administration is re-elected." [116]**
> ...Polis 1:47 PM

---

[114] *The Guardian*, "How has the US been spending other people's billions?," July 20, 2004

[115] *Associated Press*, "Report Links Iraq Deals to Bush Donations," Oct. 30, 2003

[116] Letter from Ret. Marine CSM and Ret. Marine Major, Aug. 31, 2004, http://bellaciao.org/en/article.php3?id_article=3117

172

More of Bush's bran' o' "freedom" These quotes from an old Paul Krugman op-ed from the NY Times:

> **"Ari Fleischer ominously warned, "[Americans] need to watch what they say, watch what they do. Patriotic citizens were supposed to accept the administration's version of events, not ask awkward questions."**

And:

> **"It's important, when you read the inevitable attempts to impugn the character of the latest whistle-blower, to realize just how risky it is to reveal awkward truths about the Bush administration....On "60 Minutes" on Sunday, [former counter-terror czar Richard] Clarke said the previously unsayable: that Mr. Bush, the self-proclaimed "war president," had "done a terrible job on the war against terrorism." After a few hours of shocked silence, the character assassination began. He "may have had a grudge to bear since he probably wanted a more prominent position," declared Dick Cheney, who also says that Mr. Clarke was "out of the loop." (What loop? Before 9/11, Mr. Clarke was the administration's top official on counterterrorism.) It's "more about politics and a book promotion than about policy," Scott McClellan said. Of course, Bush officials have to attack Mr. Clarke's character because there is plenty of independent evidence confirming the thrust of his charges."**

Good ammo for Kerry if he would only use it.

Today's "Hubris." I'm even reading it in the bathroom.

"Afghans will always take your money, but afterwards they will do what you want only if they were going to do it anyway."

"Pakistani border units...offered no opposition to al Qaeda escapees after the Tora Bora and Shahi Kowt battles, and now appear to be letting Taleban and al Qaeda forces cross the border to attack US and American Transitional Authority targets [in Afghanistan.]..."

....Polis 4:31 PM

Wednesday, September 08, 2004

For your approval, the most important speech of Kerry's life

More Kerry-speak: "the wrong war at the wrong time." Oh Jesus. The wrong war at the right time would have been better? So it wasn't the "wrong war." It was just a little early.

What Kerry is trying to say is, the Iraq war was a mistake. Without pissing-off too many people. Problem is, sometimes it can't be helped. Like your kids, give them the bad news. No more car until the grades go up. They'll get over it.

No more bombing the bejesus out of countries. People get hurt that way. No more acting like everything's fine when it's not. *You* get hurt that way.

Kerry should take a break from saying he's a more efficient warmonger.

ANOTHER DAMN SPEECH I WROTE FOR KERRY. COME ON JOHN, COUGH UP THE JOB. BY POLIS.

"In politics sometimes you want to ignore some things that

174

are being said, because you'd spend all your time responding to statements that are total nonsense, instead of telling people what your program is, for keeping American jobs in America, for out-of-control college costs, for healthcare, for winning the war on terror. But there comes a time when you have to clear something up, because your opponent is twisting things around, over and over.

It's that way with my vote for the $87 billion last year to continue operations in Iraq. This isn't rocket science: that was two bills and two votes, one took money out of tax cuts for the very rich to pay for the occupation, and the other didn't, and the president threatened to veto the one that didn't. That's right, no taking money from the very rich, the over $400,000 a year bracket. So they passed the second one, that didn't take money from the very rich, and I cast one of 12 protest votes against it. It was my way of saying that my opponent's highest-bracket friends, who have gotten the lion's share of the benefits during his four years, should kick-in a little more. Not a single soul in that chamber wasn't going to give that money at the end of the day. It was an argument over HOW to do it.

So now we hear the president, over and over, telling his favorite joke. Maybe he likes the laughs it gets. You taxpayers pay people like me and George Bush good salaries, and you should get more out of it than stand-up comedy. I may not be as funny as my opponent; I'll admit that. I'm the kind of guy who has an easier time being funny with a few friends. But you'll never find anyone who takes defending America more seriously than I do. I took it seriously when I was 25, and I take it seriously now. And some of the people who didn't take it so seriously when they could have, are now criticizing we who did. And I'm tired of it, and if it keeps up we're going to start talking about all their deferments and dodges, just to keeps things in perspective.

The other thing my opponent has a good time saying is that I agreed with him on attacking Iraq, when I voted for the Iraq War Resolution. That may be a good line for his speeches, but it's not true. If you look at the words of that resolution: it authorized him to, quote, "use the Armed Forces...as he determines to be necessary." In other words, we gave him the authority to DECIDE to make war upon certifying that three conditions had been met: that diplomacy had failed, that there was WMD, and there were ties to 9/11.

Now this is different from saying: go ahead and start a war. The president, remember, was doing everything he could to threaten Saddam Hussein to give up his supposed "weapons of mass destruction," and to leave the country. He asked for a big stick to threaten Saddam with, and we gave it to him. In good faith. Now the president is saying, it doesn't *matter* if Saddam had any WMD, what's important is that a tyrant is gone. He doesn't tell you the other side of that trade: we traded the tyrant for an incubator anti-Americanism. [117] We've got over 100,000 troops tied up in Iraq while Al Qaeda and bin Laden run free in the border regions of Pakistan and Afghanistan, and around the globe. I call that bungling the war on terror.

I've been asked if, knowing what I know now about WMD and the absence of links to Al Qaeda, would I have still have voted for the war resolution. And my answer is, an American president should always have the tools to conduct the diplomacy he desires, including, as president Ted Roosevelt said, a big stick. But what he does with that stick is something that it is proper for the president to have to answer for, to the American people.

Whether the conditions of the authorization were met is open to debate. We recall that diplomacy was abruptly halted, and the administration still maintains Saddam had strong ties to Al Qaeda despite contrary evidence. This is what you, the people, must decide." [END]

On Cheney's remark yesterday in Iowa that a vote for Kerry is a vote for a terrorist attack. Cheney's exact words were:

> **"It's absolutely essential that eight weeks from today, on November 2nd, we make the right choice. Because if we make the wrong choice, then**

---

[117] In late October Kerry did finally make this characterization of Iraq, saying "the president's miscalculations have created a terrorist haven that wasn't there before…" *Fort Worth Star-Telegram,* "Bush, Kerry take their war of words to Iowa," Oct. 21, 2004
a

the danger is that we'll get hit again, that we'll be hit in a way that will be devastating from the standpoint of the United States."

Why you mn-bdja-*^*4Fvglab!!-@!*%^fWD>#!!!! Pardon. These guys really get to you sometimes. Oh right. I'm just a Bush-hater. Well sorry, I'm not, but seems these guys do everything they can to *make* you one. A vote for Kerry is a vote for blood on the streets. Kerry's the only guy in the race who has *seen* blood, but what does he know? Some schmuck who didn't have the brains to have his daddy get him into the Guard. Get this: *he volunteered!* How do you pity a poor fool like that?

Edwards has put Bush-Cheney on the spot to apologize for this shit. But if K-E don't work it, it'll go away. Come to think of it, if voting for the opposition party can get us attacked, maybe we'd better not even have one. B-C would like that, wouldn't they?

KERRY SAY:

On the "Loony Left": "These folks think the "loony left" is anyone who doesn't want to pay companies to ship good American jobs overseas. Not just LET them do it, but PAY them to do it. These folks think the "loony left" is anyone who believes the Constitution is more than just a technicality."

Response to Kerry will 'blink' in the war on terror: "When George Bush waited 2 months to invade Afghanistan and then didn't surround bin Laden with US troops, he BLINKED in the war on terror, and we will pay for this for years to come." [118]

On Kerry's alleged "law enforcement" approach to terror: "George Bush took a "law enforcement" approach to terror when he did not follow the trail to wherever it led, and announced the secret arrest of double agent Mohammad Naeem Noor Khan. This infuriated our allies Britain and Pakistan. The New War requires us to be

---

[118] In late October the Kerry campaign did air an ad which added this point to the message, and said "In Afghanistan, the Bush Administration relied on Afghan warlords to go after Osama bin Laden. He got away."

patient, and not to divulge information just to take political credit." (See post Monday, August 16, 2004.)

LAST:

"My opponent says his choice was to trust a madman, or to remember the lessons of 9/11. But if Saddam was such a madman, why did vice president Dick Cheney help rebuild his oil fields in 1998, as CEO of Halliburton?

"Vice president Dick Cheney keeps saying it is strength that deters, not weakness. But recklessness and bullying are not the same as strength. They result in a spiral of instability, rather than deterrence. We see clear proof of this in North Korea and Iran, which have *strengthened* their nuclear programs. The president says that because Libya gave up nuclear weapons, deterrence is working. But win one-lose two is not a good record, in baseball or in foreign policy." [119]

FINAL ORDERS:

No stopping for wounded. Hit Bush's "we took the fight to the enemy." Anonymous ("Imperial Hubris") and other Al Qaeda experts say the Iraq war took the fight AWAY from Al Qaeda. They don't need Saddam Hussein's WMD, which he didn't have anyway, because they can just steal some from Russia, or better yet our buddies in Pakistan. What they DO need is Muslims hating Americans because they invaded a Muslim country to steal its oil. And lots of pictures on Al Jazeera of Iraqi kids shot up at roadblocks and killed by cluster bombs.

---

[119] In a presidential debate Kerry also made this point for the first time, saying "Iran and North Korea are now more dangerous."

Thursday, September 09, 2004

Kerry shakes up his campaign staff, but you've got to hand it to him: K. sticks to saying nothing better than anyone. He thinks slight tweaks in the message are all he needs, and come November the voters will just decide mommy's little precious should be president. John, you have no idea what these punks are like. They kick below the belt. They bite.

Kerry's prep school manners are out of place here. These kids wear leather jackets. Their old men beat them. They drank when they were 8. They're mean.

Today, Kerry's latest foray into a new message: focus on the *cost* of the Iraq war. Geez, make up your mind. [120]

The *real* lessons of 9/11 are to not put your head in the sand while your government makes doo-doos all over the world, then pretend a bogeyman is responsible for all your problems.

...Polis 1:22 PM

Monday, September 13, 2004

His name is Michael Scheuer. From the Toronto Sun, article on Scheuer and his book "Imperial Hubris; Why The West is Losing the War on Terror." Basically Scheuer says 'If we want to win the war on terror, here's what you have to do. I don't think you'll do it, but now you can't say I didn't tell you.' Scheuer is also one heck of a writer.

If you want to read a lot of horse manure, read Sam Huntington's "Clash of Civilizations," which says people blow

---

[120] *International Herald Tribune*, "Kerry faults Bush over cost of Iraq war," Sept. 9, 2004

179

themselves up because McDonald's and women voting offends them. If you want to know what's going down in the street, read "Imperial Hubris."

AN EXCERPT FROM THE TORONTO SUN REVIEW OF "IMPERIAL HUBRIS"

> **"None of bin Laden's reasons for waging war on the U.S. have anything to do with our freedom, liberty, and democracy (as President George Bush claims), but everything to do with U.S. policies and actions in the Muslim world," notably unlimited support for Israel's repression of the Palestinians and the destruction of Iraq....Ironically U.S. and British military intervention in Afghanistan and Iraq "are completing the radicalization of the Islamic world," a prime bin Laden goal. Bush's misbegotten invasion of Iraq was "icing on bin Laden's cake.""**

...Polis 2:48 PM

Tommy Franks, come on down! Seig Heil! From a NewsMax report:

> **"Gen. Tommy Franks says that if the United States is hit with a weapon of mass destruction that inflicts large casualties, the Constitution will likely be discarded in favor of a military form of government...[Franks said] "It means the potential of a weapon of mass destruction and a terrorist, massive, casualty-producing event somewhere in the Western world – it may be in the United States of America – that causes our population to question our own Constitution and to begin to militarize our country in order to avoid a repeat of another mass, casualty-producing**

event.""[121]

Yes, *that* Tommy Franks, the one who just endorsed George Bush for president. This only made the news in the blogosphere.

Adbusters, the Canadian artist's project and magazine, post-nuclear issue. Teen gangs rule the streets with AK-47s and rocket launchers, Baghdad in America. No central government anywhere. The dollar is a memory, back to original currency: cigarettes, coffee, and weapons. Items that always hold their value. Burned-out warehouses and oil drum fires are home; the rich have gone to islands or behind high walls, Green Zones in America. Rival gangs fight for turf, drugs, and women. The Afghan model of society. All that's left when Jeb Bush, the last president, was done with the country.

...Polis @ 2:48 PM

Tuesday, September 14, 2004

Before the meltdown. States that were in the Kerry column now moving toward Bush. Michigan, Wisconsin, Minnesota. Former Gore campaign manager Donna Brazile says "Bush right now is smelling blood." Kerry about to crash-burn, we gotta hep 'im, to quote Strom Thurmond.

More bitching first. Kerry's interview with TIME this week is dismal. His big chance to attack Shrub's get-them-before-they-get-you foreign policy, and what does he talk about? Don't lay-off firemen.

That's right John! Just say the thing that will make the least people mad, for *heaven's* sake don't tell them the president doesn't *know what he's doing!*

A cross between Howard Dean and Kerry's war medals would have been an unstoppable robo-candidate. Howard would have told

---

[121] "General Franks Doubts Constitution Will Survive WMD Attack,"
http://www.newsmax.com/archives/articles/2003/11/20/185048.shtml

181

them where to get off. Kerry only got the nomination because he's a war hero, and everyone knew, even then, that Bush would go straight for your patriotism. We just didn't know how dirty he'd get.

What they criticized Dean for is what they love about Bush. Blunt, you-know-where-I-stand-even-if-you-might-not-like-it, hell I'm not even really a politician, just a regular good-old-boy. *They don't like it when we good-old-boys tell them liberals how it is, do they folks?* Howard would have said, *what's so good-old-boy about Andover, shit-head?* Even Yale has more poor boys than that place.

The Dean scream would have blown over. Howard's problem was he did the scream all wrong: YEAAAH! If he had jumped on a table and done a Southern-style rebel yell he would have picked up a few votes. YEEEE-HAAAAW! *That's* how you do it.

Kerry needs a dramatic speech. Tomorrow, I'll post the emails of some players in the Kerry campaign (all public record, so I can't get in trouble) so you, my kind and indulgent readers, can forward this. We need to bother them *now*. They're doing it all wrong and they're going to lose.

Flypaper, take the fight, get them there not here, good metaphors even though they're all wrong. Kerry doesn't have a single good metaphor. Not a single one. He's fighting with superlatives, "America is not AS SAFE as we ought to be after 9/11. We can do a BETTER job at homeland security. I can fight a MORE EFFECTIVE war on terror." You see what I'm saying, John? Hate to say it man, but you're boring.

You have an opening about a man wide in the defensive line. Run through it. Say a vote for brinksmanship is different from a vote to start a damn war. Get up and fight, goddammit. Would John Kerry have "left Saddam in power?" How about: "Maybe he wouldn't have been in power if Dick Cheney and Halliburton hadn't helped him rebuild his oil fields. If they hadn't helped him slaughter Kurds and Shiites when they rebelled!" What the fuck, can we get some *truth* going here? At least it would make the race fun again.

Domestic issues. George Bush, leader of the "haves and

182

have-mores," stop sending jobs to countries where the biggest draw is no organizing unions unless you want a bullet in the head.

Last, Kerry should tell his "don't make them mad" centrist advisors, like Bill Clinton, to take a hike. Bill wants him to talk about the economy more, but he's giving him bad advice because he wants it for Hillary in 2008. Wants to live in the White House again, wimin and likker. And this time Hillary will be too busy to care.

You guys are great. You must be emailing this stuff around, because today Paul Krugman of the NY Times picked up some of our talking points. An example (emphasis mine):

> Krugman: **"Can Mr. Kerry, who voted to authorize the Iraq war, criticize it? Yes, by pointing out that he voted only to give Mr. Bush a *big stick*."**

> Polis, suggested speech, Sept. 8, 2004 post: "The president, remember, was doing everything he could to threaten Saddam Hussein…asked for a *big stick* to threaten Saddam with, and we gave it to him in good faith."

Tomorrow I post the emails of two key players in the Kerry campaign, so you can forward this and tell them to come alive.

…Polis @ 2:24 PM

Wednesday, September 15, 2004

Today: the K. campaign trips. Kerry slammed Bush for distorting his position on Medicare, on the very same day that 9/11 widows endorsed Kerry. So the Medicare story took the headlines, pushed the 9/11 widows story below-the-fold. Goddammit! The 9/11 widows story hits Bush where he lives! That's big news! Kerry shoots himself in the foot. A reader emailed me and said, "they are incompetent, aren't they?"

183

To the folks who read this and care about the future of our country, and want Kerry to start doing the right things, his close friend and advisor Tom Vallely is at Harvard, in the public Harvard directory. Look him up. Maybe an email from you urging the campaign to consider the advice in this blog will help. I've tried calling and emailing these assholes myself for months, no response. With seven weeks before the election and Kerry 11 points down, we have nothing to lose.

FLASH:

--- tom_vallely@-----.net wrote:

Dear Ralph,
Thanks for your voice mail. The campaign is aware of your blog polis polis and the language there is good stuff. I'm on the road a lot so it's hard to get me. But in a few days you'll be able to get me in the Cambridge office and the number there is 617-------- and ask for my assistant Amy ---- to set up an appointment (it'll be after the election).
>
> Tommy

UPDATE 9/16: I took these emails down, since we've made contact at a high level and know that the campaign is aware of this site. No sense swamping their boxes. You guys email me with your thinking, and I'll email them. Better yet, post it as comments. Bloggers love comments.

The sound of a car bomb is something you must get used to in Iraq, reporting from there must be a hoot. We're here at the Ministry of BOOM! oh yea that's just another one…

..Polis 11:33 AM

Thursday, September 16, 2004

Help

I'm really sorry, but you want to scream at these Kerry people. We'll never know conclusively if Bush fulfilled his National Guard duty, so drop it. We DO know that Bush leapt to the head of thousands of guys to get a coveted slot in the Guard, a virtual guarantee you weren't going to the Nam. Now the story is that Dan Rather and the Big Bad Liberal Media forged documents to besmirch our beloved Fuehrer.

Rumors of an elaborate Karl Rove set-up. This has pushed the son-of-privilege story to the back page. CBS saying 'the documents may be forged but what they say is true,' is like saying this is counterfeit money, but it's such a good copy it ought to be worth *something.*[122]

Let's talk about how you got into the Guard in the days of the Vietnam draft. After '72 they abolished deferments. It didn't matter who you were. That's what stopped the war, if you ask me. You were going and that was that. Unless you got into the Guard, lucky duck.

Not-so-Anonymous Michael Scheuer quotes Colonel Theodore Draper, who was writing about Lee's Army of Northern Virgina when he wrote this passage. Think of those guys in Afghanistan fighting us in white pajamas and barefoot in the snow. Scheuer thinks we're going to lose in Afghanistan because we pissed everything away in Iraq:

> **"[A] more sinewy, tawny, formidable-looking set**
> **of men could not be. In education they are**

---

[122] Memory refresher. This story was broken by bloggers. The memo Rather based his story on turned out to be a forgery. The first thread began to unravel when a blogger noticed that typewriters did not have raised "th"s after dates in those days, as in "May 25th". Some expensive models did, but a backwater military base was not likely to have one.

185

certainly inferior to our native-born people, but they are usually very quick-witted within their own sphere of comprehension; and they know how to handle weapons with terrible effect. Their great characteristic is their stoical manliness; they never beg, whimper, or complain; but look you straight in the face, with as little animosity as if they have never heard a gun." [123]

...Polis @ 1:48 PM

Saturday, September 18, 2004

I think John should do the Jay Leno show, but here's the twist: with daughters Vanessa and I the forget the other's name. Her. I can't take credit for this idea. A woman thought it up. Said her woman's intuition told her that he'd loosen up with his girls there and everyone would see what a great guy he is. Hmm. Personally I bet John's a fun guy to have a beer with (I knew your type at Yale, John. You're a party animal) but he's fighting this "stiff Brahmin" bit. Some guys only loosen up around friends and family. Guys like me.[124]

Good move yesterday on Kerry's secret Reserve call-up remarks in Albuquerque, N.M. Maybe this will wake up those young "four more years" dudes I keep running into. The draft is next, baby. This is not a video game. No college exemptions? Universal draft? Still want to vote for Bush, meat-head? Take off your hat. You're inside.

General News: Fallen Soldier's Mom Arrested At First Lady's Rally. Two days ago in Hamilton, NJ, from AP:

"A woman wearing a T-shirt with the words "President Bush You Killed My Son" and a picture of a soldier killed in Iraq was detained

---

[123] *Civil War Quotations*, P.G. Tsouras, (ed.)

[124] Two nights later Kerry made an appearance on the David Letterman Show. Alone.

after she interrupted Mrs. Bush's speech. Police escorted Sue Niederer of Hopewell out of the rally after she demanded to know why her son, Army 1st Lt. Seth Dvorin, 24, was killed in Iraq. Dvorin died in February while trying to disarm a bomb...As shouts of "Four More Years" subsided, Niederer, standing in the middle of the crowd of about 700, continued to shout about the killing of her son. Local police escorted her out of the event, handcuffed her and placed her in the back of a police van. The first lady continued speaking, and several people shouted back at Niederer. One woman yelled, "Your son chose to fight in that war.""

There's an element in this country I have been unaware of since birth, and it took Bush to bring them out from under their rocks. I never thought a Nazi takeover could happen in America, but now I'm not so sure. As long as you call it something else.

Sunday, September 19, 2004

Bush says questions about CBS-Dan Rather fiasco "need to be answered." Are these people crazy? Come on, Kerry: "That's right, and while we're at it, questions about Valerie Plame need to be answered. Questions about WMD in Iraq NEED TO BE ANSWERED. Questions on how you got into the Guard during the Vietnam draft NEED TO BE ANSWERED!" NEED TO BE ANSWERED! NEED TO BE ANSWERED!

Tuesday, September 21, 2004

Bush took the bait. Getting tons of hits suddenly, 5,000 in one day. I think Buzzflash or someone gave me a link.[125] Thaaank yoou!

---

[125] Buzzflash.com

187

Kerry did it! Said:

"Saddam Hussein was a brutal dictator who deserves his own special place in hell. But that was not, in itself, a reason to go to war. The satisfaction we take in his downfall does not hide this fact: We have traded a dictator for a chaos that has left America less secure."

Friggin' about time.

Bush responds, says Kerry "apparently woke up this morning and has now decided, 'No, we should not have invaded Iraq,' after just last month saying he still would have voted for force even knowing everything we know today."

That's the wording Kerry is looking for: voting for the war resolution = voting to invade. Step in for the kill! SPEECH! BIG SPEECH!

KERRY SHOULD SAY:

"Voting to authorize force, to give a president the tools he needs to conduct diplomacy, is different from launching an attack and occupation of a country the size of California. This fits into a pattern of my opponent insulting your intelligence and thinking you won't know the difference. He counts deficit reduction and pro-middle-class votes as tax-hikes, even though many in his own party approved them. He says a vote that stood up for the middle-class was actually a vote against body armor. Mr. President, you have nothing to teach me about body armor. I wore it, for real, not make-believe.

"Knowing everything I know now, would I have voted to place faith in an American president's diplomacy? I say yes. I'm running because THIS president has broken that faith, on a non-existent, non-imminent threat, on non-existent links to Al Qaeda, on what it would take to win this war, on what this war is really all about. Here's the Kerry doctrine, and you can take it to the bank: Pre-emptive war is justifiable if it is TRULY pre-emptive. WAR BASED ON ARROGANCE, PRIDE, AND WISHFUL THINKING, IS NOT.

War can create more problems than it solves, and usually does. No, Mr. President, we do not need a permission slip to defend ourselves. But we do need to understand who the enemy is, and who he is not.

"The president says he had a choice to make: to trust a madman, or to remember the lessons of 9/11. He had a third choice: to hunt Al Qaeda to extinction without creating another terrorist haven in the Middle East. He says the point was to deny the enemy sanctuary in Iraq, but it has done exactly the opposite. Meanwhile, Al Qaeda runs free and is getting stronger.

"My opponent says criticism sends a 'wrong message to the troops.' This also fits a pattern of this administration, of silencing and trying to intimidate critics, by questioning their patriotism, or smearing their character. This includes generals who disagree on numbers of troops needed in Iraq, dedicated public servants like Richard Clarke and Paul O'Neill. Even ordinary citizens have been arrested for wearing anti-Bush tee shirts at a rally, in West Virginia. That's not what my America is about. Look at our events: we are challenged constantly, but we treasure free speech. I say this: *No American ever need fear speaking his or her mind to John Kerry!*

"Resolve "to stay the course" is not a good thing if it's three in the morning and you wanted the Parsippany exit but now you're headed toward Fort Apache, the Bronx." (Don't worry, New Yorkers will forgive, just say no diss to the Bronx - Hey! We Love New York! No further comment, thank you!) [END]

Remember!:

-Flip-flop stuff = Bush insults YOUR intelligence
-'wrong message to troops' = draft-dodgers questioning patriotism, telling you to shut up.
-Pre-emptive war vs. pre-EMINENT war : There's a difference.

Okay dammit, just put me up there, I'll do it myself. Only 5 more weeks till election. I can't take this anymore.

Keeping Sudan in the news, good, it shows Bush's rank

hypocrisy. There's a bona fide genocide going on as we speak. Where's all the good versus evil stuff now?....Polis 1:32 PM

Wednesday, September 22, 2004

Another lost news day; CBS-Dan Rather story takes the front pages. Kerry back to being Kerry; this is like pulling teeth. Dribbling and fiddling, dawdling and diddling, won't go for the hoop. He's waiting to see how "should not have invaded" plays out, waiting for the polls to come back. No time for this shit. All Bush has to do is run down the clock and he knows it. Big buzzer goes off and the game's over. Bush soundbite today clean, at the UN: "There is no safety in looking away."

Kerry quote today: "He [Bush] does not have the credibility to lead the world, and he did not and will not offer the leadership in order to do what we need to do to protect our troops, to be successful and win the war on terror in an effective way."

Arrggh!

Boston Globe today: some Kerry advisors worry he'll be seen as the "anti-war candidate." Those simple boobs.

There are two wars going on here, the RIGHT war (Al Qaeda) and the WRONG war (Iraq.)

Say "THE IRAQ DIVERSION."

You have reported for duty, lieutenant. Fine, fine. Now storm that bunker! That's a direct order!

More mail from readers:

"I hope that soon Kerry will respond to the "He would have left Saddam in power" jabs from Bush by saying that Bush has chosen to leave the actual terrorist who attacked us on 9/11, Bin-Laden in power."

190

"Kerry should say that unlike Bush, he would have removed the REAL imminent danger to the US and the world from power and THEN dealt with Hussein."

"Kerry might also point out that contrary to Bush's statements, the sanctions against Iraq WERE working. That's why even though Hussein might have had a desire for WMD, not even a teaspoon of WMD were found in Saddam's possession."

"Bush has made more enemies than he has defeated, lost far more jobs than he has created."

If my readers were running the K. campaign we'd win.

....Polis 1:00 PM

Thursday, September 23, 2004

Those poor kids in Iraq Hell. By the time you are 21 all you want to do is go fishing and sit quietly looking at mountains. You've seen all the excitement you ever want to see in this life. At 21. I cut out a picture from the Boston Herald and taped it to my wall. It's 3 soldiers in Iraq hunkering down behind a wall, helmets looking way too big for their heads, and the looks on their faces say GET ME OUT OF HERE! The *faces* are the story - What the hell am I doing here this is DANGEROUS! – this I do not like! One minute you're in back seats of cars trying hard to lose your virginity, the next minute everyone is trying to kill you.

I oughta be there dammit, an old man safe while my little brothers are dodging car bombs, what's wrong with me? Writing this crap no one is ever going to read, hoping it might wake people up, so we can impeach the man and get our boys out of there. If age counts for anything, knowing a bit more about the human race and tribal manners and all that, then they *need* us old guys in a place like that. It's a crime to send young men to war. In the world I see it's all the

191

old guys who go first, congressmen and senators and me and the head of Viacom, if he isn't in jail. And Blair and Putin and Sylvester Stallone. That would be my New World Order. Hell, the adrenaline rush might charge us up like young bulls. The wives would love it.

It would be interesting to see if wars got off the ground. And the young guys could have a crack at doing a little living, like we did. Dancing and fornicating and making kids for a while. Now that would be *fair*. Bush sits and says we must stand firm. What do you mean *we*, buddy? I don't see your ass on the line.

I taped that picture to my wall so I can look at it anytime I'm feeling sorry for myself. Worried about the next rent or whatever. I look at that and cut the crap. These guys have a good day if they're still in one piece at the end of it. May Bush rot in hell for putting them there.

Yaser Hamdi released from Gitmo, this week, the American Taliban dubbed "enemy combatant." He joined the Taliban in Afghanistan way before 9/11, on some kind of extreme thrill-seeking thing. Very dumb. You've snowboarded down Everest? Well check these pictures out... So this week the Bushies let Hamdi go after saying he was "too dangerous" to be allowed to see a lawyer for the last 2 years.

One thing you can't say about the Bushies is they aren't creative when it comes to handling this "rights" business. The catch for Hamdi is he must give up his US citizenship. He was born here. They've floated this one before - stripping Americans of their citizenship, in a draft of Patriot Act II. [126] It didn't get anywhere that time but they knew it wouldn't. The point was to get it in place for the next time, the next attack, when the world will be their oyster.

...Polis 2:42 PM

---

[126] *The Dallas Morning News,* "Conservatives, liberals fear broader anti-terror powers - sides unite to protest Justice's push," April 13, 2003

Friday, September 24, 2004

Kerry has busted out! They had him pinned down in those rocks over yonder but it looks like he's given a signal and they're charging! Wait, lemme wipe off my binoculars they're getting all fogged up and I can't see anything! Looks like they made it to the ledge behind the grassy ridge!

A few hours ago at Temple University Kerry gave a speech that said "The invasion of Iraq was a profound diversion from the battle against our greatest enemy, al-Qaeda." The Bush-Cheney reaction is what you want to watch. They're turning purple with rage and quivering. Kerry touched a nerve. Cheney sputtered that Kerry is trying to "tear down everything we've done." Now that's interesting. What's "everything we've done"? All the elaborate lies they told us to get us into this war? All that beautiful spin and distortion? I'd sure like to know what Dick-o meant by that. I guess if I thought I had pulled-off the greatest hoax in human history and some punk just blew the lid off, I'd be mad as hell too.

Pat yourselves on the back. We got through.

Exit strategies: The problem is the insurgents and the regional powers want our nose good and bloody before they let go our pants leg trying to get out. That's their only insurance against us trying something like this again. We may have to fight our way out of this bar. It's okay. Repeat: We liberated you assholes, we won, you're on your own now. Bad guys everywhere beware.

My man Scheuer, page 92:

"15 December 2001: After two weeks of US air bombardment of al Qaeda forces in the Tora Bora mountains, the Northern Alliance fails to fully engage al Qaeda; bin Laden, al-Zawahiri, and most of their fighters escape to Pakistan...bin Laden says, "if all the forces of world evil could not achieve their goals on a one square mile area against a small number of mujahadeen...how can

these evil forces triumph over the Muslim world?"

Polis 1:01 PM

Saturday, September 25, 2004

Keep moving up the hill! No stopping for wounded! Had a chance to see the full text of Kerry's speech at Temple University yesterday. This is a whole new John Kerry. Of Al Qaeda he said:

> **"They want to provoke a conflict that will radicalize the people of the Muslim world, turning them against the United States and the West. And they hope to transform that anger into a force that will topple the region's governments."**

At last he's getting the point, according to Scheuer in "Hubris," which he must be reading on the plane. Bin Laden is betting that once one government falls, Saudi's or Pakistan's, the rest will go like dominos. Jeopardy, answer: George Bush's invasion of Iraq. Question: What did Osama never dare to hope for to tie us down in a no-win war that would unite Muslims against us?

Check out what the Freepers are saying.[127] Naturally it's the most dumbed-down way of looking at things. One thread is called "Scheuer's answer: just surrender." I want to argue with that a minute. You may want to put on your hip waders 'cause I've got that poopy feeling.

First off, I didn't know having troops in the Middle East was one of our goals to begin with, so how is abandoning something we don't really want a "surrender?" I'd rather fight and kill Al Qaeda than do all that stuff.

"Surrender?" "Appease?" Who gives a shit? No one ever asked me if I wanted to own a chunk of the Middle East and its problems, and the same goes for everyone else I know. If they had

---

[127] Far right-wing website FreeRepublic.com

194

asked I would have said no. So I'm not "surrendering" anything.

Okay, just kidding. Let's kick ass, have an empire, and oppress as many people as we like.[128] Forget the other stuff; I just wanted to see what you'd say. I'm with the program. So shouldn't we be smart enough in the 21st century to not make the first mistake every empire makes? Over-extension? Can we get the debt under control and educate our kids for a while? Then we can kick even *more* ass. Hey, I want to fall back because I *do* want to be an empire. And GWB is screwing it up for me.

Saddling our kids with the tab for our free lunches. Now those are some fine moral values.

Put troops in places where they get killed, then say, ok, now it's my way or they died in vain. I'm getting the hang of it. I'm ready to be a war prezdent.

Muslim scholars deeply divided over issues in Islamic law. They need to work this out for themselves. Why do we think everyone has to look like us?

Story time. Tell me your crazy dreams and I'll tell you mine. Years before 9/11, a dream I was on a helicopter on the way to the White House, I don't know why, you know how dreams are. But when I looked down there was rolling countryside and we were flying over high walls like the Great Wall of China, new white walls, and on them were guys in black suits toting machine guns along the top. It was Virginia horse country. I wondered why everything had moved, the Capitol, the White House, everything. That's it. That was the dream. I told you I'm shoveling it like crazy today.

Background material, Kerry war room circulate to press or gimme a job and I'll do it:

---

[128] In a February '05 article in the *Boston Review*, "A New Grand Strategy," a prominent Neoconservative thinker is quoted as saying: "Every 10 years or so, the United States needs to pick up some small, crappy country and throw it against the wall, just to show the world you mean business."

October '04 Atlantic Monthly, "The Long Hunt for Osama" by Peter Bergen, EXCERPT:

"With only a small number of American "boots on the ground," the U.S. military chose to rely on the services of local Afghan proxies of uncertain loyalty and competence, a blunder that allowed many members of al-Qaeda, including Osama bin Laden himself, to slip away."

October '04 Atlantic Monthly, "Bush's Lost Year" by James Fallows, EXCERPT:

"Let me tell you my gut feeling," a senior figure at one of America's military-sponsored think tanks told me recently, after we had talked for twenty minutes about details of the campaigns in Afghanistan and Iraq. "If I can be blunt, the Administration is full of shit. In my view we are much, much worse off now than when we went into Iraq. That is not a partisan position. I voted for these guys. But I think they are incompetent, and I have had a very close perspective on what is happening. Certainly in the long run we have harmed ourselves. We are playing to the enemy's political advantage. Whatever tactical victories we may gain along the way, this will prove to be a strategic blunder."

This man will not let me use his name, because he is still involved in military policy. He cited the experiences of Joseph Wilson, Richard Clarke, and Generals Eric Shinseki and Anthony Zinni to illustrate the personal risks of openly expressing his dissenting view."

Newsweek, "'Staying the Course' Isn't an Option," by Retired Air Force Col. Mike Turner, a former military planner who served on the U.S. Central Command planning staff for operations Desert Shield and Desert Storm. EXCERPT:

196

"If the Bush administration remains in power, failure in Iraq is a virtual certainty. "Staying the course" during a crisis spiraling rapidly downward will cost thousands of American and Iraqi lives, will continue to sap the operational readiness of this nation's armed forces, and will continue to strengthen Al Qaeda's hand. To paraphrase FDR, it's time to change horses. The one we're on is about to drown."

And in the "Couldn't have put it better myself" department: A Republican "elder statesman" says in Newsweek this week that

"this administration's [nuclear] nonproliferation strategy consists of flailing around with a two-by-four." [129]

Today's last grating, annoying, unwanted advice: Roll up the sleeves and loosen the tie a little, John. You don't always want to look like you just stepped off the cover of GQ. Sweat stains are good; Sixpack likes that. Wear a flag pin like Bush, not all the time, but just to let the bastards know they don't own it.

"Hubris:"

"Homeland"-an odd, unnerving word to use to refer to America, reminiscent, as it is, of phrases used by Hitler and Stalin in World War II."

....Polis 1:00 PM

Sunday, September 26, 2004

More coincidence maybe, but I saw Kerry with a flag pin in a recent photo-op. Where the hell is the covering fire? They're getting cut to pieces! Kerry needs a party behind him, DEMANDING

---

[129] "War-Gaming the Mullahs," *Newsweek,* Sept. 27, 2004

ANSWERS   Valerie Plame - Dresser Industries - Noor Khan.
Goddammit! Over!

There's plenty to talk about. From the June 25, 2003 Las
Vegas Review-Journal:

> **"WASHINGTON -- When President Bush took
> office in January 2001, the White House was told
> that remote-controlled Predator spy planes
> recently had spotted Osama bin Laden as many as
> three times.**
>
> **Officials were urged to arm the unmanned planes,
> first demonstrated north of Las Vegas at Nellis
> Air Force Range, with missiles to kill the al-Qaida
> leader. But the administration failed to get drones
> back into the Afghan skies until after the Sept. 11,
> 2001, attacks, current and former U.S. officials
> say."**

The reason Bush didn't arm the planes and kill bin Laden is
there was some kind of budget dispute. What isn't disputed is that
Don Rumsfeld was "actually on Capitol Hill on Sept. 9, threatening a
veto of a $600 million diversion from "Star Wars" to
counterterrorism." [130] Star Wars missile defense, you know, the one
that doesn't work. Boeing, Lockheed Martin, TRW and Raytheon
together account for 60 percent of all the money that has been flushed
down the Star Wars toilet.

More good stuff: Vincent Cannistraro, a former chief of
counter-terrorism at the C.I.A., told New Yorker reporter Jane Mayer
that, although he believes many bin Laden family members have cut
off all contact with Osama, "an interconnectedness" remains. On Feb.
26, 2001 bin Laden attended his son's wedding in Afghanistan. Also
in attendance were bin Laden's mother, two brothers, and a sister.
This is 3 months after bin Laden took credit for bombing the USS
Cole. A poem was read aloud during the wedding which celebrated

---

[130] *Fort Worth Star-Telegram,* "Through the 2004 looking glass" by Molly
Ivins, Apr. 04, 2004

the attack:

> **A destroyer: even the brave fear its might.**
> > **It inspires horror in the harbour and in
> > the open sea.**
> **She sails into the waves**
> > **Flanked by arrogance, haughtiness and
> > false power.**
> **To her doom she moves slowly**
> **A dinghy awaits her, riding the waves.**

Cannistraro told Mayer that as recently as Spring 2001,

> **"an allied intelligence agency had seen two of
> Osama's sisters apparently taking cash to an
> airport in Abu Dhabi, where they are suspected of
> handing it to a member of bin Laden's Al Qaeda
> organization."** [131]

Mayer writes that even after 9/11, according to Cannistraro, "Saudi sources observed several of Osama's children traveling between Saudi Arabia and Afghanistan without restrictions." [132]

Flash back to the Bush administration allowing charter flights to whisk bin Laden family members out of the US shortly after the airspace had re-opened after 9/11, after *token* interviews (not after *no* interviews, as Michael Moore's critics claims he said.) After any big crime it's normal for family members to be pulled before a grand jury to determine if they are material witnesses. Would Bush count this as a "big crime?"

More good stuff: Paul Krugman of the NY Times says:

> **"The Wall Street Journal confirmed an earlier
> report that in 2002 the military drew up plans for
> a strike on the base of the terrorist leader Abu
> Musab al-Zarqawi in an area of Iraq not under**

---

[131] Jane Mayer, "The House of Bin Laden," *The New Yorker,* Nov. 12, 2001
[132] ibid

199

Saddam's control. But civilian officials vetoed the attack - probably because they thought it might undermine political support for the war against Saddam. So Mr. Zarqawi, like Osama, was given the chance to kill another day." [133]

Go to the original WSJ issue that Krug is referencing, Oct. 25, 2004 and you find:

"Lisa Gordon-Hagerty, who was in the White House as the National Security Council's director for combatting terrorism at the time, said an NSC working group, led by the Defense Department, had been in charge of reviewing the plans to target the camp...Ms. Gordon-Hagerty said she wasn't part of the working group and never learned the reason why the camp wasn't hit. But she said that much later, when reports surfaced that Mr. Zarqawi was behind a series of bloody attacks in Iraq, she said "I remember my response," adding, "I said why didn't we get that ['son of a b-'] when we could.""

And it's people like Mike Moore who are attacked. The truth-tellers. These are the most dangerous people. Columnist Molly Ivins says the 2004 presidential race is "already bizarre beyond belief. [Former counter-terrorism czar] Richard Clarke is now under ferocious attack for stating both the obvious and the already known."

Here's what I say: I'd be proud to be called part of the "Michael Moore wing of the Democratic party" anytime. Damned straight.

Kerry's finding his groove, but not fast enough. Ralph Nader predicts a big Bush win, big enough so they can't blame him. This worries me. Nader is nothing if not a savvy bookie.

---

[133] *New York Times*, "It's not just Al Qaeda," Oct. 29, 2004

"War is nothing but lies" –Sun Tzu

....posted by Polis 1:20 PM

Monday, September 27, 2004

Three days until the first debate. Getting Meetup.com e-vites to Democrat debate-watching parties. One says "Munchies! Beer! Come watch Kerry kick Bush's ass!" They're all over town. You can take your pick from bashes in Cambridge to cocktails at nice addresses on the North End waterfront. Kerry HQ by the Fleet Center is a beehive. You can walk in anytime and be processed in batches every 10 minutes or so, with other walk-ins, then you get put on-deck for the next phone line that opens up for phone banking. Very efficient.

Then you have war stories from people going door-to-door in New Hampshire, the closest swing state. People getting chased by dogs, getting lost on dark country roads, cars dying, all that good stuff. And here I am stuck trying to swamp Kerry with email to get his act together, or what's left of it in the fourth quarter. I'm really nervous GWB will win. Oh my God. I promise I'm not an egomaniac, who am I to tell K. how to "get his act together?" I'm saying that almost anyone who's not a complete half-wit could be doing a better job. C. told me even her elderly and not-very-political mother once mused "Why did we invade Iraq? I'd rather spend $87 billion fighting Al Qaeda."

Kerry prepping for the debate so we're getting dead air, as they call it in the radio business. No good soundbites coming through. Dead air is the mortal sin of radio because people start changing their dials by the thousands, and it's everyone's job right down to the receptionist to yell "dead air! dead air!" when you notice nothing coming out of the lobby speakers. Fun business, radio.

Weird scenes inside the goldmine, as the Lizard King would say. Hurricane scenes in Florida. Someone should tell these people that Bush pulling out of the Kyoto global warming treaty is not helping this sort of thing. No matter how many federal dollars he

201

sends. Neither does giving creepy Orwellian names to slash-and-burn laws: Clean Skies, Healthy Forests, why not call drilling for oil in the Arctic Refuge the "Caribou Preservation Act?"

MY SUBMISSION FOR A TV AD FOR KERRY, "STRAW MEN"

Kerry's center-rightists won't like this. They think you can win a fight by doing the rope-a-dope. Maybe against some guys, but not against these gutter-fighting hoods.

Kerry: I'm John Kerry and I approve this message.

Announcer: In 2003 John Kerry sponsored an alternative resolution for Iraq funding which would have forced the very highest income brackets to pay more. Under threat of veto by the White House, this resolution was defeated, and a heavier burden fell on the middle class. George Bush calls John's two different votes on these two different measures a "flip-flop."

[graphic: "$87 billion for Iraq: PASSED 87 to 12. Alternative resolutions defeated.]

George Bush says John is "wrong on defense" for opposing some weapons systems, such as the F-16 fighter, the M1-Abrams tank, and the B2 Stealth bomber. But these SAME weapons systems were all opposed by Dick Cheney, Donald Rumsfeld, or George Bush Senior.[134]

[pictures of weapons and these three guys interposed.]

George Bush says that John Kerry wants to "negotiate" with terrorists, part of what the New Republic calls "a campaign of straw men, half-truths, and baseless attacks."

[New Republic cover here]

---

[134] "John Kerry's Defense Defense," by Fred Kaplan, http://slate.msn.com/id/2096127

"...in plain language endlessly repeated," says the New Republic, "Bush paints a picture of the world and his opponent that is *unhinged from reality...*"

[UNHINGED FROM REALITY, white letters on blackout screen]

John Kerry understands the reality of what it takes to win the war on terror. John Kerry. Tested Leadership. Tested Courage.

[END: a nice 3 or 4-shot collage of Kerry in committee, on the trail, etc. and yes, of Vietnam but lightly! And not that same goofy once-we-were-brothers photo with Kerry showing his scrawny chest and dogtags. Put on a shirt, John!]

"Hubris":

"And because our elites are so full of themselves, they think America is invulnerable; cannot imagine the rest of the world does not want to be like us; believe an American empire in the twenty first century is not only our destiny, but our duty to mankind, especially to the unwashed, unlettered, undemocratic, unwhite, unshaved, and antifeminist Muslim masses."

....Polis 5:08 PM

Tuesday, September 28, 2004

Kerry suddenly switching the soundbite to "Mission *not* accomplished." He's supposed to be saying *"Iraq war was a diversion."* Man I'm tired. I can't talk to this guy anymore.

Howard Dean's interview on Charlie Rose yesterday. He managed to squeeze all these points into 30 minutes, and Charlie wasn't making it easy:

-Iraq war was a diversion from the real, global war on terror

203

-George Bush's mind was made up that he was going to overthrow Hussein from the day he took office. Dean cites former Bush Treasury Secretary Paul O'Neill on this. Careful to emphasize that O'Neill is a Republican and former Bush cabinet member, the "impeccable source" strategy. Another thing Kerry doesn't do: cite Republicans who support his points. Chuck Hagel, Doug Bereuter. Bush would call it the Zell Miller strategy: criticism coming from your own side makes folks think twice.[135]

-Two states, Iran and North Korea, have become nuclear powers "on Bush's watch." Beautiful! Why have Iran/N. Korea become nuclear? They're scared, and they think they need a "Bush deterrent."

-It's high time George Bush be held accountable for what his brand of politics is doing to the country. Dean says we're "swirling lower and lower into the gutter," nice hand gesture here. The smear war on Vietnam veterans, Max Cleland, John McCain, now Kerry.[136] The smear war on critics, Clarke, O'Neill, Zinni, Shineski. Vote-Bush-or-die.

Howard Dean on Charlie Rose Show: A+

Rove at work again, planting pieces in the New York Times, what Valerie Plame subpoenas could do to the "freedom of the press." ("Reporters Put Under Scrutiny in C.I.A. Leak" 9/28/04) Rewind. Stop. Play. When the press embarrasses politicians: good. When the press gives secrets to the enemy: bad. Especially when the traitor is in the White House. Plame's undercover identity was a *secret*. A for-real one, not a political one. She ran networks to track down WMD.

---

[135] In the second presidential debate on Oct. 8, 2004 Kerry did begin his response to a question on the Patriot Act by noting that two prominent Republicans thought it had to be "fixed," Republican Party chairman Marc Racicot and Congressman Jim Sensenbrenner. Zell Miller is the Democratic senator who attacked Kerry in his keynote Republican Convention speech.

[136] In an ad against Cleland during his race for re-election to Congress, the Republicans threw pictures of bin Laden and Saddam onto the screen and questioned the triple amputee's commitment to defending America. Cleland lost the election to Republican Saxby Chambliss.

Someone in the White House must go to jail. Stop. Rewind. Play.

M. says Kerry doesn't understand basic things. Nobody likes to fight, but if you're in a fistfight and a dude pulls a knife, you pull your knife. If he pulls a gun, you run home and get yours. The thugs are pulverizing Kerry with everything they've got and everything they can make up, and it's making Kerry tho mad he could just slap them.

Scheuer-bits, "Imperial Hubris":

"Frankly, America does not have many friends in its war on bin Laden, and none are willing to share all they hold on al Qaeda."

....Polis 4:58 PM

Wednesday, September 29, 2004

Debate number one, countdown, zingers for tomorrow tonight.

Kerry: Give the media *one word* to blare on the front page: "BLUNDERED." "When a commander commits a serious blunder, he is relieved of his command. I ask the American people, why should we rehire a commander-in-chief who has erred a thousand times greater than Gallipoli?"

Now the media sheep are off asking "what's Gallipoli?" It's a famous World War I fiasco in which British generals lost 80,000 men for nothing. Trivia catagory, history. For $500. The blunderer and architect of the Gallipoli disaster was none other than the young Winston Churchill. An eager-beaver new Lord of the Admiralty, he was frustrated that the army was getting all the action in this war. His Gallipoli brainchild was designed to get the Navy back into the picture. One third of his ships were sunk on the first day. Shit-for-brains.

Stand by. Debate countdown, 26 hours...

On time-table for Iraq withdrawal: "The president says talking about a time-table for withdrawal sends a message of weakness to insurgents. But a time-table sends the right message to the Iraqi people. A Kerry administration will talk about time-tables sensibly, and I'll not be called weak by someone who didn't pick up a real rifle when we could have used him. Where were you Mr. President?"

Zinger: Bush says: "A president has to *mean* what he says." Kerry shoots back: "He also has to *know* what he's doing."

ALSO:

"The president diverted resources from the real global war on terror, he bungled the capture of bin Laden and the Qaeda leadership at Tora Bora, sparked nuclear proliferation in Iran and North Korea, and made the world a more dangerous place. Ladies and gentlemen, I volunteered to fight for my country as a young man. Many disagree with what I said when I came back, but I feel I earned the right to say it."

"I'm not saying I'm perfect, but I believe from the bottom of my heart that I can lead our nation into safe waters in these turbulent times, which began on that terrible morning in September in 2001. Give me that chance. No, Mr. President, supporting the troops is never complicated, we all support the troops. But making a problem sound simple doesn't make it go away. Only hard work and clear judgment do that."

Stop saying "as safe as we should be!"

Debate countdown, 25 hours...

Good luck, John, forget what everyone says and listen to your heart. It's a great one.

...Polis 1:23 PM

Friday, October 01, 2004

206

Mission accomplished

The noise from my apartment must have sounded like football season. We were bloodthirsty animals screaming YES!, pumping our fists and stomping our feet. Kerry spanked Bush all across the board in the first debate. Took him to school. This changes everything. An alternative vision for how to win the war on terr'. All because Kerry read Michael Sheuer (and maybe us. Anyone say nice shot?) The Neocon spin operation was at work before the debate even ended. But if Kerry doesn't hammer message, no one will remember what he said by election day. The BOOHIES can make you confuse up for down.

Put it on videotape and mail it out free to anyone who wants it in the swing states.

WORK IT:

-Iran and North Korea have become nuclear states because Bush scares them.

- The invasion of Iraq was an enormous DIVERSION and strategic blunder in the real war on terror. Iraq and Al Qaeda are two different things.

-We will hunt Al Qaeda and kill him.

The only big point not hit is the Neocon "flypaper" theory. This says, even if the invasion was unjustified, it serves a purpose. It draws terrorists so we can fight them there rather than here. Cartoonish Neocon thinking at its best. Who says they can't come here too? And now they have on-the-job training in killing Americans. Great.

Bush sweating bullets, voice high and nervous. Hunched-over in a defensive posture. John: careful with the shark-like grin when you're taking notes to finally nail this SOB who's been trashing your combat record while his ass was safe in Alabama. You look like you're about to eat him alive, and you did. YEA!

207

Next debate: it's the middle-class, stupid.

Now that you know I'm a smart-aleck expert on everything, with a Napoleonic complex to boot, I may as well tell John how to win the second debate too. I wanna be the goddamn general.

For every good general I bet you have nine brush-heads with a fifth-grade education, who excel at covering-ass. One guy told me that at basic training once they were jogging ten miles down a road, and to make them run faster they had a helicopter drop 50 pound bags of flour around them, which split in the road and rotted. He was thinking: why not rocks or something? Flour? They don't care, they didn't pay for it. You did.

A rising tide does not raise all ships unless you have a strong middle-class. Shrub brags about adding jobs, but look at what they are. You'll see a big chunk in retail, hotel, and restaurant. Shit jobs. McJobs. The ones with good bennies aren't coming back as fast as we're losing them. I'm talking white-collar jobs. Now if your business plan doesn't have an outsourcing component, you're a non-starter for venture capital.

I say hit the decline of college opportunity for middle-class kids. Forget our generation, we're screwed. We're all going to be eating dogfood when we're old unless we're fluent in Chinese. But we can make sure our kids do better, by going to the best college they can get into, with a big social program to take care of it. Did I say that dirty word? Social program? Oops, scratch that, this is an OPPORTUNITY program. That's in bold on the talking points sheet. We want to position these Republican swine square against the AMERICAN DREAM!

More of Bush's brand of "freedom" : An Army officer in Iraq wrote a highly critical article on the the Bushies's conduct of the war, and now he's being investigated for disloyalty -- if charged and convicted, he could get 20 years. First published on Salon.com, Operation American Repression:

"Lorentz's essay contains no classified

information but does include a starkly critical evaluation of how the Bush administration has conducted the war. "Instead of addressing the reasons why the locals are becoming angry and discontented, we allow politicians in Washington DC to give us pat and convenient reasons that are devoid of any semblance of reality," Lorentz wrote." [137]

For saying that, 20 years. The fascist bastards.

Crossgates Mall, Guilderland, New York. Man arrested at for refusing to take off a tee-shirt that said "give peace a chance." Agree with me or die. Where are these Nazis coming from?

....Polis 11:48 AM

Tuesday, October 05, 2004

Stem cell research? The mind of this campaign truly baffles me. After a debate victory on national security and a possible comeback, what does Kerry do? He changes the subject. Meanwhile Bush is hammering that Kerry-is--unsafe-for-America. Kerry's new poll strength already softening.

I can see Bush changing the subject, but Kerry? Kerry shoots himself in the foot again, wandering all on his own into treacherous God, guns, and gays country. Stem cell research? I'm not even sure how I feel about it myself.

If you want to show Bush's medieval mind, bring up global warming. A lot more people even know what it is. There is a Republican mole in the Kerry camp feeding him bad advice.

Now is *not* the time to have a biology class!

---

[137] "Operation American Repression?" by Eric Boehlert, Sept. 24, 2004, http://www.commondreams.org/headlines04/0929-20.htm

Precious newspaper column inches ceded to Bush again. Message-of-the-day score in the national papers: Bush- 10, Kerry- 0.

Bush refining his lines of attack on Kerry, for "flip-flops," on middle-class tax cuts, and his vote against Gulf War 1991, said:

"That means Saddam would not only have been in his palaces, that means he would have been in Kuwait as well. The policies of my opponent are dangerous for world peace. If they were implemented, they would make this world not more peaceful, but more dangerous."

Despite debate defeat Bush stays relentlessly on-message. Kerry can't or won't drive home Bush's own responsibility for making the world more dangerous, by letting bin Laden/Al Qaeda slip away. I see Bush having the lead in the polls again in 7 days....Polis 1:05 PM

Wednesday, October 06, 2004

Greatest hits

Best Kerry lines from the first debate September 30:

-**"I will hunt down and kill the terrorists, wherever they are."**

-**"This president has made, I regret to say, a colossal error of judgment. And judgment is what we look for in the president of the United States of America."**

-**"I'm proud that important military figures who are supporting me in this race: former Chairman of the Joint Chiefs of Staff John Shalikashvili; General Eisenhower's son, General John**

210

Eisenhower, General Admiral William Crown; General Tony McBeak, -- all believe I would make a stronger commander in chief. And they believe it because they know I would not take my eye off of the goal: Osama bin Laden. Unfortunately, he escaped in the mountains of Tora Bora. We had him surrounded. But we didn't use American forces, the best trained in the world, to go kill him. The president relied on Afghan warlords and he outsourced that job too. That's wrong."

-"The president talks about Iraq as a center of the war on terror. Iraq was not even close to the center of the war on terror before the president invaded it."

-"I've met kids in Ohio, parents in Wisconsin places, Iowa, where they're going out on the Internet to get the state-of-the-art body gear to send to their kids."

-Colin Powell, our secretary of state, announced one day that we were going to continue working with the North Koreans. The president reversed it publicly while the president of South Korea was here. And the president of South Korea went back to South Korea bewildered and embarrassed because it went against his policy. And for two years, this administration didn't talk to North Korea. While they didn't talk, the fuel rods came out, the inspectors were kicked out, the television cameras were kicked out. And today, there are four to seven nuclear weapons in the hands of North Korea.

-"It's one thing to be certain, but you can be certain and be wrong."

...Polis 1:28 PM

Thursday, October 07, 2004

The New Republic: is Kerry helping kill American troops?

I knew it would come to this. Was saying so the minute the Neocons said Al Qaeda preferred Kerry. This was after the Spanish people threw out their warmonger-bums after the Madrid train bombing (see post April 2, 2004.)

EXCERPTS From "Speech Impediment," by Peter Beinhart, The New Republic, 10/11/02:

> **"This column should not be necessary. A more decent president would not accuse his opponent of assisting terrorists and harming American troops merely because he criticizes U.S. policy. A more decent conservative movement would call such accusations anti-democratic, rather than mindlessly parroting them, as National Review Online's Jed Babbin did this week. But the president is who he is. And so are his supporters. And so, in response to John Kerry's increased criticism of U.S. policy in Iraq, Bush and his surrogates have essentially accused Democrats of helping insurgents kill American troops....**
>
> **Bush's argument is stupid and repugnant. It's stupid because it involves unsupported assumptions about how the Iraqi insurgents think. Bush suggests that, when Kerry says America is losing in Iraq and must therefore change strategy, he makes America look irresolute - and thus emboldens the killers. But one could just as easily make the opposite argument...perhaps bin Laden -**

like his fellow murderers in Iraq - thinks Bush has been good for business....

After all, as London's International Institute for Strategic Studies recently asserted, Al Qaeda recruitment has increased since the Iraq war. In his book, former counterterrorism czar Richard Clarke...imagines the terrorist kingpin desperately hoping America will invade Iraq and thus divert resources from the hunt for him. So maybe bin Laden would cast his absentee ballot for Bush, in the hopes of getting more of the same....

Maybe hearing Kerry call for a new strategy makes them fear America will fight the war more effectively - which disheartens them....

At a recent rally in Columbus, Ohio, Bush said, "These people don't need an excuse for their hatred. I think it's wrong to blame America for the anger and the evil of the killers." But evidently, it's OK to blame John Kerry....

But the biggest problem with the president's latest talking point isn't that it's dumb; it's that it's anti-democratic. When Bush says Kerry's Iraq criticism emboldens America's enemies, he's essentially saying that - for the good of his country - Kerry should shut up....

A more decent president would be ashamed."

Of course if it were me I'd just keep it short and simple. Bush has brought this so low that Kerry is within his rights to just say he won't have his patriotism questioned by a draft-dodger. No, make that "a damned draft-dodger."

Today's "Imperial Hubris" fix, Scheuer knows his shit:

"Freedom is neither a spontaneous nor a universal

aspiration. Other goods captivate the minds of other people from other lands, order, honor, and tribal loyalties being the most obvious."

....Polis 1:52 PM

Monday, October 11, 2004

Since we know from the Duelfer report that Saddam was "gaming" the UN oil-for-food program to buy weapons now killing our troops, is it possible that some of that same money found it's way to Dresser Industries?[138] Yes, I'm back to that. We will not rest we will not falter and we will not fail. To expose Dick Cheney and George Bush as traitors, hypocrites, and enemies of the US Constitution they are sworn to defend. I am Polis and *j'accuse.*

Washington Post Special Report:

"[Halliburton] returned to dealing with Iraq after the council established the "oil-for-food" program in December 1996, permitting Iraq to export oil under U.N. supervision and use the proceeds to buy food, medicine and humanitarian goods. The program was expanded in 1998 to allow Iraq to import spare parts for its oil facilities."

Saddam's UN oil-for-food abuses should lead naturally to questions on the legality of Halliburton evading sanctions laws. And to questions on whether Halliburton was profiting from the same scam Saddam was using to stock-up on rocket launchers.

Kerry getting all tangled up in the sheets again, trying to explain, if Saddam needed to be "disarmed," how that makes this the "wrong war at the wrong time." Don't ask me. I have no ideas on how to help him with that one. I had a co-worker once who's talent was taking something you thought you were perfectly clear on, and

---

[138] "Bush defends Iraq invasion in face of new weapons report," by John J. Lumpkin, Associated Press, October 7, 2004

214

by the end of five minutes of talking to him you'd leave his office thoroughly confused. That's Kerry.

Bush focusing on Saddam's future intentions. Okay so we didn't find any weapons of mass destruction – so what? - he would've done something, somehow, sometime. We go to war for *that?*

More on how Bush let Al Qaeda get away, from "The Long Hunt for Osama" by Peter Bergen, The Atlantic Monthly:

> "...according to CNN, not until this past spring [2004] were U.S. satellites ordered to survey the Afghan-Pakistani border region twenty-four hours a day, seven days a week."

From "Bush's Lost Year" by James Fallows, The Atlantic Monthly:

> "It is hard to find a counterterrorism specialist who thinks that the Iraq War has reduced rather than increased the threat to the United States..."

> "The Administration apparently did not consider questions like "If we pursue the war on terror by invading Iraq, might we incite even more terror in the long run?" and "If we commit so many of our troops this way, what possibilities will we be giving up?" But Bush "did not think of this, intellectually, as a comparative decision," I was told by Senator Bob Graham, of Florida, who voted against the war resolution for fear it would hurt the fight against terrorism. "It was a single decision: he saw Saddam Hussein as an evil person who had to be removed.""

> "Soon after the attacks President Bush created an interagency Campaign Coordination Committee to devise responses to al-Qaeda, and named Clarke its co-chairman. Clarke told me that this group urged a "rapid, no-holds-barred"

215

retaliation in Afghanistan, including an immediate dispatch of troops to Afghanistan's borders to cut off al-Qaeda escape routes."

Memo; second debate: Bush stomping around the stage like an idiot.

...Polis 1:40 PM

Wednesday, October 13, 2004

Norm Ornstein, presidential scholar at the conservative American Enterprise Institute, on Bush's extraordinarily dirty campaign: "I've not seen a president do what this president has done."

The closest I can think of is Nixon's 1972 campaign against McGovern. They had posters of a grinning, joint-smoking, sunglass-wearing McGovern with the caption: "Vote for Acid, Amnesty, and Abortion." It was funny. I liked it. I think now it's a collector's item. Tricky Dick starts to look like a moral giant compared to these Repubs. He always looked kind of shifty and defensive, which means he might have at least been *capable* of feeling guilt. Not these guys. Even Tricky Dick didn't accuse his opponent of helping kill American troops in Vietnam.

...Polis 1:33 PM

Friday, October 15, 2004

No John, we don't know. That's what an Ohio viewer of the third and last debate said about Kerry's answer to flip-flopping. K. said: "you can always play with votes, everyone knows that."

No John, we don't know. Explain it to us please. John could say: "Lookit, when you watch C-Span you'll see back-to-back votes on the same bill or slightly different bills, and you'll see the numbers coming up a little different each time. People are changing their votes to make a point. That's not flip-flopping. The president is trying to

216

fool you by comparing apples to oranges."

Oh, like in C-Span! Put things the way people can understand it. TV.

Cheney's livid that Kerry mentioned Cheney's lesbian daughter Mary in the debate. She's an activist and manager of Coors's corporate relations for the gay and lesbian market. That's funny. I didn't even know Coors *had* a gay-lesbian market. None of the gay people I know will drink that piss. The Kerry daughters booed on the stage by Repug thugs in Florida, at the MTV music awards. A wing-nut yells into the open door of Teresa Kerry's limousine "Teresa, how could you kill a baby?" dredging up a near-abortion for medical reasons 30 years ago (she miscarried.) [139] They dragged John McCain's adopted daughter into the 2000 South Carolina primary. [140] People who wear band-aids over purple hearts to mock the wounds of a man who still has shrapnel in his leg, who lost friends in Vietnam, now their delicate sensibilities are offended. These savage hypocrites don't wike it when someone hurts their widdle feewings...

One hit like 9/11 turns them into scared, trigger-happy Nazis. Makes them lose their cool, their grasp of the situation. Wusses. And they vote for the captain every company prays they don't get, because his men wind up dead. Every army has them, every company dreads them, everyone knows who they are. They'll order you into a crossfire and make the same mistakes over and over, the swaggering, blustering shit-for-brains...

"...the pathetic, under-seige look of the White House..." – Michael Scheuer

"Farenheit 9/11" now on video/DVD

Lots of people haven't seen it because they live in the sticks or they don't like Michael Moore and don't want to give him ten

---

[139] *Boston Globe,* "Report says Bush sought Vatican help," June 14, 2004
[140] See April 2, 2004 post.

217

bucks at the theater. So as of Oct. 5th you can rent it at your local video store. Maybe grandpa wouldn't make the trip because he heard it's "propaganda," but he'll watch it if he can relax in his own chair (and there are no good ballgames on.)

I'm almost done with "Imperial Hubris." Here's what Scheuer has to say about the Disneyland in Iraq Magic Show:

> **"[President John] Adam's warning-that championing the cause of democracy for foreign peoples whose culture, politics, and society America does not understand would entrap the United States abroad "beyond the power of extrication"-ought to give pause to Americans in this year of our Lord 2004."**

> **"...our youngest voters have...never learned the nature and length of the arduous and often bloody struggle Americans have waged to get to their present stage of self-government. American democracy began not in Jamestown in 1608, or at the Continental Congress in 1776 but-to pick a plausible date- in 1215 when the English barons reduced King John's arbitrary powers at Runnymede."**

> *Breaking News: Platoon defies orders in Iraq[141]*....Polis 1:42 PM

Monday, October 18, 2004

No draft, huh? Simple math. They're yanking grandpas out of retirement and slapping Kevlar helmets onto them; you tell me there will be no draft. Link this to any Young Republican "Four more years!"-type blog you can find. Keep it up, meat-heads, you'll be soorreee... Telegram from Army catches 57-year-old retiree off guard, from the online Progress-Index:

---

[141] *Mississippi Clarion-Ledger*, "Platoon defies orders in Iraq," October 15, 2004

218

> "County resident Cleveland Rodgers, who served
> 36 years in the Army, was comfortably retired and
> was teaching supply soldiers at Fort Lee. He was
> enjoying civilian life and, despite some health
> concerns, the last thing he expected was to be
> recalled by the U.S. Army, having served in the
> Army until he was 55...The retired master
> sergeant figures, if sent to Iraq, the Army will
> likely have him working on chemicals." [142]

Flu shots. Now Kerry's off gabbing about flu shots. *And if what I've said so far doesn't grab you, vote for me and I'll get you your flu shots!* They have two weeks. Like Tom Wolfe said, a desperate salesman is a dead salesman.

The following article is so damned important for understanding the war on terror that I'm going to risk running afoul of copyright laws by posting big chunks of it. The article is "Idea Man" by Spence Ackerman in the October 25, 2004 issue of the New Republic. Sorry, Spence. Can we settle this over a beer?

"Idea Man" (abridged)

> "An Annenberg poll released last week found
> that, by a 14-point margin, respondents trusted
> President Bush more than the Massachusetts
> senator to protect the nation from Al Qaeda. And
> it's not just Kerry's strength that is in question--
> it's his judgment. When Kerry accused Bush of
> "diverting [his] attention from the real war on
> terror" against Al Qaeda by invading Iraq, the
> president's surrogates shot back that Kerry
> possessed an insufficiently broad understanding of
> the war. "The idea that somehow you kill Osama
> bin Laden, and maybe Al Qaeda wraps up, and
> then you're done with the war on terrorism could
> not be further from the truth," Condoleezza Rice

---

[142] http://www.zwire.com/site/news.asp?brd=2271&nav_sec=57584

told CNN. Conservative New York Times columnist David Brooks dismissively wrote that Kerry "defined the enemy in narrow, concrete terms."

It's true that Kerry conceives of victory in the war on terrorism chiefly in terms of destroying Al Qaeda. But what Kerry understands--and the administration disastrously does not--is that Al Qaeda is not "narrow," nor, increasingly, is it "concrete."

The president's chief contribution to the ideological struggle has been the occupation of Iraq, which has horrified the very Muslims it was supposed to draw to America's side. Beyond Iraq, the president has done little to promote Middle Eastern democracy beyond giving speeches to domestic audiences. In its final report, issued this July, the 9/11 Commission practically begged the Bush administration to "engage the struggle of ideas" in order to "prevent the continued growth of Islamist terrorism." Little wonder, then, that the perpetrators of the Madrid train bombings, the Abu Hafs Al Masri Brigades, proclaimed themselves "very keen that Bush does not lose the upcoming elections" in a March statement to an Arabic newspaper.

Kerry would take the exact opposite tack. Far from imposing democracy from the top down, Kerry told a Los Angeles audience in February, "We must support human rights groups, independent media, and labor unions dedicated to building a democratic culture from the grassroots up." In this, Kerry has increasingly echoed Senator Joseph Biden, a leading candidate to be Kerry's secretary of state. Biden says he will tell regimes whose repression has indirectly bred terrorism, "I want to see you at least squint toward democracy.... John Kerry would have been funding openly, and supporting any way he could, democratic movements in these countries."

Nor does Kerry intend to shy away from a cardinal source of funding for the madrassas-- Saudi Arabia. Biden in particular is prepared to confront the Saudis over their troublesome ideological adventures. "Our policy should be: Cease and desist, or we've got to figure out new relationships here," he says. "Am I going to invade your country? Hell no. Are we going to depose you? Hell no. But let me tell you: Are we going to supply the physical security for your continued existence? *I don't know."*

Bush's approach is different. Ever since his September 20, 2001, address to Congress, and especially in his 2002 State of the Union address, Bush has emphasized the need to attack state sponsors of terrorism at least as much as actual terrorists. "One of the principal strategic thoughts underlying our strategy in the war on terrorism is the importance of the connection between terrorist organizations and their state sponsors," Undersecretary of Defense for Policy Douglas Feith explained to Nicholas Lemann of The New Yorker shortly before the invasion of Iraq. "Terrorist organizations cannot be effective in sustaining themselves over long periods of time to do large-scale operations if they don't have support from states. They need a base of operations. They need other types of assets that they get from their connection with their state sponsors--whether it's funding, or headquarters, or, in some cases, the use of diplomatic pouches and other types of facilities."

Simply put, this does not remotely describe Al Qaeda. When bin Laden lived in Sudan and

Afghanistan from the mid-'90s until 2001, Al Qaeda effectively propped up the ruling regimes rather than the other way around. Nor did Al Qaeda's jihadists require sympathetic governments to support them as they planned and executed attacks: The September 11 hijackers proved murderously productive during their stays in Germany and the United States. Bin Laden and Zawahiri are believed to be in the lawless Northwest Frontier Province of Pakistan, but the presence of a hostile regime in Islamabad hasn't prevented them from inspiring attacks in places like Bali, Riyadh, Istanbul, and Madrid. Even if the United States overthrew every regime that so much as batted an eyelash at bin Laden, Al Qaeda's lethality in the three years after losing its Afghanistan sanctuary proves that a policy focused on ending "state sponsorship" will never destroy the network.

Kerry, by contrast, understands that the threat from Al Qaeda is not state-centric. Asked where the "center" of the war on terrorism is, [Kerry advisor] Rand Beers immediately replies, "There isn't one." He explains, "What Al Qaeda did during its Afghan period was to create a jihadist movement on a global basis. While Al Qaeda certainly has the financial wherewithal, the organizational skills, the tactical wherewithal to conduct significant operations à la the dual embassy bombing in Africa in 1998 or the World Trade Center-Pentagon attack in 2001, the fact that the major events since then have been conducted by organizations which were able to operate at a distance from and, to at least some degree, independent of central direction from Osama bin Laden is an indication. I wouldn't say that it's Al Qaeda 2.0, I'd say it's Global Terrorism 2.0. That means we're going to have to have a much broader and a much more comprehensive campaign that goes beyond the decapitation strategy that seems to excite George Bush."

Eliminating Al Qaeda means using force in the area where a significant portion of the network has entrenched itself since the fall of Kandahar in 2001. "The Al Qaeda-Taliban-[Afghan warlord Gulbuddin] Hekmatyar nexus along the Pak-Afghan border represents an area of activity that we have to attend to," says a senior Kerry adviser. "One, we want to ensure that Afghanistan doesn't again become a sanctuary. And two, we want to ensure that the fundamentalists who have gained political power in the Northwest Frontier Province and who have some degree of allegiance to bin Laden don't become a more dominant political movement in Pakistan more generally." Adds Biden, "What I think you would see is John Kerry doing everything he can to build a greater consensus worldwide that will allow us, if need be, to even consider using force in conjunction with the Pakistanis against Al Qaeda in Pakistan."

Kerry's advisers won't map out everywhere they intend to use force. But they understand that the ideological campaign will bolster the military one. Policymakers in a Bush administration, a Kerry administration, or any subsequent government, will always have to consider the prospect that using force in a given situation could swell Al Qaeda's base of support instead of diminishing it, as the Iraq invasion has. But, though Al Qaeda will always portray U.S. action as a crusader's strike against Islam, when the political legitimacy of American power is on display, Al Qaeda's appeal is significantly diminished. As Biden says, "Remember all the talk that the Muslim street was going to rise up if we went into Afghanistan?" One reason it didn't was the near-unanimity of the international community in support of the invasion. What Kerry's ideological warfare is designed to do is expand the political space available to use force--which is further enhanced by expanding the stealthy and deadly capability of Special Forces. It's no accident that one of Kerry's earliest and most persistent critiques of Bush is over his failure to use American troops in December 2001 at Tora Bora, where the United States had both the political legitimacy and the military opportunity to strike a decisive blow against Al Qaeda forces. The strategy Kerry is proposing resembles nothing so much as a classic counterinsurgency campaign, where political and military measures reinforce one another against a shadowy and dispersed enemy. Against Al Qaeda, it's the only strategy that makes sense."

Subscribe to The New Republic and tell them Polis sent you!

....Polis 5:44 PM

Tuesday, October 19, 2004

Bush says Kerry doesn't "share our commitment to victory in Iraq." Wow. That sort of talk used to get you called out to a duel. He's calling him a traitor. Does Kerry sulk off sometimes and fantasize about clocking this guy? In the park at midnight, Mr. President. Take off that commander-in-chief jacket. Just you and me, bare fists. I'm bigger so I'll give you the first lick.

Democrats still won't do a Lewinski on Plame – Noor Khan - Dresser Industries. Remember when it was all Monica all the time? In a sane country that's what we'd be seeing, if not a televised hanging of someone in the White House for giving secrets to the enemy. If they let Bush get away with it and we get attacked again, now the Democrats will be to blame too; they're the ones who said nothing about Bush's betrayals. Just on general principles I'd say about the half those guys up there, from both parties, sitting in jail sounds about right.

The draft-dodger is having a wonderful time slicing little pieces off Kerry, slow and painful, and is probably amazed the Dems don't get mad. Not for long, anyway. With friends like these... It's downright unnatural.

ANOTHER TV AD THAT WILL NEVER BE MADE:

Kerry: I'm John Kerry and I approve of this ad

Thirty or forty-something soccer mom: "I'm voting for John Kerry because I think he's the best man to win the war on terror. He's tough, he's a decorated combat veteran, and the debates convinced me that he knows what he's doing. [Turn to the camera, pause.] I want my children to be safe. I took another look at John Kerry after that debate, and I liked what I saw." [Make sure she has a Midwestern accent.] Tag: John Kerry. The right man for the job. /END.

Bush: 75% of Al Qaeda leadership killed or captured? John can we hear from you here? When Bush said this in the debate you didn't say a damned thing. Al Qaeda creates new leaders as soon as old ones are killed, so that's flat-out wrong. Spence Ackerman in The New Republic on this:

> **"Bush boasted that "seventy-five percent of known Al Qaeda leaders have been brought to justice."...But, even if Al Qaeda weren't able to replenish its leadership positions, and even if Al Qaeda weren't able to attract new terrorist recruits, this figure would still not represent a significant diminution in the network's latent potency...based on intelligence estimates from American and European officials, 20,000 "potential terrorists" received training in Al Qaeda's Afghanistan camps; 2,000 have been killed or captured. This means that, even under the incorrect assumption that the number of jihadists is static, Al Qaeda will survive Bush's first term with 90 percent of its potential**

manpower intact." [143]

Sorry, more armchair quarterbacking. Kerry soundbite Bush is "out of touch" just doesn't rock me. How about Bush lives in "fantasyland" or "Alice in Wonderland?" My buddy Steve, who sold "Impeach punk-ass Bush" bumper stickers around town and only had his table tipped over twice by knuckle-draggers, pointed out that the element of *ridicule* is key against people who don't argue rationally. Your facts just don't matter to them. They keep repeating themselves. Charlie Chaplin understood this when he made the film "The Little Dictator."

....Polis 7:43 PM

Wednesday, October 20, 2004

The Polis lines

I've been following the firefight very closely, and can only say we need more OOMPH. These are the lines I'd like to put in Kerry's speeches, and feed to the media, one a day. If he listened to our suggestions, he'd win.

LINES:

"There are a range of folks, from respected conservatives at publications like the New Republic to former chairmen of the Joint Chiefs of Staff, who say I'm the best man to win the war on terror. What does George Bush give you? Fear, false attacks, and distortions."

"Nuclear proliferation happened as a result of their belligerent policies, strengthening hardliners in Iran and North Korea. That's a failure in statesmanship." (Screw Kerry's soundbite that Bush was "on the sidelines." He was in the middle of it and it's his fault!)

---

[143] Spence Ackerman, "Idea Man," *The New Republic,* October 25, 2004

226

"Our brave soldiers deserve a commander-in-chief who can navigate treacherous passages and see through stormy weather, not one who heads blindly for the shoals."

"We have many issues on which we're going to move America forward. They only have one big issue: More fear."

"Winston Churchill inspired us by saying we have nothing to fear but fear itself. All they can say is 'be afraid.'"

"They say there will be no draft, no social security privatization. They also swore up and down that Saddam had WMD, that they didn't do nation-building, and that they believed in fiscal responsibility."

Stay tuned for more. Add your own! Democracy is fun!

...Polis 8:03 PM

Thursday, October 21, 2004

"Imperial Hubris":

"Bin Laden, at day's end, has turned Clausewitz on his head. Indeed, bin Laden has no center of gravity in the traditional sense-no economy, no cities, no homeland, no power grids, no regular military et cetera bin Laden's center of gravity, rather, lies in the list of current US policies toward the Muslim world because that status quo enrages Muslims around the globe-no matter their view of al Qaeda's martial actions-and gives bin Laden's efforts to instigate a worldwide anti-US defensive jihad virtually unlimited room for growth."

Blunders dammit

I always thought there would be no writing more carefully crafted than president writing, just goes to show we're all flying by

227

the seat of our pants. Kerry headline on Iraq today: "terrible mistakes." Omigod, what a yawn. Say blunders, John, BLUNDERS.

Quote Bush. The Shrub gives verbatim Kerry quotes then plays off them, skillful and effective. To rebut Kerry's calling the Iraq war a diversion, Junior said something about Zarqawi, to wit: "If Zarqawi and his associates were not busy fighting American forces in Iraq, does Senator Kerry think he would be leading a productive and peaceful life?"[144]

The Shrub is pulling in, without saying it, the "flypaper" theory, which, if you can believe it, says we invaded Iraq to keep terrorists "busy." Good. Good and wrong.

The straw man. Bush says Kerry believes that Zarqawi "would be leading a productive and peaceful life" if we had not invaded Iraq, something Kerry never even remotely suggested. The challenge of rebutting Bush is that so much nonsense is thrown at you in such a short space that it's hard to know where to start.

WHAT KERRY SHOULD SAY, AND MAKE SURE IT HITS ALL THE PAPERS:

"Yesterday the president suggested the Iraq invasion was not a diversion, because we are keeping Zarqawi "busy," that's what he said, "busy," there rather than here. The problem is now there are more Zarqawis; now they are busy creating more terrorists. And nothing says they have to stay there, which is why we're in greater danger as a result of this president's policies."

This attacks the core of the Bush statement. As for the straw man, a "would [Zarqawi} be leading a peaceful and productive life," you do what a bull does to the waving red cape once it has spotted the part of you it wants to gore: ignore it.

---

[144] On October 29 Kerry did start quoting Bush, saying in Columbus "Yesterday, George Bush said, and I quote him, "a political candidate who jumps to conclusions without knowing the facts is not a person you want as your commander in chief..."" Reaction in the blogosphere was that Bush had just endorsed Kerry.

News:

A reader reports "The World According to Bush" now out on DVD, a more objective look at the administration than Mike Moore. Get it sent from Amazon to your swing state grandpa.

....Polis 2:16 PM

Friday, October 22, 2004

Hep me

I'm looking for help getting this published. If they pay I'll kick you a third, no no, fair's fair. Thanks.

"What a Fresh Start Means"
by Polis

Down here on the ground in the presidential campaign there is a barrier Kerry cannot seem to break: What exactly is he going to do to get us out of Iraq ? In a conversation with a customer service agent for my cellphone company, I casually steer the chit-chat toward the presidential debates. I never miss an opportunity to take the pulse of my countrymen, this one in El Paso, Texas. The very nice lady on the line tells me: "I'm a Republican girl, and the whole time I just listened for one thing from Kerry, how is he going to get us OUT OF THERE. And I didn't hear the answer." Door-to-door workers in swing states relate similar experiences.

Forget for a moment that this logic befuddles me. If a CEO runs his company into the ground, his days are numbered. No one asks what each candidate for the job would do differently. He's gone. If there's one thing we're beginning to agree on, it's that Iraq is a mess and we're in trouble. My gut is to say: why would you trust the person who got us into this mess to get us out? But that dodges the question.

In some ways the question is not fair. A candidate Kerry is not privy to the military and political intelligence on the ground that a president Kerry would be. But that's another dodge.

What makes Iraq so dangerous for America is that ordinary Muslims around the world who are not yet terrorists see proof of an attack on their religion. According to experts on Al Qaeda, such as CIA analyst and "Imperial Hubris" author Michael Scheuer, the invasion is a massive propoganda victory for bin Laden. "Capitalizing on growing anti-US animosity, Osama bin Laden's genius lies not simply in calling for jihad, but in articulating a clear and convincing case that Islam is under attack by America" Scheuer writes. In order to win the war on terror, this propoganda victory must be diluted, and its recruiting power halted or reversed.

German Defense Minister Peter Struck recently re-affirmed what many Americans suspect: the major allies want no part of combat operations in Iraq. Why would they want to be getting killed instead of us? Especially after Donald Rumsfeld dissed them as "the old Europe?" President Bush is pinning his hopes on newly-trained Iraqi army and police units, but this is a classic quagmire. As in Vietnam, you're not sure if you are training a true national army, or simply funneling weapons and intelligence to the insurgents. The first order of business for an insurgency is to infiltrate the ranks of the opposing force.

In a convoy ambush in Tikrit, a truck with Iraqi soldiers suddenly stopped and refused to follow. Moments later an IED exploded near an American Humvee. The Iraqis knew it was coming. Already we have seen Iraqi units refusing to fight, and their officers arrested for links to insurgents. As did the Viet Cong, the insurgents view anyone who works for or cooperates with the occupiers as collaborators. They know about "with us or against us." We cannot simply withdraw, for fear of civil war, but the longer we stay the longer we bleed. Dilemmas like these are among the reasons specialists in insurgencies are calling this one hell of a mess.

A possible part of the solution is Muslim peacekeeping troops under a UN flag. The Islamic world is vast, and with units that are neither Syrian, nor Turkish, nor Jordanian, nor Indonesian, but UN, the gravest humiliation to the insurgents can be removed. Armed, gibberish-speaking infidels with no knowledge of Arabic custom or

230

religion, searching homes and patting down Muslim women is creating terrorists, and American troops are admitting it. There is no guarantee such a course will bring immediate peace. But it is the beginning of a political strategy to parallel the military one. When President Bush says, "freedom is a gift from the Almighty," he does untold damage to our cause. Although he declares that the Christian God and the God of the Koran are "the same God," the Muslim world knows it's not true. Christian theologians have also angrily denounced this remark as an incorrect Biblical interpretation.

There is no easy way out of Iraq. As Colin Powell said "you break it, you own it." Bush broke it, now we own it, and there are no good options, only less bad ones. Peter Beinart of the New Republic writes: "for the Bush administration to slam Kerry for lacking a convincing plan for victory in Iraq is like dropping him in the middle of he desert and slamming him for lacking a convincing plan for finding water."

The question we must ask is, who is best suited and equipped to navigate the way out? Bringing in the Muslim world will entail challenges in statesmanship like we have never seen before. It will require extraordinary finesse, titanic resolve, and above all, credibility with the world. It will require "thinking outside the box" in foreign relations, and one of the most creative peace efforts in human history.

CIA analyst Scheuer tells us the greatest disservice the administration performs is promoting the fiction that we were attacked on 9/11 for who we are, rather than what we do. He tells us Al Qaeda cares nothing for our freedom or belief in separation of church and state. Bin Laden lays out the case that we support tyrannical regimes in the Middle East in order to obtain favorable terms for Arab oil, and that we are Crusaders who want to convert them. Showing the Muslim world we are not interested in attacking their religion, or stealing their oil, will be a blow that will leave Al Qaeda and the terrorists vulnerable. Neutralizing the Iraq front will allow resources to go where they belong: in hunting down the enemies who attacked us on 9/11.

Tuesday, October 26, 2004

Bush doing a good job of blunting Kerry attack that he lost bin Laden's trail at Tora Bora. Blew the chance to decimate Al Qaeda. The trademark Bush spin-with-the-punch sidestep maneuver: Says Kerry is "blaming our military." A good kick-boxer homes-in on the spot where he knows he has bruised his opponent, hits it again and again. It will buckle. Instead Kerry flails around and talks about flu shots.

Kerry's lack of fighting skills costing him dearly. Bush says:

"Last week in our debate, [my opponent] once again came down firmly on every side of the Iraq war. He stated that Saddam Hussein was a threat and that America had no business removing that threat. Senator Kerry said our soldiers and marines are not fighting for a mistake - but also called the liberation of Iraq a 'colossal error.'...He said he wants to hold a summit meeting, so he can invite other countries to join what he calls 'the wrong war in the wrong place at the wrong time.'"

And Kerry opened himself up to every bit of this, trying to play it cute.

KERRY BE DONALD TRUMP, PUT THIS INTO YOUR STUMP SPEECH, BY POLIS:

"The Bush administration has micromanaged this war from the start, even against the advice of our generals, and now they're trying to back-off. These were not ordinary explosives. These were WmD, weapons of major destruction. One pound can blow-up a jetliner.[145] They knew exactly where they were since 1991, and they

---

[145] This refers to the infamous missing HMX high explosives in Iraq, another crisis weathered by Bush. As Sun Tzu might have said, Bush chose ground that was "high and sunny" in order to have the advantage in deflecting attacks from the flanks. Bush staked-out the ground of Lord-Protector in the war on terror. Kerry had to knock him off that perch. In different military

were warned to secure them. One WMD expert says this was, and I quote, "like invading the US to get rid of [weapons of mass destruction] and not securing Los Alamos laboratory." The president says he supports the troops, but the fact is he failed the troops. Troops will die as a result of this.

Yet the president keeps repeating the same old distortions, trying to get you to believe that we think terror is a "law enforcement problem," and that we don't even know we're at war. He says I was, quote, "criticizing our commanders" for having failed to choose the war plan that would have destroyed most of Al Qaeda in Afghanistan, but who said anything about criticizing our commanders? I was criticizing *him*, and the decision it was *his* and *his* alone to make, to go in "slow and small." These are the words of former counter-terrorism czar Richard Clarke. Richard Clarke is the hero who once foiled a terrorist attack on Los Angeles airport.

The president says he will "never relent," but he *did* relent. And the other day the president said "If Zarqawi and his associates were not busy fighting American forces in Iraq," he would not be leading, quote, "a productive and peaceful life," and, quote, "that is why Iraq is no diversion." But if Zarqawi were not fighting us in Iraq, he would be a nobody like before, with no platform and no recruits. Iraq gave him recruits and a terrorist haven. A dictatorship is bad, but that's not a threat to the United States.

Mr. Bush will say anything, distort anything, blow any amount of smoke to keep his job. Now he says we're trying to nationalize healthcare. That's a ridiculous statement to be coming from the president of the United States. IT'S TIME FOR THE AMERICAN PEOPLE TO BE DONALD TRUMP, AND SAY: YOU'RE FIRED!"

Headline today in the Boston Globe: "Bush has exploited attacks of 9/11, [Jimmy] Carter asserts."

---

terms, Bush had the advantage of a strongpoint that has a clear field of fire for thousands of yards. It has to be taken before any other attack plan is possible.

And if Kerry says Bush "took his eye off the ball" one more time I'm going to vomit. No he didn't, John. He took his eye off AL QAEDA! OUR ENEMIES!

....Polis 8:46 PM

Thursday, October 28, 2004

HOW CAN THEY NOT KNOW?

This is a new Kerry/Edwards and they just might win. All punches are landing squarely, from "our heroic troops are doing their job, president's not doing his." Kerry's devastating dissection of Bush excuses:

> **"The Bush Administration first tried to convince the American people that this was not a big deal -- not a big deal that 380 tons of high grade explosives were now likely in the hands of terrorists and insurgents. Then, White House officials said guarding explosive dumps was not a high priority -- but guarding the Iraqi Oil Ministry apparently was. As more information was revealed in the press, the White House switched to their most comfortable position – the situation was bad but it was not their responsibility..."**

The blood is flowing. But these two thrusts weren't picked up by all news outlets, including USA Today, which went with Kerry's weaker "Kennedy-Bay of Pigs" soundbite. Don't give them a choice! Settle on the soundbite then repeat it for them in case they didn't get it right! "He said, "TROOPS DOING BEST, IT'S BUSH WHO'S FAILING!"" *Here, I'll write it for you!* Clog up their fax machines until they get it right!

If it ain't in USA Today, it didn't happen.

Hit: Now they DO blame the troops, Rudy "I thanked God George Bush was president as I watched someone jump from the towers " Giuliani said: "No matter how you try to blame it on the

234

president, the actual responsibility for it really would be for the troops that were there."[146]

HOW DARE THEY BLAME THE TROOPS! Bush MUST RESIGN!

Next step: Bush is trying to "Dan Rather" this; says Kerry went and shot-off his mouth before he "knew all the facts." Whoa, *they* are supposed to know the facts, not Kerry. The explosives "might have" been removed while Saddam was in power? HOW CAN THEY NOT KNOW?

KERRY HERE'S YOUR ATTACK, SAY IT!!!:

"They keep blowing smoke with all this flip-flop stuff. Sometimes politicians have good reasons for changing their votes or their positions, because conditions change. Now let's get back to the real issue they're trying to ignore, that in Iraq our troops our doing their job but the commander-in-chief isn't doing his. Now they're telling you *they don't know* when those high-explosives were stolen. That proves my point, HOW CAN THEY NOT KNOW?

They were warned repeatedly that they were there, and now they say they don't know how long they've been gone. They don't know because they didn't bother to check until now, until someone told them to. A small amount of these explosive can turn over a Humvee or a Bradley, and we're missing 380 tons of it. This is not a blunder, this is a disaster, and the commander-in-chief is directly responsible, not the troops. Just as he's responsible for letting most of Al Qaeda getting away at Tora Bora.

Now they say we made that up, about Tora Bora, just to get elected. But that's the assessment of some of the world's foremost intelligence experts. Bungling is bungling is bungling and their political attacks can't change that. They talk about supporting the troops but they have failed our brave heroes."

---

[146] *USA Today*, "Democrats try to turn Giuliani's weapons remark against Bush," Oct. 28, 2004.

235

GREAT JOB! ATTACK! ATTACK, GODDAMMIT! I WANT EVERY MAN UP THAT HILL!

Friday, October 29, 2004

Essay: Be Safe, Vote Against Bush

R. says I'm sounding full of myself. Foock's sake, how else are we going to get through to these knuckleheads? I'm really scared of Bush winning. We have to face that possibility. What the hell will we do??! Canada's too cold.

The minute the news showed the first cruise missiles exploding in Baghdad, my first thought was, I'm ashamed to say, not for the innocents being slaughtered at that moment alongside the hapless Iraqi army, but for my own hide. Now we're really going to get hit by terrorists, I thought. I flat-out didn't believe George Bush's breathless hyping of WMD in Iraq. His self-righteous demonization of a man who "committed mass murder" and who "had rape rooms" infuriated me. I knew that our government, including his father, had sponsored rape rooms, mass murder, and the torture of children, under Reagan/Bush in El Salvador and Guatemala. I knew that Bush the Elder coddled Saddam while he was gassing Kurds and slaughtering Shites, and that the tears for Iraqis were crocodile tears. I knew that Iran had spent 20 years under the boot of America's ally, the Shah, and that the Shah's torture methods were demonic.

It occurred to me that Bush talked to the people who didn't know these things. Now we know that Americans are divided not by blue or red, conservative or liberal, but by two different versions of reality. A report by the Program of International Policy Attitudes shows 75% of voters for Bush believe Saddam was involved in 9/11. 72% of Them believe Saddam had WMD programs. 51% even believe Bush supported the Kyoto treaty. Do these people ever pick up a newspaper?

Which means, this election is a war of ideas. Since few people outside the candidate's bases are excited about either of them, this is a referendum on the biggest issue of the day: George Bush's

236

idea of pre-emptive war.

If Iraq was truly a imminent threat, then the attack, despite all setbacks and incompetence, was a visionary and politically courageous act. If it disrupted a chain of events that would have resulted in WMD in the hands of bin Laden, then "winning the peace" be damned. They were going to hit us, we hit them first, and that's that. We'll get out the best way we can. But if we boosted Al Qaeda's manpower without significantly diminishing its ability to obtain weapons of mass destruction, then the invasion was an enormous strategic blunder.

Hunter Thompson told us that, since 9/11, America is suffering a collective nervous breakdown. The unspoken core of the Bush message is that the definition of a "credible threat" has changed since that morning in September. He invokes "the lessons of 9/11" as a way of delivering a jolt to nervous system. Whatever the "lessons of 9/11" are, we want to have learned them. Since this enemy has no formations, no missile silos or tank battalions that can be seen from the sky, we'll just have to believe the president about everything, period.

In March '03 Bush "ordered" Saddam to leave Iraq within 48 hours, a move aimed at humiliation rather than diffusing a crisis. After the invasion Bush said with a smirk, "a president has got to mean what he says; Saddam Hussein now knows that I mean what I say." The flight-suit aircraft carrier stunt gave me further evidence that none of the stated reasons for going to war were true. The evidence was the nature of this man standing before me: arrogant, gloating, self-glorifying. When you catch someone in a little lie, it's hard to believe him about anything else. Forget WMD, forget connection to Al Qaeda, write them off to a level of uncertainty. Bush said during the campaign that John Kerry wanted to "negotiate" with terrorists, which can be looked up and it's just not there. I don't look for the big lies, I look for the little ones. They tell me everything I need to know about the rest.

Bush attacked the wrong people, and when you attack the wrong people, you have the enemy you had before, plus brand new ones. This war has put us in grave danger without making us one iota

237

safer. For every civilian we kill we make potential terrorists out of grieving loved ones and new generations. To think otherwise is to deny other people are human, who love theirs as much as we love ours, who thirst for revenge, *just like us*. What kind of animal could see his family slaughtered by American bombs and not want to kill Americans? George Bush has accused critics of racism. "Do people think the Middle East is not ready for democracy, because their skin is brown?" he asked at a March 2004 press conference. But by treating Iraqi husbands, fathers, and brothers as not fully men who will avenge their loved ones, whatever the cost, he is the one who is racist. We've touched-off new cycles of revenge while barely touching those who attacked us on 9/11. This is why Iraq is so wrong.

Bush's latest swing state ad cuts to the chase: "why take the risk?" we hear as a woman stands alone with her conscience in a voting booth. But I'm voting against George Bush for exactly that reason: I want to be safe, and with his Iraq war he has put me, personally, in mortal danger. Otherwise I'd be with Nader, Cobb, or the Libertarian. A vote against Bush, for Kerry, will protect my hide. If we elect Bush this time, as George Soros says, we will ratify by popular vote, before the world, Bush's idea of pre-emptive war, and its slaughter of civilians: men, women, and children just as innocent as those who died on 9/11. That means a part of the world that so far hates our government, but not us, will begin to transfer that hatred. And that scares the hell out of me.

"See you tomorrow, folks. You haven't heard the last of me. I am the one who speaks for the spirit of freedom and decency in you. Shit. Somebody has to do it. We have become a Nazi monster in the eyes of the whole world, a nation of bullies and bastards who would rather kill than live peacefully. We are not just Whores for power and oil, but killer whores with hate and fear in our hearts. We are human scum, and that is how history will judge us . . . No redeeming social value. Just whores. Get out of our way, or we'll kill you...Who does vote for these dishonest shitheads? Who among us can be happy and

proud of having all this innocent blood on our hands? Who are these swine? These flag-sucking half-wits who get fleeced and fooled by stupid little rich kids like George Bush? They are the same ones who wanted to have Muhammad Ali locked up for refusing to kill gooks. They speak for all that is cruel and stupid and vicious in the American character. They are the racists and hate mongers among us they are the Ku Klux Klan. I piss down the throats of these Nazis. And I am too old to worry about whether they like it or not. Fuck them."

--Hunter S. Thompson, "Kingdom of Fear, Loathsome Secrets of a Star-Crossed Child in the Final Days of the American Century."

....Polis 8:25 PM

Wednesday, November 03, 2004

No unity

George Bush was true to his game plan right through to the end: make Kerry's trustworthiness the issue. It worked. The gain to Bush is America's loss. We enter a new era of gutter politics. Karl Rove's "genius" is his bet that fear, innuendo, and character assassination trump reason. The black art of veiled smear, distortion, and guilt-by-association is soaring like a comet. Rove, the Dark Prince, has won the battle for the soul of the Christian nation.

The Democrats made a decision early on not to question Bush's own trustworthiness, in the face of widely-reported and well-documented incidents. Now we have four more years of George Bush. The administration does not deny that the Plame leak originated from the White House, it merely says it doesn't know who it is. British and Pakistani officials are on-record expressing outrage at the Noor Khan fiasco, and no one has ever questioned Dick Cheney on Dresser Industries. No extensive investigation is required; no digging for something incriminating. Ninety percent of the case against George Bush on the national security can be Googled in ten minutes. But the tree that falls in the forest makes no sound if there is no opposition party to hear it. John Kerry spoke of holding this administration accountable, but in the end, hold it accountable, he did not.

I thank you dear readers for the kindness and honor you have done me by visiting my blog. The blog winds down, but the fight goes on. Let's remember that Newt Gingich and the Republicans, when they were the minority party, played hard and played for keeps. They slammed Clinton for behavior that besmirched the presidency, but never endangered the national security. Gingrich hammered until he crippled Clinton's presidency and nearly took him down. By putting forth a clear agenda, the ten-point Contract for America (Contract on America), repeating it, and then fighting like wildcats about everything else, the Republicans won their first majority in over 30 years.

The fact is, this election shouldn't have been close. If there is any silver lining, it will be the demise of the center-right-triangulator wing of the Democratic party who don't believe in anything but polls and not getting anyone too upset. Often referred to as centrists, this fiction really describes the right and the far-right. The real center is *us*, and all those Republicans who voted against Bush, the fiscal conservatives who are furious at the national debt, the conservative generals like Wes Clark who call this administration "the nastiest, most imperialistic administration in living memory." The center is many socially conservative Christians who don't think Bush acts very Christian. The center is now championless. We're completely on our own.

The center-right-triangulator wing equates putting up a fight with left-wing radicalism, and warns against appearing as a far-out fringe. Even after Republicans attack with an audacious hypocrisy that can only be described as psychotic, such as attacking a Silver Star winner's war record when their own candidate avoided combat, by equating criticism with treason as John Ashcroft did when he said to critics of the Patriot Act, "to those who scare peace-loving people with phantoms of lost liberty, your words only give comfort to the

240

enemy," beyond short flurries of Democratic indignation, the so-called centrists confuse fighting back with going negative. This even though the Republicans make them pay dearly for every slip of the tongue.

The lawyer corporate-lobbyist wing of the Democratic party have shown their true colors. They can work with Republicans. It's us middle-class and poor slobs they can't stand.

Kerry said: "I'll never rush to war without a plan to win the peace." Does that mean it's ok to rush to war if you do have a plan to win the peace? Or that not having a plan is ok as long as you don't rush? Why didn't someone tell him that line stinks?

My biggest personal surprise is I thought that if Bush won, I'd have a negative view of America. But what I've seen astonishes me. 9/11 widows like Chris Britweiser stepped forward to speak out against George Bush, public officials like Richard Clarke, Michael Scheuer, and Paul O'Neill put their careers on the line and invite certain, vicious personal smear to warn the American public. We've seen soldiers risk jail time for refusing to "kill poor people in Iraq." We've seen artists like Michael Moore make films which now earn them daily death threats. We've seen so many acts of unexpected and breath-taking patriotism. But working at the polls, I also saw too many people who didn't know they had to register before they voted. This is new to a lot of people. And most of them wanted to vote against Bush. So this is not the end. This is the beginning.

The Democrats must retool their platform into a clear, consistent agenda, which includes a limited and carefully chosen list of items such as killing the $100 billion Star Wars pork barrel.

Star wars is a debate we can win, because even its inventors, like MIT's Ted Postel, say it's a waste of money. Star Wars says that we are going to allow countries take nuclear potshots at us, rather than do what we have always promised to do: obliterate them. Even John McCain thinks it's a waste of money, and last year he said: "This incestuous relationship between the contractors and the Pentagon and the lawmakers is just the worst."

The money from Star Wars should go toward buying whatever protection the troops are missing in Iraq, like armored Humvees, and you'd have plenty left over, for making college affordable again, no matter what college you get into. Some Democrats will say challenging anything in the military budget is political suicide, all they are saying is they don't have the stomach for a fight. Good. Let someone in who does. We don't like throwing money at education or social problems. Why should we throw money at defense? Less money for pork barrel weapons systems so there can be more for something else does not equal "weak."

Which means that highest on the agenda should be holding our representatives accountable for not representing us. Public office is a high honor because you have been chosen by the voters to speak for them, to "represent." So speak. Your job is not to call for unity, not to be bipartisan unless it's in our interest. It's to represent the people who pay your ample salary. You do not go to Washington to be liked.

The tools to start bridging the cultural divide have been created in this last election, with websites like Main Street Moms Oppose Bush and the Swing State Project. They put us in touch with our fellow citizens in other states, to discuss, share information, and respectfully disagree. Reaching one person in one rural county, and discussing the issues and exchanging information, I believe, is one of the single most powerful things one person can do in the next four years. George Bush won the election despite sky-high disapproval ratings, so there's plenty to talk about.

As for holding our Democratic congressmen accountable for rolling over and playing dead in the face of administration misdeeds and possible crimes, let a thousand primary challenges bloom. We can win. There's nothing a politician hates like a challenge, because it means he might have to go out and debate someone. And that might mean looking stupid. Boy they hate that.[147]

---

[147] As of this writing, a list of Democratic senators who have voted with Republicans on such Bush administration triumphs as drilling in the Arctic Wildlife Refuge, tort reform, and bankruptcy include: Bayh (D-IN), Bennett (R-UT), Biden (D-DE), Bingaman (D-NM), Cantwell (D-WA), Carper (D-

Let's not feel sorry for ourselves because we made phone calls to voters and knocked on doors and we still didn't win. Remember, the first American Revolution didn't end with the Battle of Lexington. It was a ten year slog in which men spent many hard winters camped out, often with their feet wrapped in rags. Fort Ticonderoga, Valley Forge. Think of that. Between what they had to do then and what we have to do now, I'll take our job any day. So let's get re-organized, and get back to work.

DE), Conrad (D-ND), Dodd (D-CT), Feinstein Inouye (D-HI), (D-CA), Johnson (D-SD), Kohl (D-WI), Landrieu (D-LA), Lieberman (D-CT), Lincoln (D-AR), Nelson (D-NE), Obama (D-IL), Reed (D-RI), Reid (D-NV), Rockefeller (D-WV), Salazar (D-CO), and Schumer (D-NY). See "Democrats: MIA," *The Nation,* April 11, 2005.

Mom, Apple Pie, and the Iranian Revolution

Mom, Apple Pie, and the Iranian Revolution

By Ralph Lopez

Working under Prof. Jeremy Pressman, "American Foreign Policy," Harvard Extension School, Master's program, 2003.

On September 20, 2001 president George W. Bush declared unequivocally that the September 11 attacks were the work of those who "hate us for our freedoms," thus absolving past and recent administrations of all Middle East policy failures. The declaration also paved the way for debate over the East-West, Cold War paradigm versus the North-South, neocolonial one. If East-West, US versus. USSR Cold War containment theory does a fairly good job of explaining US policy, including that which resulted in blowback, then American foreign policy could hope to be partially forgiven as miscalculations of the times. If the North-South, rich nation vs. poor nation theory of US behavior prevailed, the implications were far more disturbing. The possibility lay open that parts of the world, and the attackers, most assuredly hated "us" for reasons other than our "freedoms." The first American overthrow of a Middle Eastern government, that of Prime Minister

245

Mohammed Mossadeq in 1953, raises questions which seem to be better answered by a North-South interpretation of that covert action than by a "domino theory" defense of it. New York Times journalist Stephen Kinzer argues forcefully that, not only was Dr. Mossadeq *not* a threat to the US strategic position; in the eyes of many policy makers, including presidents Truman and Eisenhower, his democratic nationalism represented the best bulwark against Soviet designs ("All the Shah"s Men, An American Coup and the Roots of Middle East Terror," John Wiley and Sons, Inc., Hoboken, New Jersey 2003) Kinzer presents ample evidence that Iran"s relations with the British Anglo-Iranian Oil Company (AIOC) were of a purely neocolonial nature, that Mossadeq disdained the Russians as much as he did the British, and that the Tudeh Party, Iran"s communist party, was weak and no match for the broad National Front coalition put together by Mossadeq.

The plan to overthrow Dr. Mossadeq was conceived by the British and championed by various US State Department and CIA hawks, such as Theodore Roosevelt grandson Kermit Roosevelt, and General Walter "Beedle" Smith, even before the Dulles brothers took power under the incoming Eisenhower administration in 1953. The flashpoint was Mossadeq's nationalization of the Iranian oil industry, which was 51% British-owned and which extracted and sold Iranian oil at 84% of profits compared to the 16% that went to the Iranians. This prompted an observer to remark that there was more money being paid in taxes to the British treasury on the British share than Iran's entire share. In addition, it was AIOC policy never to open the books to the Iranians, so even this splitting of the take was questionable. Although sleights such as stark differences between the living conditions of Iranians and those of British executives were everywhere, including fountains marked "not for Iranians," the Iranians at first centered their demands on a 50-50 split in oil revenues, the right to inspect the books, allowance of Iranians onto the company"s board of directors, and the training of more Iranian technicians. The demands were rejected outright by the British, and in retaliation the Iranians, led by Mossadeq, proposed nationalization of AOIC. Of the tens of thousands of Iranian employees of the AIOC, the *Jerusalem Post* reported: "They lived during the seven hot months of the year under the trees. In winter times these masses moved into big halls, built by the company, housing up to 3,000-4,000 people without walls of partition between them. Each family occupied the space of a blanket.. There were no lavatories."

Iran"s history is inextricably bound to the contest between neocolonial Britain and Czarist Russia, culminating in a 1907 treaty in which the powers, without consulting the weak and corrupt Qajar ruler, simply divided it between themselves. The British were in the south, the Russians in the north, and a neutral zone separated them. Both British and Russian troops were present to enforce it. However, the British had long established a stranglehold on the country's resources, the terms of which were described by British Foreign Secretary Lord Curzan, in 1919, as "the most complete and extraordinary surrender of the entire industrial resources of a kingdom into foreign hands that has probably ever been dreamt of, much less accomplished, in history." With its proximity to Britain's Indian colony, Curzon also declared:

> "If it should be asked why we should undertake the task at all, and why Persia should not be left to herself and allowed to rot into picturesque decay, the answer is that her geographical position, the magnitude of our interests in the country, and the future safety of our eastern Empire render it impossible for us now" to disinherit us from what happens in Persia."

With the turmoil and exhaustion brought on by the Bolshevik Revolution, Russian power and immediate interest in pursuing the contest waned, and in 1917 the Bolsheviks renounced most of their rights in the country and canceled all debts owed by Iran to the fallen Czarist government.

In his defense of "analogical reasoning" in statesmanship, political scientist Yuen Foong Khong quotes

248

Arthur Schlesinger: "the historian can never be sure-the statesman himself can never be sure, to what extent the invocation of history is no more than dignifying a conclusion already reached on other grounds." Proponents of the Cold War, East-West confrontation explanation of the US conspiracy with royalist elements in Iran to overthrow Mossadeq might be correct in pointing to the superheated Cold War atmosphere of the times: the US had just "lost" China, the North Koreans in 1950 had poured over the 38th Parallel, and the USSR had recently brought Latvia, Estonia, Lithuania, and Poland into its orbit. However, as Jerome Slater suggests, merely looking at a map and counting the red patches can represent "a failure of intellect, a substitute for historical observation and careful analysis." The eminent Thomas Paterson notes that during this time: "Most upheaval actually sprang from indigenous sources-colonial, tribal, ethnic, religious, cultural, economic. Yet Americans posited a mechanistic "domino theory.""

Paterson, however, also contends that Secretary of State John Foster Dulles' reputation as a "simplistic, hardline, rigid thinker" was at odds with "what one saw around the table within the department arguing about what should be done." This is at odds with the account of at least one participant around such a table, the man appointed to implement the overthrow of Mossadeq, Kermit Roosevelt. Roosevelt notes that at the meeting called by Foster Dulles to

249

decide Mossadeq"'s fate, the decision was one which Dulles "clearly, he had already made." At the close of the momentous meeting, Roosevelt, who was then 36 years of age, recalls:

> "It was with mixed feelings that I left his office. On one hand, it was good to have our project approved. The manner of its acceptance to my mind implied not only support of the Shah but also confidence in the Agency-and in me personally. This I had to regard as flattering. On the other hand, this was a grave decision to have made. It involved tremendous risk. Surely it deserved thorough examination, the closest consideration, somewhere at the very highest level. It had not received such thought at this meeting. In fact, I was morally certain that almost half of those present, if they had felt free and had the courage to speak, would have opposed the undertaking."

Roosevelt remembers that Foster Dulles "waved us from the room" and picked up the phone. "I hoped that perhaps he was calling the White House, that he was making an appointment to get the president"'s concurrence. But I never knew." Paterson has made pointed note of the McCarthyite purges that Foster Dulles conducted of his State

Department, which in effect eliminated all who disagreed with his analysis, such as one China hand who offered his professional opinion that the American-backed Chiang Kai-shek would probably lose. Dulles' inquisition took this to mean that the professional was plotting to defeat Jiang. The effect, says Theodore White, "was to poke out the eyes and ears of the State Department on Asian Affairs, to blind American foreign policy."

Mossadeq was first and foremost a nationalist, as both Truman and Eisenhower understood. Author William Blum notes that he "had campaigned successfully against lingering Soviet occupation of northern Iran after World War II, and in October 1947 had led Parliament in its rejection of a government proposal that a joint Irano-Soviet oil company be set up exploit the oil of northern Iran." Kinzer writes:

> "Two central beliefs shaped Mossadeq"s political consciousness. The first was a passionate faith in the rule of law. The second was a conviction that Iranians must rule themselves and not submit to the will of foreigners." In his book *Iran and the Capitulation Agreements* Mossadeq argued that "Iran could develop modern, European-style legal and political systems if it took one vital step. It must impose the law equally on

everyone, including foreigners, and never
grant special privileges to anyone."

Rising Third World nationalism at this time was often modeled on American ideals. Kinzer relates an anecdote in which, after a long conversation with an older Iranian woman, she became agitated for the first time when he mentioned Mossadeq, and said:

> "Why did you Americans do that
> terrible thing? We always loved America.
> To us, America was a great country, the
> country that helped us while other countries
> were exploiting us. But after that moment,
> no one in Iran ever trusted the United States
> again. Why, why did you do it?"

In contrast to the hated British, Americans were well-liked, among all strata of society. The U.S. had, in 1919, criticized Britain"s ruinous Anglo-Persian Agreement, and championed Iran"s claim for compensation for the wartime occupations of Britain and Russia during World War I.

The British dependence on Iranian oil was complete, supplying the Royal Navy with fuel at a fraction of market price, which fueled victory for the British in both World Wars. British Foreign Secretary Ernest Bevin acknowledged that without Iranian oil, "there was no hope of our being able to achieve the standard of living at which we are aiming in Great Britain." The *Jerusalem Post* recounts that the usual response from Bevin's British colleagues when arguing that the British were making a mistake by not being more flexible was: "We English have had hundreds of years experience on how to treat the Natives. Socialism is all right back home, but out here you have to be the master."

The British position on AIOC infuriated the Truman administration. The administration called AIOC's stubbornness "one of the greatest political liabilities affecting the United States/UK interests in the Middle East," and called the company's policies "reactionary and outmoded." The company's attitude was "a handicap in the control of communism." Averill Harriman remarked, upon a tour of the Abadan refinery complex, the largest in the world, that the British had "a completely nineteenth century colonial attitude." Upon news of the nationalization British Prime Minister Winston Churchill wanted to shell Iranians from warships immediately.

In describing Mossadeq, the "communist danger," and the threat of a Soviet takeover, Kermit Roosevelt says in his memoir: "The British motivation was simply to recover the AOIC oil concession. We were not concerned with that but with the obvious threat of a Russian takeover." What stands out in Roosevelt's account is use of words such as "obvious" in making his claims. Roosevelt's arguments, and those of the State Department, are put forth as axiomatic, unquestionable, and articles of faith. Foster Dulles often referred to Mossadeq as a "lunatic," a "madman," and a "fanatic." In the momentous meeting that would change the course of history, Foster Dulles employs the tone of a "school master," according to Roosevelt:

> "First, gentlemen you do know, I assume, where Iran is and what it is. Persia, as it used to be named, has been throughout history the bridge between Far Eastern Asia and the lands of the Mediterranean and Europe."

Blum notes of the Roosevelt memoir that "it would be incorrect to state that Roosevelt offers little evidence to support his thesis of the communist danger. It would be more precise to say that he offers *no* evidence at all." In 2000 the New York Times published a leaked official, and secret, CIA history of the overthrow of Mossadeq, which read:

> "By the end of 1952, it had become clear that the Mossadeq government in Iran was incapable of reaching an oil settlement with interested western countries, was reaching a dangerous and advanced stage of illegal deficit financing; was disregarding the Iranian constitution in prolonging Premier Mohammed Mossadeq's tenure of office; was motivated mainly by Mossadeq's desire for personal power; was governed by irresponsible policies based

on emotion; had weakened the Shah and the Iranian Army to a dangerous degree; and had cooperated closely with the Tudeh (Communist) Party of Iran."

This fantastic document (which I recommend to anyone as reading more hair-raising than Stephen King) neglects to mention that it was the British, not Mossadeq, who were uncompromising on an oil settlement, that it was a British blockade driving the country to financial ruin, and that Mossadeq had once gone as far as suppressing the Tudeh Party, which was in any event far weaker than the Mossadeq's National Front which was "a coalition of highly diverse political and religious elements including right-wing anti-communists," who may have agreed on little else but Mossadeq's honesty and integrity, and on his drive to get a fair oil deal for Iran.

The CIA history employs the language of NSC-68, which, as Paterson asserts, "glossed over complexities and ambiguities, treated communism as a monolith, [and ignored] differences within the communist community." It made sweeping assumptions about Soviet motives and capabilities without evidence. The report, in short, exaggerated the "threat." This mode of argument was not lost on Mossadeq himself, and in a UN "debate" with the British in an effort to resolve the crisis, he said: "I have not made actual count of the pejorative words used by Sir Gladwyn Jebb [his British opponent] in his various statements, but as you leaf through the pages of the record, defamatory word after defamatory word springs to the eye."

In explaining US foreign policy during the Cold War, proponents of the East-West model might cite the importance of what Columbia's Robert Jervis calls, "state actors" perceptions of each other." The implication is that the difference between those opposing overt and covert military action in any given instance, and those in favor, was whether or not the Soviet Union was perceived as aggressive and expansionist. This theory loses its explanatory power in this instance, however, because both presidents who opposed Mossadeq's ouster believed the Soviets were indeed aggressive, and would start trouble if they could. Yet Truman was "unalterably opposed" to the overthrow of Mossadeq. Eisenhower, who only late and reluctantly gave his assent, asked at one meeting of the National Security Council, why wasn't it possible "to get some of the people in these down-trodden countries to like us instead of hating us?"

In a little-remarked upon twist to the Cold War logic which held sway in the minds of the Dulles brothers, Truman believed that rising nationalist movements in the Third World were not only *not* a threat to the U.S. strategic position, but potentially beneficial. Truman liked and admired Mossadeq, and "had nothing but contempt" for the Anglo-American Oil Company. A Cold Warrior who refused to negotiate with the Russians and had fulfilled the Truman Doctrine by intervening in Greece, Truman made a distinction between armed leftist minorities and popular indigenous movements which reflected the legitimate aspirations of a people. Truman thought movements like Mossadeq's would result in positive social change and mature democratic institutions, and be the best "bulwark" against communism. Eisenhower said Mossadeq was "the only hope for the West in Iran." "I would like to give the guy ten million bucks," Ike once said to British Ambassador Anthony Eden, who was attempting to broach the subject of the proposed coup.

There is now evidence that the Dulles brothers may have subverted the judgment of Eisenhower by telling him that Iran was sliding into anarchy under Mossadeq, presenting a tempting opportunity for the Russians to intervene, in order to win his grudging approval for Operation Ajax. What they neglected to tell their boss, and what he may have not known even up until his death, was that the anarchy was being paid for with Company money. Evidence indicates that the early stages of Operation Ajax were set into motion without Eisenhower's approval. Knowing well Eisenhower's views and his abhorrence of the plan, it will be for other scholars to debate whether this constituted gross insubordination that should have earned for Foster Dulles a fate similar to General MacArthur's fate under Truman, when Truman declared he would "fire the son of a bitch" for insubordination, and did.

One question to be asked is clear: would Eisenhower

have nevertheless eventually approved of Operation Ajax, essentially a British brainchild presented to the Americans with vigor once the Eisenhower administration had taken office, had he understood the true situation on the ground? This again is a question for other scholars to engage.

Khong asks rightly, of the argument made by skeptics of analogical reasoning in foreign affairs, that if policy makers invoke history, such as "appeasement" in 1938, to justify conclusions "already reached on other grounds," just what are these "other grounds?" I have already suggested that the North-South neocolonial paradigm is a better fit than the East-West, and merits further study. In the case of 1953 Iran, the extent of British oil dependence, the skewed terms of the oil contract, and the willingness to use force against a much poorer and weaker population to enforce it, all bore the hallmarks of a neocolonial arrangement, even in the words of many American policy makers such as Averill Harriman. It has become fashionable to trot out George Kennan's, former head of the State Department Policy Planning Staff, PPS23 in support of theories of US empire, but no document written at such a high level can be ignored. Penned with respect to the Far East in 1948, it is nevertheless another window into policy makers' thinking, and contains now well-known gems as:

"We have about 50% of the world's wealth but only 6.3% of its population. Our real task in the coming period is to devise a pattern of relationships which will permit us to maintain this position of disparity without positive detriment to our national security. The day is not far off when we are going to have to deal in straight power concepts. The less we are then hampered by idealistic slogans, the better."

In the division of the spoils after the overthrow of Mossadeq, the AIOC held 40 percent of the shares of a newly formed consortium, five American companies held 40 percent, and the rest was shared by Royal Dutch/Shell and a French company. In order to enforce the division of spoils, the Shah of Iran was made dictator and given full US backing and support, even as he instituted one of the most corrupt and ruthless regimes in modern history. Blum says: "life under the Shah was a grim tableau of grinding poverty, police terror, and torture." In 1976, three years before the Iranian Revolution, Amnesty International reported that the US-backed Shah had: "a history of torture which is beyond belief. No country in the world has a worse record in human rights than Iran." The methods of his secret police included pulling of teeth and nails, electric shock, and the forcing of boiling water into the rectum.

Slater notes that economic interest does not always fit the instances in which US interventions take place, such as Grenada or Nicaragua, which have no natural resources to speak of. But former State Department employee Blum argues, disturbingly, that the greater challenge felt by the responsible policy makers is to stamp out a principle, "as a warning to others," that what the US "always feared from the Third World was the emergence of a good example" in the form of a flourishing, non-aligned society independent of the US military and economic sphere.

Kinzer writes that "It is not far-fetched to draw a line from Operation Ajax through the Shah"s repressive regime and the Islamic Revolution to the fireballs that engulfed the World Trade Center in New York." The Iranian Revolution in 1979 provided safe haven and an ideology for unsavories such as Hamas, bin Laden, and the Taliban during the 1980s and 1990s. Although useful as an explanatory device, the effect of placing too much emphasis on East-West relations and the Domino Theory is to say that, although the effects of US foreign policy were sometimes unfortunate, they were necessary to defeat a greater evil, the Soviet threat. This enables us, as Jervis implies, to continue our perceptions of America as "mom and apple pie." Similarly, our perceptions of others can be colored by distrust, fear, and uncertainty, unless and until the "other" becomes human, takes human form. One anecdote on Mossadeq seems a particular favorite of Kinzer, as he uses it to conclude his book. Under virtual house arrest by the Shah Mohammed Reza Pahlavi until the end of his days, living at his family's estate, a woman recounts the only time she ever saw Dr. Mossadeq get angry, as he lived out his days in study, treating villagers" ailments, and conducting farming experiments. A peasant had been beaten by the local police in order to get information on Mossadeq's habits and conversation, and he complained to Mossadeq. Kinzer, who interviewed the woman on her memories, reports that she said:

> "It was the only time I ever saw him [Mossadeq] get angry. He called the police chief and shouted at him to come to the house immediately. When he got to the house, Mossadeq pushed him against a wall, held his cane against the guy's throat and shouted: "You are here to watch me, and you have no right to abuse anyone else. If you have a problem, you come to me and only me! Don't ever, ever lay a finger on one of my people again!" This was a Savak officer [the Shah"s secret police] and not a nice man at all. After that, the police never went near us."

Mossadeq was close to eighty at that time. When the Iranian Revolution broke out in 1979, giving rise to the hostage crisis, seas of demonstrators carried placards bearing the likeness of Mossadeq, who had died 12 years before, at the age of 85.

www.ingramcontent.com/pod-product-compliance
Lightning Source LLC
Chambersburg PA
CBHW030259290526
45785CB00001B/151